# MAJOR OPTIONS

# MAJOR

# OPTIONS

### The Student's Guide to Linking
### College Majors and Career Opportunities
### During and After College

## BY NICHOLAS BASTA

PRODUCED BY

THE STONESONG PRESS, INC.

AND

ALISON BROWN CERIER BOOK DEVELOPMENT

HarperPerennial
*A Division of* HarperCollins*Publishers*

ISBN   0-06-271506-2—0-06-273023-1   (pbk.)
Library of Congress 90-55997
91  92  93  94  95  DT/RRD  10  9  8  7  6  5  4  3  2

*To my parents, Nick and Herta Basta,*
*my first teachers about work and careers*

# CONTENTS

# ACKNOWLEDGMENTS

Dozens of recent college graduates shared their experiences and thoughts with me, and dozens more older graduates provided perspective and comments on their experiences since attending college. Some of these interviews were conducted electronically, through the facilities of Compuserve Information Services (Columbus, OH) and several other electronic networks. As this medium can be challenging to use, the interviewees who took the time to key in their answers to my questions deserve an extra tip of the hat (ironically, one of the least responsive of the professional forums I accessed was that of professional educators!). These interview subjects gave this book the real-world perspective that makes all the difference.

I was in contact with a number of college professors to discuss certain aspects of college and career planning; in particular, I'd like to mention David Soles of Wichita State University and Steven Ross of Columbia University. The career-placement and alumni-relations offices of Hartwick College, Bryant College, Drew University, Tulane University, Washington University in St. Louis, Occidental College and Concordia College (Minnesota) were especially helpful.

A number of schools were generous in supplying me with general bulletins or undergraduate catalogs, which formed the basis of the "Sampler" sections in the academic program descriptions. These include: Eastern and Western Kentucky Universities, Hofstra University, Tulane University, Boston University, Bucknell University, Santa Clara University, Bard College, Colby College, New Mexico State University, Case Western Reserve University, the New School for Social Research, New York University, Concordia College, Ohio University, the School of Visual Arts of New York, Allegheny College, Illinois Wesleyan University, Georgia Institute of Technology, University of Maine, University of Denver, New York Institute of Technology, Pepperdine University, Denison University, Washington University in St. Louis and the Baruch College of the City University of New York. Permission to reprint course descriptions from their catalogs is gratefully acknowledged.

The efforts of the Office of Educational Research and Improvement, US Department of Education, represented by Dr. Vance Grant, and the Office of Employment Projections, US Bureau of Labor Statistics, represented by Mr. George Silvestri, are deeply appreciated. "Washington bureaucrats" are continually berated by almost everyone, but I have found these offices to be generous with their time and insightful with their analyses. Someone has to keep the score on what is going on in American education and employment, and these folks keep the numbers coming.

Similarly, the Higher Education Research Institute, together with the American Council on Education, develop great data on what college students are thinking about as they go into college and as they come out. The use of their data is gratefully acknowledged. Another group of college-related organizations—the College Placement Council, the Collegiate Employment Research Institute at Michigan State University, and the Lindquist-Endicott Report of Northwestern University churn out invaluable data on job placement and salaries every year.

An extensive number of professional organizations were generous with membership survey data, historical documents, and other resources. These include: American Institute of Aeronautics and Astronautics; Public Relations Student Society of America; National Press Photographers Association; National Association of Broadcasters; American Women in Radio and Television, Inc.; The International Radio and Television Society; American Society of Landscape Architects; The American Society of Microbiology; Industrial Biotechnology Association; National Association of Purchasing Management; The American Physiological Society; American Optometric Association; The American Society for Information Science; Society of Manufacturing Engineers; Special Libraries Association; National Resident Matching Program; American Society for Medical Technology; National Health Council, Inc.; Direct Marketing Association, Inc.; National Investor Relations Institute; Data Processing Management Association; Institute for Certification of Computer Professionals; Association of Information Systems Professionals; International Council of Shopping Centers; Society of Real Estate Appraisers; Institute of Real Estate Management; Operations Research Society of America; National Association of Social Workers, Inc.; American Medical Association; Association of Ground Water Scientists and Engineers; National Water Well Association; National Association of Environmental Professionals; American Academy of Environmental Engineers; American Society of Safety Engineers; National Association of Accountants; The Institute of Internal Auditors; American Institute of Certified Public Accountants; Administrative Management Society; The National Management Association; Mortgage Bankers Association of America; National Association of Tax Practitioners; The Institute of Certified Financial Planners; International Association for Financial Planning; Association of Executive Search Consultants, Inc.; Life Insurance Marketing and Research Association, Inc.; Institute of Management Consultants, Inc.; Acme, Inc.; American Compensation Association; Employment Management Association; American Society for Industrial Security; American Ceramic Society, Inc.; Human Factors Society; American Historical Association; American Political Science Association; and the American Home Economics Association.

# FINDING A CAREER DIRECTION

This is your how-to manual for transforming your academic studies into a satisfying career.

Most college graduates, looking back on their school years, will remember college as the place where they found themselves, where they made the transition from youth to adulthood, from dependency to independence. Then, in the next breath, they will unanimously state: "College helped me start my career."

It has been a cliche that college is the ticket to a rewarding career, but that cliche has never been truer than today. Current and projected growth rates for professional careers out-distance the rates for semi-skilled labor by a wide margin, and, for the many types of work where a college education is optional, more and more employers are insisting on degreed job candidates. Finally, there is the cold, hard, cash argument: College graduates average lifetime earnings a half-million dollars greater than those without degrees.

If you're reading this book right now, you've probably already entered college, or have made a serious commitment to it. You've heard the justifications again and again, and you've made your decision. What do you do now? How do you turn this airy promise of a better life into an actual career?

The answer is to find the links between a major that interests you and a career that you will enjoy. The major will develop skills, abilities, interests, or specific knowledge that the career demands or rewards.

Like most college students, however, you may find it difficult to see into your future and choose a direction. Many people change their majors midstream; some several times. Part of the problem is that you're still growing as a person—an important part of college in itself. But part of the problem is that you don't know your options. In this book, you can look inside the most common college majors and dozens of attractive careers. You can envision your future many different ways, and see what feels right.

If a particular discipline appeals to you, you'll learn all the places that major might lead—both the justifiably popular choices and the inviting roads less traveled. The key to the transition is skills. All college programs, even rarefied ones that seem to pursue learning for learning's sake, offer skills that are desirable or essential in today's job market. For example, a major computer-software company makes a point of hiring graduates with degrees in philosophy or music as programmers. This company believes that the rigorous training in logical structures and analytical thinking makes better workers.

Employers look for dozens of skills among college graduates. This book will help you uncover these skills and the professions they apply to. Often, however, it is up to the college graduate to demonstrate the value of the skills and experiences gained in college. Sometimes an employer has restrictions when hiring. Some requirements make sense, for example, some professionals must be certified to practice. All too often, though, an employer is making a judgment call based on out-of-date information, on traditions that die hard, or on simple biases for or against certain types of training. In this book, you will learn how others have successfully made a pitch for being hired, and which of your skills will be most attractive to employers.

Many academic programs, especially in the liberal arts, develop similar skills. For example, if you want to be a writer, an English, history, or philosophy program would prepare you to roughly the same degree. If you are most interested in developing traditional liberal arts skills like writing and clear thinking and speaking, then consider also your personal interests when choosing a major. The experiences of former students interviewed for this book show that many successful professionals once chose their majors because they thought the department was great, because some courses in their major were fascinating, or even because it was easy to meet the requirements. But by a direct or circuitous route, they were able to link the skills and interests of their majors to the skills and interests of their careers.

After all, it makes no sense whatsoever to attend college unless you can study things that interest you. Survey after survey has shown that professionals feel the same way about their jobs,— "interesting work" is their number-one requirement. What a wonderful parallel!

---

# How to Use This Book

*Major Options* has two parts:   a compendium of majors and a compendium of careers.

The first part profiles the most common programs of concentration for 4-year college degrees, from accounting to visual arts. Each starts with an enrollment boxscore, an overview of the program, and a list of concentrations within the major. Next a course sampler provides a selection of the courses you could expect to take, giving you a clearer picture of the academic program (generally the course numbers indicate the academic level—100s for first-year courses, 200s for second year, etc.). Several graduates then assess the value of the program for their own careers. We interviewed hundreds of former students who graduated years ago or quite recently, asking them questions such as "What career path did you follow to your present job?" and "How would you rate the helpfulness of your major in landing you your first job?" Each profile ends with a list of the careers directly linked to that major, leading you to the entries in Part Two.

The second part profiles careers where a college degree is necessary or advisable. Each entry answers questions like:   What are the day-to-day activities? What skills will I need to excel? What are the short-term prospects for expanding opportunities and career growth? What does this profession pay? Each entry includes the address and phone number of one or more professional associations that can give you more information if the career sounds attractive. Each entry lists the academic majors common among people in the field, so you can start your inquiries either with the major or the career.

This entire book would be an academic (ha, ha) exercise without an assessment of the numerical trends in academic programs and jobs. So at the beginning of each section there are some very important numbers that can help you make your choices—the latest figures on which majors students are choosing and which fields are growing. It pays to study the lists closely. If a particular academic program is growing dramatically, that says something about how well today's students feel they are being prepared for professional work by taking that major; if a program is shrinking, the reverse holds true. However, keep in mind that there is a certain amount of faddishness about academic choices—at various times certain programs are "in," and certain ones "out," for reasons independent of the quality of the programs or the job possibilities they generate.

A special effort has been made to get the very latest data available, and to incorporate the latest news on business and job trends. There are monumental problems in doing this; for example, the statistics showing how many college students graduated with each degree, compiled by the National Center for Education Statistics, lags behind current events by 2 years. Also, there is an inherent inertia to the college/career combination; many students choose an academic program based on the job market when they enter college, and at graduation some find that the sheepskin that once looked like a meal ticket now looks like yesterday's news.

To counter these problems, we have provided historical and projected data that help put the numbers into perspective. Statistics on college programs are traced back to 1979 and forward to 1989, and data for job markets are current as of early 1990. Where possible, data on trends that have affected the job market in previous years are included. The US Bureau of Labor Statistics produced forecasts of job markets through the year 2000; this forecast is extremely valuable for career planning, but its predictions need to be analyzed carefully.

All these numbers will help you make choices—among majors and among careers. Which comes first: the choice of an academic program at college, or the choice of a career that then dictates what program to follow? There's no one answer. For the blessed minority that know exactly what they want to do in life, the two choices are made simultaneously. Others, knowing that they want to attend college, but in the dark about what happens after, choose the academic program that seems most interesting. Another group, suspecting that a major in one particular field will lead to interesting work possibilities, chooses a program and then, as graduation looms, begin to wonder about how to apply what they have learned in the working world.

The first group of college students will probably depend on the compendium of careers more than the compendium of academic programs. The second group will probably want to study the majors part first, to learn the academic possibilities in college, then read the careers part to see how those majors can be transformed into a career. The third group will probably be interested in both sections equally.

# Thinking About Careers

Fitting a person to a job, and a job to a person, involves a long list of questions and decisions. The first set of decisions is internal and individual. What am I good at? What am I interested in? What kind of working conditions am I comfortable with? What are my monetary goals?

A variety of tools can help you approach, if not actually answer, such questions. A number of psychological tests are available through college career centers, counseling centers, and private career consultants. One of the oldest tests, called the Myers-Briggs Type Indicator, puts individuals into one of sixteen boxes based on character traits like extroversion and introversion, sensing and intuiting, thinking and feeling, judging and perceiving. You then match the personality type with those that exemplify various professions to see how your skills and interests fit with actual careers.

Kate Wendleton, an experienced corporate job counselor and seminar leader in New York, says that tests like the Myers-Briggs are useful in their place. She feels, however, that it is unrealistic to expect all of humanity to fit into 16 pigeonholes. Instead, she uses an exercise called "The Dream." On a sheet of paper, you outline exactly where you want to live and your professional and financial goals, for now, for 5 years in the future, then 15, 25, and on up to 40 years from now. This is a thought exercise and game that should be fun to do. "When you have finished the exercise, ask yourself how you feel about your entire life as laid out in the plan," Ms. Wendleton says. "If you don't like it, you are allowed to change it—it's your life."

Going through a battery of exercises, personal counseling, and the like can be time-consuming. At some point, a feeling inevitably seeps in: "What's the point to all this? It's a waste of time. I need a job!" Nevertheless, it's strongly recommended that you try at least some of the testing and evaluation. If you approach it with an open mind, you may learn some surprising things about yourself. On a more practical level, you can turn the results of this process into a top-quality resume.

In the final analysis, your willingness to invest time and care in career planning simply becomes a reflection of how important a career is to you personally. Some people live to work—their career is the broadest expression of who they are, and what they value. Others work to live—their career is simply the means to afford all the things that make a life complete. I don't recommend one attitude over the other; it's purely a personal choice. But in both cases, it makes a lot of sense to choose careers carefully. Almost half of your waking existence will be spent at the job—why not put that time into something of value to you?

Once you have looked within, it's time to talk to other people about their career experiences. To start, in the Assessment sections of the Majors part, you will learn about the career paths that some recent graduates have taken following graduation. A few words of guidance are in order concerning these profiles: You will find that many unusual careers have resulted from the various majors; conversely, some very typical career paths—studying education, for example, and then becoming a teacher—have apparently been overlooked. These careers weren't profiled in order to encourage you to make the same career choices, and to pull you away from obvious paths. Rather, the intent is to show how a particular major can be adapted to different careers. Because the most obvious career paths are just that—obvious—I have generally not profiled such graduates.

Then you need to build a network of contacts—the most powerful resource in analyzing potential careers. At first, your network will be comprised of people you know personally: friends and family, teachers, advisers. Your network will really begin to grow when you add contacts who don't know you personally, but are in a position to provide assistance. You can acquire some of these contacts through "information interviews." It has become common in the professional world to go to, or be asked for, an information interview, simply to provide information and possible job leads. Think of the many college graduates interviewed for this book as a network; would you want to ask these professionals about their work, how they got their jobs, and why they do what they do? Build your contacts with people who are actually working in the careers you are considering.

Statistics showing demand and growth of a field is one type of information that is helpful in career planning. You will find many such figures throughout this book. Trends in these numbers may suggest directions your career might go. For example, say you want to pursue a career in education. The demand, projected growth rate, and pay will vary depending on whether you choose to apply your degree in elementary or secondary education, or instead in corporate training. These kinds of figures can also help explain why it is sometimes worthwhile to adopt a particular industry rather than a specific job. Let's say you are most interested in construction. In the early 1990s, this industry is in a slump, but the projected growth for property managers is above average. You could work for a few years as a property manager, gaining valuable experience in the building industry, and then move into construction later.

Remember, these statistics should be a *guide* to informed choices, not the *rule* for choosing. Even if you decide on a major that tens of thousands of students graduate from, and seek an occupation with a low projected growth rate, it is worthwhile to give it your best shot—you may be one of the lucky ones. Keep in mind, too, that regardless of the projected growth rate of a profession, most types of job openings occur because of retirements or other transfers out of that profession, rather than the predicted increase in number of openings.

## Thinking About Employers

Years ago, the career ladder for most professionals was well defined. You joined a large company, worked as a trainee, and knew who occupied each rung on the ladder above you. If you were talented and/or ambitious, you would steadily climb up this ladder.

There are professions where such ladders are still so clear-cut. A lawyer in a private firm, for example, starts as an associate, then after a set number of years may become a partner and eventually a senior partner or a leader in the firm. Today, in the course of a career, most professionals change employers, shift lines of work, or jump from one industry to another. Employers say that the new generation of professionals are much less loyal to their firms; at the same time, it is incontrovertible that employers are much less committed to their employees.

So don't think of your career as one job with one employer. Think of related lines of work, related industries, related skills. The job descriptions in the Careers section were written with this in mind. For example, corporate MARKETING MANAGERS work day in and day out with advertising agency ACCOUNT EXECUTIVES. Newspaper or magazine JOURNALISTS get the information they report from PUBLIC RELATIONS SPECIALISTS. DESIGN ENGINEERS work with MANUFACTURING ENGINEERS to develop marketable products. There are many more examples. The important point here is that you often get valuable experience in one type of employment by working in another. One job advisor makes the point this way: select your first job with the next one in mind.

Certain college degree programs—education administration, for example, and most of the science and engineering occupations— account for the bulk of the entrants to those professions. Where this is the case, it pays to check the college enrollment data in the table called Degrees Awarded and Trends. Where you find that enrollments in these programs are flat or declining, yet the projected growth for the relevant occupation is above average, there's a real potential for a rapid upswing in numbers of job offers or starting salaries.

Besides the type of industry and type of work, you must choose your environment. Large, multi-national companies? Small, entrepreneurial outfits? Private employment versus public or non-profit employment?

Like salary needs, the arena where we work is a very personal choice. Conventional wisdom states that big companies provide security, the opportunity to gain experience, and the satisfaction of working for a well-known entity. Small companies are supposed to provide lots of responsibility fast, and the chance to make a lot of money overnight—or to lose one's job overnight.

That's the conventional view, but today's dynamic job market presents many exceptions. Large companies, especially conglomerates of far-flung operations, can be as entrepreneurial as a new start-up. Small companies dominated by their founders can be stultifying. Conversely, large companies have proven themselves to be unpredictable employers, hiring and firing personnel rapidly, while small companies can be steady job generators that grow smoothly and successfully.

The best advice is to check the specific employer carefully. Look up articles about the firm in the business press, going back a few years to get a sense of perspective.

Over the past decade or so, small companies have been the source of most new jobs, while large companies were shrinking. These trends can, however, reverse themselves quickly.

It remains true, though, that more varied experience can more often be obtained at a small company than at a large one. Large firms have large staffs organized into special-function groups. Getting something done often comes down to coordinating the actions of these staffs. Small companies, lacking the special-function groups, require their employees to wear several hats and take on a variety of responsibilities.

Meanwhile, don't overlook the non-profit or public-service sector. Non-profits usually can't afford to pay as well as for-profit companies, but they do offer numerous high-paying positions. Their business and administrative duties can be every bit as demanding as those of for-profit firms. Some non-profits are among the best-run organizations in the country.

Another, quite new, type of employer is the overseas corporation that sets up shop here in the United States and hires Americans. Nearly 3.5 million workers are employed by such companies. Many of these companies are huge—in fact, many of them are bigger than all but a handful of the biggest US companies. Should you consider a job with them?

Yes—especially if you are starting down a path to a career. The rap against foreign employers is that they reserve the top positions for natives of their home country. You won't be immediately in line for the presidency or chairmanship of any large company—

US or foreign—at the outset of your career anyway. So what is there to lose?

What is to be gained, however, is potentially of great value over the course of a career. The trend toward globalization—worldwide trade in goods and services—is now all but unstoppable. The US is exporting more goods, and the push is on for a higher level of expertise in international trade activities, increasing the demand for professionals with international experience.

# The Job Hunt

If, by writing a book, I could guarantee you a good job, I'd be either filthy rich or godlike in my omniscience (I'm neither!). Even an automotive how-to manual doesn't guarantee that your car will work perfectly after just reading it. *You* have to get moving, put the work in, and make the *right* moves.

Reading this book *will* get you started on two things:   selecting a major (if you haven't already) and choosing a potential career. You are also directed to other sources of information about careers.

The foremost source of information about potential employers is your network of professional contacts. The same network that helped you further define your career options is also the best source of leads on potential job openings. It takes effort to identify people who might share your professional interests, and to keep in touch with them, but the investment will pay off in the form of a quicker route to your ultimate career.

The next key task in starting a job hunt is to write a resume. People with jobs have business cards in every pocket; people who want jobs should have a resume that can be handed out as readily as a business card would be offered. There are plenty of good books about resume-writing, and there are many advisors and consultants ready to help. The classic problem for college students is that they have little work experience to list. The books and consultants can help anyone find something credible to write about, even someone who's been doing little more than breathing air and eating food. At this point, the exercises and evaluations at the start of the career-planning process come in handy. By analyzing the results, you should be able to come up with key skills and interests. You can also get some insights from the ways the people interviewed in this book used their academic training to succeed in the work they do. If your interests have been demonstrated by activities (in school, or through hobbies, sports, or other activities), so much the better. Took a lot of math courses? That demonstrates numerical skills. Wrote a long history paper? That demonstrates communication skills. Aced your freshman science-laboratory class? That demonstrates problem-solving skills.

The last step to getting a job is the interview. Again, there are numerous books and advisors who can help prepare you for interviewing. Companies take many different approaches to the interviewing process. Some give tests; some play subtle mind games to try to expose the type of person you really are. Many companies still hire on the basis of one executive's feelings about how the candidate will function on the job, based on sitting across the table from each other and having a talk.

I have two general comments about interviews: first, always try to determine who it is that is interviewing you. It's better if it's a line or business manager. Too many human-resource professionals who interview college students have only a vague idea of what it is that company does or what the job entails. Second, extensive research is the antidote to the stage fright that can afflict job hunters. By researching a company as thoroughly as you would an academic paper, you can gain confidence.

And you should be confident. You've done your homework—making informed choices about your college major and your career. You've looked for the answers inside yourself, in the academic world, and in the business world around you. Now you're ready to go for that first job.

# PART I

# THE

---

# MAJORS

# ACADEMIC PROGRAMS
# BY THE NUMBERS

This section describes dozens of the most popular college majors. To help you put it all together, here are some helpful statistics that compare the whole range of possible choices.

First, some general statistics about colleges and their programs. Each year, roughly 2 million young adults, and a few hundred thousand older adults, begin their studies at colleges across the land. Each year, about $150 billion is expended—by the federal government, employers, universities, and students themselves—in paying for a college education.

Those 2 million or so college freshmen represent slightly over 50% of that age group. About 1 million of them will graduate with a baccalaureate degree 4 years later. (An indeterminate additional number will obtain their degree in 5 or more years.) Looking back to previous years, we find federal data that show that 18.9% of the adult American population has 16 or more years of schooling.

Thus, a little less than one out of five adult Americans has a college degree of some sort; this proportion has been rising by a couple percentage points per decade, and eventually, if current trends hold, just over one out of four adults will have a college degree in the late 1990s.

There are about 3400 junior colleges, colleges, and universities spread across America. About three out of four students are attending a public university; about 60% attend full-time.

The total number of programs offered changes rapidly. The Department of Education counts about 450 programs. This section describes those that are most significant, in terms of size, intellectual content, or career potential.

Three sets of data follow. The first is a 10-year trace of the programs selected by incoming freshmen. The next table shows how these intentions worked out for the classes of 1987 and 1989. As you can see, engineering, health professions (non-MD) and the fine arts were the big losers in retaining students; the social sciences, history and political science, and education were the big winners. Data from the 1989 class (taken in 1987) has been included to provide a better perspective on the trends; if an academic program grew for both the 1987 and 1989 classes, it is a sign of health.

The third set of data shows the 5-year trend for degrees awarded. Included here are a number of professionals (law, medicine, etc.) who enter the working world only after completing graduate-level work. (A close reading of the last table will reveal many academic programs that rely on a master's degree to win a job assignment. Such programs as journalism or education administration have more master's graduates than bachelor's graduates.)

Showing bachelor, master's, PhD and "professional" jobs raises the question of just what an academic degree is anyway. Most liberal arts students obtain a bachelor of arts degree in their chosen field. A smaller number label their degrees "bachelor of science," and some schools offer both a bachelor of arts and a bachelor of science degree. Generally, the latter has a higher technical content, with more science courses and more technical subjects like math.

In the descriptions of majors that follow, by and large, each academic program is different from the next. However, many schools have structured major/minor programs, in which a student selects a major, and also takes enough classes to form a distinct minor degree in another academic program. Some students choose closely related fields, such as English (major) and theater (minor). Others attempt to straddle the job market by choosing two dissimilar programs, say science and accounting. These major/minor programs tend to blur the distinction between academic programs.

Similarly, many schools offer "concentrations" or "joint" programs between two related academic departments. The school may offer a concentration when it has insufficient resources (or student interest) for a full-fledged, independent program. Some schools offer a concentration in, for example, women's studies, as part of a degree-generating department such as sociology or political science.

Finally, the dual-major program has proven popular among

many students. By taking extra courses (perhaps extending the undergraduate program by a year or so), a student can graduate with two degrees. Employers like to see job candidates who are multi-talented and hard-working; a dual major certainly proves these two characteristics.

Whether you choose one major or some combination thereof, your choice of academic programs will open up many different career paths—including some that you have never suspected. The following descriptions will help you make the choices that are right for you.

# ACCOUNTING

|  | 1983 | 1985 | 1988 |
|---|---|---|---|
| **Enrollment** BS or BA | 45,732 | 47,005 | 42,886 |
| **Boxscore** Master's | 3,046 | 3,207 | 3,101 |
| PhD | 66 | 59 | 57 |

**Overview**

What grammar is to English composition, accounting is to business. Keeping track of the flow of funds into and out of an enterprise is a basic task of business managers; for many, a solid grounding in the principles of accounting is the first step up the rungs to corporate chiefdom.

Most business administration or economics programs require or allow for a couple of semesters of accounting so that students will learn how to read a balance sheet and keep a ledger. Students who major in accounting, however, go much farther, learning the theories behind accounting procedures, the famed "generally accepted accounting principles" (GAAP), and the ways accounting standards are applied in different types of businesses.

A lot of math is involved, but in general, the level of mathematical complexity is not high—usually, the ultimate math course is calculus. Instead, the major stresses the meaning behind business and financial concepts. Another important element of accounting

"Academic Programs" continued on p. 12.

## FRESHMAN CHOICES IN COLLEGE MAJORS, 1979–89

| MAJOR | 1979 Percent | 1984 Percent | 1989 Percent | 1979–89 % change |
|---|---|---|---|---|
| Arts and Humanities, total | 11.0 | 9.6 | 10.4 | −5.5 |
|   Fine arts, theatre and music | 4.5 | 3.3 | 3.6 | −20.0 |
|   English, literature, languages and speech | 1.6 | 1.6 | 1.9 | 18.7 |
|   History | 0.6 | 0.6 | 0.8 | 33.3 |
|   Journalism and communications | 3.4 | 3.4 | 4.1 | 20.6 |
|   Philosophy, religion and others | 0.9 | 0.8 | 1.0 | 11.1 |
| Biological Sciences, total | 3.6 | 4.2 | 3.7 | 2.8 |
| Business | 24.3 | 26.4 | 24.5 | 0.8 |
|   Accounting | 6.2 | 6.4 | 6.1 | −1.6 |
|   Business administration | 7.4 | 7.4 | 6.5 | −12.2 |
|   Finance and management | 4.9 | 6.4 | 6.4 | 30.6 |
|   Marketing | 1.9 | 2.3 | 3.0 | 57.9 |
|   Other | 3.9 | 3.9 | 2.5 | −35.9 |
| Education, total | 8.4 | 6.5 | 9.2 | 9.5 |
|   Elementary education | 2.6 | 2.8 | 4.6 | 76.9 |
|   Secondary education | 0.7 | 0.9 | 1.8 | 157.1 |
|   Special education | 1.8 | 0.8 | 0.6 | −66.7 |
|   Physical education or recreation | 2.3 | 1.2 | 1.1 | −52.2 |
|   Business, music, art and other | 1.0 | 0.8 | 1.1 | 10.0 |
| Engineering and Computer Science, total | 14.2 | 16.8 | 12.8 | −9.9 |
|   Aerospace and aeronautical | 1.0 | 1.3 | 1.5 | 50.0 |
|   Civil | 1.2 | 0.9 | 1.1 | −8.3 |
|   Chemical | 1.0 | 0.7 | 0.7 | −30.0 |
|   Computer science, data processing | 3.6 | 5.8 | 2.6 | −27.8 |
|   Electrical or electronic | 3.2 | 4.1 | 3.0 | −6.3 |
|   Industrial and mechanical | 2.5 | 2.5 | 2.3 | −8.0 |
|   Other | 1.7 | 1.5 | 1.6 | −5.9 |
| Physical Sciences, total | 2.9 | 3.2 | 2.1 | −27.6 |
|   Chemistry | 0.9 | 0.8 | 0.6 | −33.3 |
|   Math, statistics, physics and astronomy | 1.1 | 1.3 | 1.1 | 0.0 |
|   Earth, marine, atmospheric and other sciences | 0.9 | 1.1 | 0.4 | −55.6 |
| Professional, total | 16.2 | 15.6 | 13.2 | −18.5 |
|   Architecture and urban planning | 1.2 | 0.8 | 1.3 | 8.3 |
|   Home economics | 0.8 | 0.5 | 0.2 | −75.0 |
|   Health technology and therapy | 3.8 | 3.5 | 3.2 | −15.8 |
|   Law enforcement | 1.5 | 1.5 | 1.5 | 0.0 |
|   Nursing | 3.6 | 4.1 | 2.8 | −22.2 |
|   Other health-related | 3.7 | 3.8 | 3.9 | 5.4 |
|   Other professional | 1.6 | 1.4 | 1.3 | −18.8 |

FRESHMAN CHOICES IN COLLEGE MAJORS, 1979–89 (*CONTINUED*)

| MAJOR | 1979 Percent | 1984 Percent | 1989 Percent | 1979–89 % change |
|---|---|---|---|---|
| Social Sciences, total | 7.5 | 6.7 | 9.6 | 28.0 |
| Economics | 0.4 | 0.4 | 0.4 | 0.0 |
| Political science | 2.0 | 2.1 | 3.1 | 55.0 |
| Psychology | 2.6 | 2.7 | 4.2 | 61.5 |
| Sociology, social work and anthropology | 2.2 | 1.3 | 1.6 | −27.3 |
| Other | 0.3 | 0.2 | 0.3 | 0.0 |
| Technical and related fields, total | 7.0 | 6.1 | 5.3 | −24.3 |
| Building trades, drafting, electronics and other | 2.5 | 2.6 | 2.3 | −8.0 |
| Agriculture and forestry | 3.0 | 2.0 | 1.2 | −60.0 |
| Other fields | 1.5 | 1.5 | 1.8 | 20.0 |
| Undecided | 4.8 | 5.2 | 6.9 | 43.8 |

SOURCE:   UCLA Higher Education Research Institute

HOW FRESHMEN ACADEMIC CHOICES CHANGE

| | A | B | C | D | E | F |
|---|---|---|---|---|---|---|
| | Probable in 1983 | 1983 freshmen in 1987 | % change | Probable in 1985 | 1985 freshmen in 1987 | % change |
| Agriculture | 0.7 | 0.8 | 14.3 | 3 | 1.6 | −46.7 |
| Biological sciences | 5 | 5.7 | 14.0 | 5.2 | 4.9 | −5.8 |
| Business | 22.8 | 25.5 | 11.8 | 23.3 | 27.7 | 18.9 |
| Education | 6.5 | 9 | 38.5 | 1.7 | 4 | 135.3 |
| Engineering | 10.1 | 6.6 | −34.7 | 19.1 | 14.3 | −25.1 |
| English | 1.2 | 3 | 150.0 | 0.8 | 1.8 | 125.0 |
| Health professional (non-M.D.) | 11.4 | 5.9 | −48.2 | 4.2 | 1.4 | −66.7 |
| History or Political science | 3.6 | 5.6 | 55.6 | 5 | 7.3 | 46.0 |
| Humanities | 1.8 | 2.7 | 50.0 | 1.4 | 3.5 | 150.0 |
| Fine arts | 4.8 | 3.4 | −29.2 | 5.5 | 4.9 | −10.9 |
| Mathematics or Statistics | 1.2 | 1.6 | 33.3 | 2.2 | 1.5 | −31.8 |
| Physical sciences | 2.1 | 1.9 | −9.5 | 2.6 | 3.2 | 23.1 |
| Social sciences | 5.1 | 11.2 | 119.6 | 3.5 | 9.8 | 180.0 |
| Technical (other) | 9.5 | 7.9 | −16.8 | 5.9 | 4.6 | −22.0 |
| Non-technical (other) | 7.3 | 8.7 | 19.2 | 8.9 | 8.6 | −3.4 |
| Undecided | 7 | 0.4 | −94.3 | 7.6 | 0.8 | −89.5 |

NOTE:     Data are for students at four-year colleges and universities
SOURCE:   UCLA Higher Education Research Institute

## DEGREES AWARDED AND TRENDS

| | Bachelor | | | |
|---|---|---|---|---|
| | 1984 | 1986 | 1988 | %** |
| TOTAL, ALL PROGRAMS | 974309 | 987823 | 993362 | 2.0 |
| Agribusiness and agricultural production | 6020 | 5569 | 4800 | −20.3 |
| Agricultural science | 9225 | 7976 | 6392 | −30.7 |
| Veterinary medicine (D.V.M.)* | | | | |
| Renewable natural resoures | 4072 | 3278 | 3030 | −25.6 |
| Architecture and environmental design | 9186 | 9119 | 8606 | −6.3 |
| Architecture | 4567 | 4392 | 4266 | −6.6 |
| Area and ethnic studies, total | 2879 | 3060 | 3463 | 20.3 |
| Business, management, marketing, total | 230031 | 238160 | 243344 | 5.8 |
| Accounting | 47692 | 45617 | 42866 | −10.1 |
| Banking and finance | 17576 | 22483 | 26100 | 48.5 |
| Business administration and mgmt. | 68229 | 66806 | 68544 | 0.5 |
| Marketing mgmt. and research | 25055 | 27744 | 30173 | 20.4 |
| Marketing and distribution | 3416 | 3486 | 4920 | 44.0 |
| Communications, total | 38586 | 41666 | 45382 | 17.6 |
| Communications, general | 17171 | 18495 | 21337 | 24.3 |
| Journalism | 9795 | 10402 | 10891 | 11.2 |
| Radio/television | 6864 | 7233 | 6315 | −8.0 |
| Comm. technology (photo, film, etc.) | 1579 | 1425 | 1323 | −16.2 |
| Computer & information science, total | 32172 | 41889 | 34548 | 7.4 |
| Education, total | 92382 | 87221 | 91013 | −1.5 |
| Education administration, total | 101 | 51 | 9 | −91.1 |
| Special education, total | 10301 | 8206 | 6507 | −36.8 |
| Teacher education, general, total | 42164 | 43075 | 48153 | 14.2 |
| Teacher ed., specific subjects | 35868 | 32260 | 32454 | −9.5 |
| Engineering, total | 75732 | 76333 | 69505 | −8.2 |
| Aerospace engineering | 2534 | 2902 | 3092 | 22.0 |
| Chemical engineering | 7475 | 5877 | 3926 | −47.5 |
| Civil engineering | 9693 | 8679 | 7497 | −22.7 |
| Computer engineering | 1480 | 2192 | 2115 | 42.9 |
| Electrical, electronics engineering | 19943 | 23742 | 23598 | 18.3 |
| Industrial engineering | 3937 | 4162 | 4082 | 3.7 |
| Mechanical engineering | 16629 | 16194 | 14918 | −10.3 |
| Eng'g and related technologies, total | 18712 | 19620 | 19286 | 3.1 |
| Foreign languages, total | 9479 | 10102 | 10028 | 5.8 |
| Italic (Romance) languages, total | 6532 | 6815 | 6876 | 5.3 |
| Allied health, total | 13518 | 13648 | 12076 | −10.7 |
| Rehabilitative services (therapy), total | 6212 | 6726 | 6270 | 0.9 |
| Health sciences, total | 50820 | 50887 | 48019 | −5.5 |
| Health services administration | 3014 | 3154 | 3242 | 7.6 |
| Nursing | 33092 | 34097 | 31569 | −4.6 |
| Pharmacy | 5480 | 5130 | 5277 | −3.7 |

| Master's | | | | Doctorate | | | |
|---|---|---|---|---|---|---|---|
| 1984 | 1986 | 1988 | %** | 1984 | 1986 | 1988 | %** |
| 284263 | 288567 | 298733 | 5.1 | 33209 | 33653 | 34839 | 4.9 |
| 884 | 824 | 710 | −19.7 | 196 | 189 | 199 | 1.5 |
| 2228 | 2028 | 1762 | −20.9 | 749 | 784 | 726 | −3.1 |
| 2269 | 2270 | 2235 | −1.5 | | | | |
| 1066 | 949 | 1007 | −5.5 | 227 | 185 | 217 | −4.4 |
| 3223 | 3260 | 3159 | −2.0 | 84 | 73 | 98 | 16.7 |
| 1610 | 1677 | 1637 | 1.7 | 23 | 15 | 26 | 13.0 |
| 888 | 927 | 905 | 1.9 | 139 | 157 | 142 | 2.2 |
| 66653 | 67137 | 69630 | 4.5 | 977 | 965 | 1109 | 13.5 |
| 3297 | 3101 | 3101 | −5.9 | 53 | 53 | 57 | 7.5 |
| 4433 | 4872 | 5258 | 18.6 | 49 | 53 | 43 | −12.2 |
| 34917 | 36306 | 37609 | 7.7 | 425 | 433 | 541 | 27.3 |
| 1659 | 1737 | 1940 | 16.9 | 0 | 25 | 47 | |
| 46 | 70 | 149 | 223.9 | 1 | 4 | 1 | |
| 3513 | 3500 | 3685 | 4.9 | 215 | 212 | 232 | 7.9 |
| 1456 | 1447 | 1440 | −1.1 | 154 | 151 | 167 | 8.4 |
| 1141 | 1128 | 1217 | 6.7 | 33 | 27 | 20 | −39.4 |
| 294 | 312 | 291 | −1.0 | 16 | 11 | 16 | |
| 143 | 323 | 247 | 72.7 | 4 | 11 | 4 | |
| 6190 | 8070 | 9166 | 48.1 | 251 | 344 | 428 | 70.5 |
| 77187 | 76353 | 77704 | 0.7 | 7473 | 7110 | 6544 | −12.4 |
| 10151 | 10296 | 9585 | −5.6 | 1909 | 2108 | 1865 | −2.3 |
| 10547 | 9311 | 8543 | −19.0 | 239 | 245 | 217 | −9.2 |
| 15558 | 16161 | 18226 | 17.1 | 463 | 477 | 430 | −7.1 |
| 15142 | 13927 | 14948 | −1.3 | 1054 | 944 | 835 | −20.8 |
| 20094 | 21059 | 22693 | 12.9 | 2979 | 2493 | 4181 | 40.3 |
| 562 | 621 | 797 | 41.8 | 106 | 112 | 141 | 33.0 |
| 1514 | 1361 | 1103 | −27.1 | 330 | 446 | 579 | 75.5 |
| 3146 | 2926 | 2839 | −9.8 | 369 | 395 | 481 | 30.4 |
| 440 | 612 | 760 | 72.7 | 23 | 56 | 77 | 234.8 |
| 5078 | 5534 | 6692 | 31.8 | 585 | 722 | 860 | 47.0 |
| 1557 | 1653 | 1815 | 16.6 | 119 | 130 | 162 | 36.1 |
| 2797 | 3075 | 3330 | 19.1 | 319 | 426 | 596 | 86.8 |
| 567 | 602 | 733 | 29.3 | 2 | 10 | 10 | 400.0 |
| 1773 | 1721 | 1847 | 4.2 | 462 | 448 | 411 | −11.0 |
| 1035 | 1018 | 1092 | 5.5 | 214 | 216 | 205 | −4.2 |
| 2776 | 3045 | 2649 | −4.6 | 42 | 53 | 43 | 2.4 |
| 1237 | 1331 | 1365 | 10.3 | 7 | 13 | 16 | 128.6 |
| 14667 | 15579 | 15874 | 8.2 | 1121 | 1188 | 1204 | 7.4 |
| 2176 | 2549 | 2873 | 32.0 | 27 | 26 | 33 | 22.2 |
| 5744 | 6050 | 6400 | 11.4 | 220 | 277 | 283 | 28.6 |
| 6333 | 277 | 244 | −96.1 | 153 | 174 | 178 | 16.3 |

## Degrees Awarded and Trends (Continued)

| | Bachelor | | | |
|---|---|---|---|---|
| | 1984 | 1986 | 1988 | %** |
| Pharmacy (D. Pharm.)* | n/a | n/a | n/a | n/a |
| Optometry (O.D.)* | n/a | n/a | n/a | n/a |
| Dentistry (D.D.S. or D.M.D.)* | n/a | n/a | n/a | n/a |
| Medicine (M.D.)* | n/a | n/a | n/a | n/a |
| Home economics and vocational economics | 16316 | 15288 | 14825 | −9.1 |
| Food science, nutrition | 3399 | 3191 | 2838 | −16.5 |
| Law, total | 1272 | 1197 | 1303 | 2.4 |
| Law (LL.B. or J.D.)* | | | | |
| Letters, total | 33739 | 35434 | 39503 | 17.1 |
| English, general | 23434 | 24352 | 27739 | 18.4 |
| Classics | 429 | 412 | 403 | −6.1 |
| Speech, debate and forensics | 5967 | 6486 | 7131 | 19.5 |
| Library and archival science, total | 255 | 157 | 123 | −51.8 |
| Biology and life sciences, total | 38640 | 38524 | 36761 | −4.9 |
| Mathematics, total | 13211 | 16306 | 15888 | 20.3 |
| Parks and recreation, total | 4752 | 4433 | 4081 | −14.1 |
| Philosophy and religion, total | 6435 | 6239 | 5959 | −7.4 |
| Theology, total | 5914 | 5602 | 5584 | −5.6 |
| Theological professions (B.D., M.Div., Rabbi)* | | | | |
| Physical sciences, total | 23525 | 21620 | 17776 | −24.4 |
| Chemistry, total | 10704 | 10116 | 9025 | −15.7 |
| Geological sciences, total | 6549 | 4974 | 2552 | −61.0 |
| Physics | 3907 | 4180 | 4907 | 4.9 |
| Psychology, total | 39872 | 40521 | 44961 | 12.8 |
| Criminal justice and protective services, total | 12654 | 12704 | 13369 | 5.7 |
| Social work and public affairs, total | 14396 | 13878 | 14232 | −1.1 |
| Public administration | 1643 | 1452 | 1527 | −7.1 |
| Social work | 8824 | 8094 | 8471 | −4.0 |
| Social sciences, total | 93212 | 93703 | 100270 | 7.6 |
| Anthropology | 2693 | 2594 | 2907 | 7.9 |
| Economics | 20719 | 21602 | 22950 | 10.8 |
| Geography | 3195 | 3056 | 2948 | −7.7 |
| History | 16642 | 16413 | 18194 | 9.3 |
| International relations | 2927 | 3418 | 4225 | 44.3 |
| Political science | 25719 | 26439 | 27200 | 5.8 |
| Sociology | 13145 | 12271 | 13000 | −1.1 |
| Fine arts, total | 16210 | 14752 | 15480 | −4.5 |
| Music, total | 7870 | 7175 | 6703 | −14.8 |

SOURCE: National Center for Educational Statistics
* First professional degree
** % change between 1984 and 1988
n/a Not applicable

| Master's | | | | Doctorate | | | |
|---|---|---|---|---|---|---|---|
| 1984 | 1986 | 1988 | %** | 1984 | 1986 | 1988 | %** |
| 709 | 903 | 951 | 34.1 | n/a | n/a | n/a | n/a |
| 1086 | 1029 | 1023 | −5.8 | n/a | n/a | n/a | n/a |
| 5353 | 5046 | 4351 | −18.7 | n/a | n/a | n/a | n/a |
| 15813 | 15938 | 15091 | −4.6 | n/a | n/a | n/a | n/a |
| 2422 | 2298 | 2059 | −15.0 | 279 | 311 | 309 | 10.8 |
| 778 | 678 | 612 | −21.3 | 59 | 62 | 58 | −1.7 |
| 1802 | 1924 | 1880 | 4.3 | 121 | 54 | 89 | −26.4 |
| 37012 | 35844 | 35469 | −4.2 | | | | |
| 5818 | 6291 | 6171 | 6.1 | 1215 | 1215 | 1180 | −2.9 |
| 3500 | 3882 | 3877 | 10.8 | 695 | 710 | 695 | |
| 130 | 146 | 98 | −24.6 | 58 | 49 | 53 | −8.6 |
| 626 | 595 | 586 | −6.4 | 88 | 79 | 69 | −21.6 |
| 3805 | 3626 | 3713 | −2.4 | 74 | 62 | 46 | −37.8 |
| 5406 | 5013 | 4769 | −11.8 | 3437 | 3358 | 3598 | 4.7 |
| 2741 | 3159 | 3423 | 24.9 | 695 | 742 | 752 | 8.2 |
| 555 | 495 | 461 | −16.9 | 27 | 39 | 29 | 7.4 |
| 1153 | 1163 | 1098 | −4.8 | 442 | 477 | 405 | −8.4 |
| 5106 | 4467 | 4775 | −6.5 | 1202 | 1183 | 1207 | 0.4 |
| 6878 | 7283 | 6474 | −5.9 | | | | |
| 5550 | 5896 | 5727 | 3.2 | 3298 | 3551 | 3804 | 15.3 |
| 1667 | 1754 | 1694 | 1.6 | 1744 | 1908 | 1990 | 14.1 |
| 1514 | 1767 | 1530 | 1.1 | 315 | 271 | 350 | 11.1 |
| 1532 | 1501 | 1676 | 9.4 | 953 | 1010 | 1093 | 14.7 |
| 8002 | 8293 | 7862 | −1.7 | 2973 | 3088 | 2988 | 0.5 |
| 1219 | 1074 | 1024 | −16.0 | 31 | 21 | 32 | 3.2 |
| 15373 | 16300 | 17150 | 11.6 | 421 | 385 | 470 | 11.6 |
| 5032 | 4729 | 5180 | 2.9 | 139 | 84 | 106 | −23.7 |
| 8547 | 9101 | 9344 | 9.3 | 227 | 225 | 226 | −0.4 |
| 10465 | 10428 | 10293 | −1.6 | 2911 | 2955 | 2783 | −4.4 |
| 740 | 713 | 696 | −5.9 | 327 | 373 | 304 | −7.0 |
| 1891 | 1937 | 1831 | −3.2 | 729 | 789 | 770 | 5.6 |
| 583 | 564 | 572 | −1.9 | 120 | 131 | 135 | 12.5 |
| 1937 | 1959 | 2092 | 8.0 | 561 | 497 | 519 | −7.5 |
| 1149 | 1332 | 1213 | 5.6 | 63 | 51 | 63 | |
| 1769 | 1704 | 1577 | −10.9 | 457 | 439 | 391 | −14.4 |
| 1008 | 965 | 982 | −2.6 | 520 | 504 | 452 | −13.1 |
| 2819 | 2727 | 2636 | −6.5 | 147 | 154 | 139 | −5.4 |
| 3450 | 3453 | 3192 | −7.5 | 458 | 476 | 502 | 9.6 |

n/a   Not applicable

education is preparation for the certified public accountant (CPA) designation, which is necessary for licensing in a variety of accounting practices.

Without question, training in accounting is one of the best entry tickets to upper-management. Accounting professionals especially shine in the companies Wall Street calls "numbers driven" (as opposed to "marketing driven" or "technology driven"). Wall Street encourages this orientation by adding value to a firm's stock when that firm's forecasts are accurate and its finances tightly controlled.

Most academic programs focus on business settings where "running the numbers" is the key to overall success. Accountants can also specialize in government administration, non-profit organizations, or international business.

A field closely related to accounting is auditing. Rather than carrying the numbers forward to find the profitability or total cost of some project, an auditor works the calculations backwards to check whether all monies are accounted for, and whether the expense or revenue results that an organization announced actually happened.

Public accounting refers to the companies and individuals who provide accounting services for others. A public accountant is usually required to be well versed in a variety of accounting fields, such as taxation, account consolidation, and auditing. It is a definite career boost to have a CPA license, which is granted after passing an examination administered by state-chartered professional organizations.

A third specialization is tax accounting, which entails a thorough understanding of federal and state tax policies. Taxes can potentially absorb a third or more of the revenues of many corporations, as well as the incomes of individuals. Filling out tax forms and developing strategies to minimize tax bills are taught both in school and in seminars that are heavily attended by working accountants.

**Concentrations**

Most accounting programs have the same core of learning about the specifics of accounting practices. At upper-class levels, students have the chance to specialize in various application areas of accounting, such as:

Business accounting
Non-profit accounting
Public accounting
Tax accounting
Financial planning
Banking and finance

**Course Sampler**

**BUS 3501 Managerial Accounting**
Special emphasis is placed on the collection and interpretation of data for managerial decision-making purposes. A study is made of cost concepts used in planning and control, cost-profit-volume analysis, and budgeting.

*(New York Institute of Technology)*

**ACCT 361. Financial Accounting Theory I**
Problems inherent in attempts to measure in quantitative terms the resources and past performance of the corporate entity. Alternative concepts of income and wealth are studied, and their implications for the accounting problems of asset valuation, expiration, and revenue recognition are examined. Critical attention is paid to generally accepted accounting principles and to conventional manner of applying these principles to particular situations.

*(Washington University in St. Louis)*

**MGT 4040. Auditing Concepts**
Problems in certifying financial statements, including audit objectives, statistical approaches to audit scope, and auditing complex computerized data systems.

*(Georgia Institute of Technology)*

**Assessment**

A recent graduate of Kings College (Wilkes-Barre, PA) has found his groove at one of the major public-accounting firms. Having worked for 3 years as an auditor, he now handles personnel, re-cruiting, and office-management functions at a branch office. "In a way, I'm acting as an internal auditor for my own firm," he notes, because he handles the books for the local office's budget.

He started college with the intention of becoming a lawyer, but decided that accounting would be a more direct route to a job and a career, at least until he made up his mind about attending law school. "If you're a good student, you can usually count on a half-dozen job offers when you graduate," he says.

College training got his auditing career off to a fast start. "The thing I learned, and that I look for in new graduates that I hire, is a healthy skepticism about what you see in a financial record or plan. It's not that you're looking for improper results, but that you provide a correct assessment of what you are examining."

He found the accounting training rigorous at college, and says that auditing is not easy work, "but the experience is invaluable." Accounting graduates, especially those with experience at a public accounting firm, inevitably move into management positions at corporations when they choose to leave accounting. "You give up a little bit of the breadth of training that a business administration major may have initially, but you make up for it quickly in the more rigorous analysis that accountants do."

At another major public-accounting firm, a woman sees her work experience as a stepping-stone to an eventual position as a controller or financial officer. She combined undergraduate schooling in economics with an accounting option at Rutgers University, earned her CPA, and has worked as an auditor and planner. "Even with my background, fully 40% of my work is writing and communicating," she says. Now that she is no longer involved in detailed number-crunching, the additional economics courses she took have been valuable, especially the writing requirements.

She also looks back on her schooling to remember the cases that her professors studied with the class. "The experience the teachers injected into the coursework is very relevant to what I do now," she says.

**Career Options**

**Accountant,** of course!

**Actuary,** with the additional training required for employment in the insurance industry.

**Bank administrator**

**Business administrator,** and when an undergraduate degree in accounting is combined with an MBA, employment prospects are even brighter.

**Compensation analyst**

**Cost estimator**

Financial analyst
Financial planner
Insurance agent
Management consultant
Public administrator
Purchasing agent
Stockbroker
Underwriter

---

# ALLIED HEALTH PROFESSIONS

### (Medical Technology, Physical Therapy, Pharmacy, Health-Services Administration, Nursing, Public Health, and others)

| | | 1983 | 1985 | 1988 |
|---|---|---|---|---|
| **Enrollment** | BS or BA | 64,614 | 64,513 | 60,095 |
| **Boxscore** | Master's | 17,068 | 17,383 | 18,523 |
| | PhD | 1,155 | 1,199 | 1,247 |

**Overview**

In general, "allied health professionals" in hospitals, clinics, or private practices have more training than technicians or attendants, and less than doctors or nurses (there are, of course, exceptions). They are part of our $660 billion-plus national health-care system which consumes 11.5% of the Gross National Product and employs about 7.5 million workers. The largest groups of allied health-care professionals are the therapists, pharmacists, health-services administrators, and laboratory technicians. Schooling ranges from a 1- or 2-year associate degree program at a community college, to 4-year bachelor programs, graduate schools, post-graduate work, internships, and medical research.

The size and costs of the health-care industry has grown inexorably over the past decade, and this growth has naturally drawn growing numbers of college graduates. While there has been strong job growth among doctors and surgeons, growth among the occupations that assist doctors, or that administer medical or hospital programs, has been even more dramatic. Future growth among many of the allied health professions tops the charts among the occupations that the Bureau of Labor Statistics monitors.

In general, educational preparation for allied health professions combines scientific courses with extensive internships or field work. For some programs, the level of scientific training is roughly the equivalent of the first year of medical school. Upper-class courses focus more closely on the type of medical service the student aspires to. Liberal arts courses in communications, literature, or social sciences round out the programs.

The issue of certification or licensing is central to actual professional practice. Following the internships (which are usually graded), the aspiring allied health professional must take a written examination for licensure or certification. There are variations from state to state in these procedures, although in certain professions cross-licensing among states has been set up. Finally the allied health professional must keep in mind that completion of a four year program is only the beginning of the learning experience; refresher courses or new training is often required to keep certification current, and to move ahead in one's profession.

**Concentrations**

**Therapy,** which includes **Occupational, Physical, Speech and Rehabilitative Therapy** and **Audiology.** Each focuses on a different aspect of injury or handicap. The therapist helps a patient recover from a temporary physical disability or adjust to a permanent condition.

**Pharmacy,** which focuses on the function and dosages of medications; with graduate-level training, pharmacy (often called pharmacology) becomes involved in researching new types of medications.

**Health-Services Administration,** the management of hospitals and other health-care facilities. The training is a mixture of basic medical technology and business administration.

**Laboratory Technology,** which provides training in operating diagnostic and therapeutic equipment. This field has become heavily dependent on microelectronics and computers.

**Course Sampler**

**MT 495 Clinical Chemistry**
Enzymology, endocrinology, biochemistry of lipids, carbohydrates, and proteins, metabolism of nitrogenous end products, physiology and

metabolism of fluids and electrolytes, and toxicology as related to the body and diseases. The technical procedures includes colorimetry, spectrophotometry, electrophoresis, chromatography, automation, and quality control.

*(Indiana University of Pennsylvania)*

### HCM 4450. Health Care Policy

The course will examine the process by which health-care policy is formulated and implemented. Specific examples of major health-care policy issues will be drawn from federal and state sectors and will focus on personnel, financing, and health-care program development. Other critical policy issues to be examined through case studies will include genetic engineering, organ transplantation, and service competition. The impact of health-care policy will be examined through site visitation at institution or program levels.

*(Appalachian State University)*

### HPER 165. Adapted Physical Education

Selection and adaptation of activities to meet the individual needs of atypical children, the orthopedically disabled, the blind, the deaf, the mentally retarded, and emotionally disturbed. Field trips to nearby institutions specializing in the education of atypical children.

*(Hofstra University)*

**Assessment**

"Physical therapy has changed quite a lot since I was in college," says Dennis Surdi who, together with his wife, own and operate Harriet and Dennis Surdi Physical Therapists in New York. Mr. Surdi studied physical education as an undergraduate, then took an intensive master's-level program at New York University, from which he graduated in 1974. He followed that educational training with work at hospitals, nursing homes, and outpatient-care facilities, and opened his own practice in 1980. His firm provides rehabilitative training to injured or disabled people in a comprehensive facility that contains exercise machinery and specialized treatment equipment.

The academic training was "top-notch," according to Mr. Surdi, because the New York University department does extensive research. "Being exposed to teachers and practitioners at the forefront of physical therapy has been a big help to me, because of all the changes in the profession over the past decade," he says. In particular, the growth of health and exercise clubs—and the general increase in interest in exercise—has caused a specialty in sports medicine therapy to come into being. This, in turn, has broadened the appeal of physical therapy beyond the traditional patient who needs rehabilitation to recover from a disease or injury. For many people, physical therapy is now a normal part of a health and exercise program.

"It is now possible to specialize in a broad array of therapies," concludes Mr. Surdi, pointing out such specializations as neurological therapy, pediatrics, orthopedics, geriatrics, and obstetrics. "The academic training I had has enabled me to keep up with these new areas by providing the basics of physical therapy."

Physical therapy was the start of a career for a 1981 graduate from the University of Wisconsin (Madison), but his career has stretched far beyond that field. "I majored in therapy because I wanted to work with people in a helping role," he says, "but after a year of working as a physical therapist, I found that I was too impatient for results." What was successful for him though, was exposure through his internships to the loss control department of a hospital, where efforts are made to reduce the insurance costs of running the hospital by minimizing risky activities. Such "risk management" consulting spurred him to study insurance and risk management at the graduate business school at Wisconsin, from which he graduated in 1985.

After graduation, he went to the Washington, DC area, where he found plenty of opportunities working with federal consulting firms that were gearing up for a major effort in environmental regulation. All through the 1980s, the US Environmental Protection Agency, industrial manufacturers, and the insurance industry were working out methods to provide insurance coverage for activities related to the cleanup of hazardous waste sites and the disposal of toxic materials. People with a background in risk management were in high demand.

"I get about three or four calls a month from headhunters offering very substantial employment opportunities, but I'm quite happy where I am." His firm, at which he is a program director, has grown from 50 to over 300 employees in the past 5 years. "My undergraduate training in physical therapy is useful in several ways in my current work," he says. "The curriculum required quite a few science courses, which are valuable in environmental work. The training in medical recording—keeping accurate records of treatment procedures—turned me into a good writer, and that is critical to the reports, proposals, and bids that I'm involved in every day."

**Career Options**

Most of these academic programs directly prepare one for jobs in health-care, such as **medical technologist** or **physical therapist**. In addition, there are potential career possibilities as:

**Business-to-business salesperson,** especially for medical equipment and services.

**Corporate trainer,** usually in services such as "wellness" programs sponsored by corporations for their employees.

**Experiential educator,** in which physical exercise or therapy is combined with education, especially for children and adolescents.

**Health-service administrator,** particularly when graduate schooling in that discipline is obtained.

# ANTHROPOLOGY

|  |  | 1983 | 1985 | 1988 |
|---|---|---|---|---|
| **Enrollment** | BS or BA | 2,806 | 2,625 | 2,907 |
| **Boxscore** | Master's | 788 | 742 | 696 |
|  | PhD | 369 | 343 | 304 |

**Overview**

Anthropology is the study of humans, especially their physical and cultural heritages. Mention "anthropologist" to most people and they will think of someone like Margaret Mead, who won fame a half-century ago explaining how Samoan children grow up.

Traditionally, PhD anthropologists have sailed off to faraway islands or traveled through hard-to-reach mountain passes to live with, study, and report on primitive cultures. Today, however, anthropological training is being successfully applied by marketing managers in Fortune 500 companies, by advertising agency executives, international bankers, and human-resources managers. Especially when it comes to modern cultures, anthropology has many similarities to sociology (see SOCIOLOGY), and at some schools, the two fields are combined.

Anthropological training was first applied to business problems 40 years ago, according to Dr. Marietta Baba, a professor of anthropology at Wayne State University (Detroit, MI) and one of the leaders of today's "business anthropology" movement. Back then, she says, anthropologists helped manufacturers and the US government develop organizational practices for managing large staffs of workers or military units.

Increasing numbers of students were attracted to departments of anthropology through the late 1960s, when academic postings dried up. At that point, some enterprising—and probably desperate—anthropology students started striking out for new employment opportunities. Over the past two decades, anthropologists have proven their value in international marketing and advertising, especially when helping US multi-nationals market their products in other countries. Management consulting is another fruitful employment opportunity. More theoretically oriented, anthropologists are also helping such high-tech companies as Xerox (Rochester, NY) develop advanced programming techniques that help computers "think." Because many computer-programming principles are derived from logical, but human, thought processes, the expectation is that by understanding human thought processes more thoroughly, new and improved programming techniques can be developed.

A key element of the undergraduate education is fieldwork—taking a project or theme out into the world to study it in detail. This fieldwork harkens back to the days of classical anthropology, when a lone scientist would traipse to a remote location to live with a tribe, learn its language and customs, and later, report on their world view. Today, anthropology students live with, and write about, cultures located all over the world, including inner cities, factories, and offices. The powers of observation and analysis required by such field projects are often looked upon as formative experience for college students.

**Concentrations**

**Cultural Anthropology,** which focuses on social structures, cultural customs, and historical trends. Cultural anthropologists used to study only primitive cultures, believing that we could gain insight into our common heritage as humans only through studying cultures untouched by modern life. Some anthropologists still hold to that belief, but others are studying modern societies as well, including groups like corporations and governments.

**Physical or Biological Anthropology,** which examines the effects of environment on humans and puts ethnic groups into categories. Much insight is gained in physical anthropology by studying the skeletal remains of past generations. The heart of physical anthropology is "ethnographic" study—the description of various races and their physical characteristics. The investigation of human evolution also falls under the umbrella of physical anthropology.

**Archaeology,** which is exclusively the study of the cultures of the past. An archaeologist digs or explores to find traces of ancient cultures, and derives information on food-gathering, social structure, and customs from them.

**Linguistics,** the study of language: how it affects culture, and how a culture shapes it. Usually, a concentration in linguistics requires the study of a non-Western foreign language, in order to see more clearly how cultural differences can be analyzed by studying language.

**Course Sampler**

**ANTH 0100 Introduction to Cultural Anthropology**
People as both cultural and social beings; development of a systematic perspective on the nature of culture and the organization of social relations; the use of culture as a non-biological means of adapting to physical and social environments through, for example, language, technology, kinship, and religion. An examination of both Western and non-Western peoples and the different ways of life they represent.

*(University of Denver)*

**217j Race and Ethnicity: Cross-Cultural Perspectives**
An introduction to the main theories that attempt to explain race and ethnicity, including the notion that both are social and not biological entities. An examination of case studies from around the New World,

which reflect the ways that different socio-economic, political, and historical structuring contexts encourage varying forms of racial and ethnic identification. Application of principles derived from this study to understanding racial and ethnic interaction and tension in the contemporary United States.

*(Colby College)*

### 329 The Nature of Language

Language as a reflection of the human mind, and the role of language in defining the essence of humanity. Language and the expression of social values. Emphasis on analysis of primary linguistic data. Critical examination of theories of linguistic structure.

*(Tulane University)*

**Assessment**

A PhD anthropologist from New York University uses her training in a new way: helping firms determine how to market consumer goods. Employed at a market-research firm in New York, she and her co-workers win a contract from a consumer-goods firm to analyze a particular market trend—say, the use of household cleaning compounds. Then, through observation in the typical consumer's home and through interviews, general trends are uncovered that could indicate what new types of products would receive a favorable reception. Another discovery might indicate that a significant number of consumers are using the product in a way unexpected by the manufacturer; by altering its marketing and advertising programs, the manufacturer might be able to introduce this use to more consumers and therefore win more customers for its products. A key part of the investigation process is the "focus group." A carefully selected group of consumers is brought into a room and holds a discussion under the guidance of one of the researchers. The discussion might be recorded or filmed. Later, the research team confers to analyze the results.

"I've always been interested in business," she says, noting that she had worked on Wall Street as a stockbroker before taking this job. "This type of work allows me to combine my interest in cultural analysis—which was the reason that I studied anthropology—with my interest in business."

The arts can be another home for an anthropologist—as they are for Gary Dawson, a jewelry designer in Eugene, OR, who graduated from the University of Oregon in 1982 with a BA in anthropology. Gary designs and fabricates gold and gemstone jewelry that he sells at craft shows and from a storefront. "I see my work as an extension of my interest in anthropology," he says. "I use ancient techniques which tie me into the past, and I feel that my designs are both an outgrowth of, and influence on, current culture." As an operator of a small business, he points out that he must wear many hats—a salesperson's, a business manager's, a manufacturer's:  I think the interpersonal skills learned in anthropology classes were important training for me."

**Career Options**

College professor, liberal arts
Foreign language teacher
Human-resources manager
Job counselor (when specific counseling training is obtained).
Journalist
Management consultant, particularly with regard to human-resources issues.
Marketing manager, especially when additional coursework in business is obtained.
Marketing researcher
Media planner, and similar statistics-rich professions, assuming that one has spent extensive time analyzing data while studying anthropology.
Vocational teacher

# ARCHITECTURE AND URBAN DESIGN

### (Interior Design, Environmental Design, Landscape Architecture)

| | | 1983 | 1985 | 1988 |
|---|---|---|---|---|
| **Enrollment** | BS or BA | 9,823 | 9,325 | 8,606 |
| **Boxscore** | Master's | 3,357 | 3,275 | 3,159 |
| | PhD | 97 | 89 | 98 |

**Overview**    Shelter is one of the fundamental necessities of humans, and as a result, architecture has been a basic professional interest for centuries. In today's society—and on today's college campuses—the decisions about how a building should appear are greatly affected by its immediate environment, whether it be an office skyscraper in a city's center or a shopping mall in suburbia. Thus, there are new programs in urban planning, which introduce the traditions of city planning and new theories of how to address the social, commercial, and physical needs of cities and other populated areas.

Just as the relationship between the exterior of a building and its environment has come under more scrutiny, so has the relationship between the outside of a building and its inside. More attention is being paid to interior design, and architects are learning, both professionally and academically, to work more closely with interior designers.

The requirements for the practice of architecture are very specific. Licensing is required early. Schools offering architecture degrees have a 5-year professional program that prepares students directly both for employment and for the licensing examinations that are required for professional work in many states. Other schools offer a 4-year program (sometimes called architectural technology), which does not lead as directly to employment as an architect (some of these graduates work as architectural assistants; some go on to earn a master's degree).

Both architects and interior designers must be skilled in design and drawing. Their rigorous training in design can often be applied to widely different lines of work, such as industrial design, product design, and art or fashion writing and criticism. Architects spend a lot of time studying materials and construction techniques; interior designers study the materials for furnishing rooms or interior spaces.

Architecture students spend an enormous amount of time at the drafting table, developing structural designs. Programs in interior design and urban studies offer the more usual college experience of attending classes, doing research in the library, and taking tests.

In urban planning, economics, political science, and other social sciences form the basis for an understanding of how cities work and how people live together. The perspective of real estate developers is also analyzed. Career paths range from civil service, to real estate sales or development, to social services.

| | |
|---|---|
| **Concentrations** | **Architecture,** on a 4- or 5-year plan. |

**Concentrations**

**Architecture,** on a 4- or 5-year plan.
**Architecture Technology,** which can focus on construction technology, computer-aided design, and building design.
**Urban Planning,** sometimes labelled **Urban Studies.**
**Interior Design**

**Course Sampler**

**ARCH 4601-2-3. Architectural Design Studio I, II, II**
Introductory studio problems in architectural design with an emphasis on architectural representation, history, morphology, and technology and their relationships.

*(Georgia Institute of Technology)*

**Arch 235. Architectural Graphics**
The study of architectural graphic theory and practice:   an examination of the relationship between architectural design and early sketches, the reinforcement of architectural memory through the sketching of important artifacts, and the more refined graphic presentations of developed designs. Drawing types include the referential sketch, the first design sketch, the study drawing, and final presentation formats.

*(Washington University in St. Louis)*

**V99.0232 Law and Urban Problems**
Examines the interrelationship between the legal process and some of the major urban problems facing New York City. An interdisciplinary introduction to the law as it interacts with society. An analysis is made of problems in such areas as housing, zoning, welfare, and consumer affairs, emphasizing the underlying social, economic, and political causes of the problems, and the responses made by the laws and courts. Readings are drawn from the law and social science. No specific knowledge of law is required.

*(New York University)*

**Assessment**

"I was exposed to building management early in my life, because my parents are owners of a number of buildings where I grew up," says Kate Hewlitt, a 1983 graduate of Hartwick College. "I helped out with renovating them, including complete gutting, doing construction labor, and overseeing a crew. She took an independent studies program and received what amounts to a degree in urban studies. Now she works as the assistant manager of a large condominium association in Chicago, handling the building's needs and overseeing the suppliers and contractors that provide services.

"The courses on business and budgeting that I took are a help to me in my work," she says. "At the time I was in school, I thought that a science class that I was required to take—geology —was a complete waste of time. But now, when a contractor shows me problems with the stone walls in the complex, I can understand what he's talking about."

One architect in Los Angeles studied architecture as an undergraduate, and then urban planning as a graduate. His firm now specializes in designing large commercial complexes, such as a combined commercial/retail/hotel complex in California, and a hospital complex in Utah. "My interests have always been with how a building relates to its environment, and that's one of the reasons I chose to study urban planning," he says. He also studied in Japan, where he honed this sense of buildings and their environment. The success of his firm, which is relatively small, in obtaining large, complex, design projects hinges, in part, on the quality of his planning.

If you believe that the bosky, tree-laden lawns that adorn your college campus just happened, then you haven't met a professional like Dennis Nola. Mr. Nola, whose title is Assistant Director of the Campus Development Office of the University of Maryland, is a landscape architect. At the university, he deals day in and day out with a staff of designers, with construction crews and contractors, and with the administration on the university. On his own, he is a partner in a design consulting firm, Gemini Group, Inc., that specializes in landscape architecture for recreational facilities such as golf courses.

Mr. Nola, a 1979 graduate from Pennsylvania State University sums up his college education this way: "I'd say I learned about 40% of what I need to know to be a good landscape architect while in college." In particular, the problems of actually constructing what one has designed, and those of dealing with clients, selection committees, and vendors, are not evident to the student.

After school, he worked for a couple of years as a landscape architect for the Maryland Department of Highways and then moved on to the University of Maryland. His projects included developing athletic facilities, walkways, and parking facilities, and maintaining the trees and plants that adorn the campus. "What I *did* learn in school was how to solve problems creatively," he stresses. "Landscape architecture is a combination of aesthetic judgment and the practicalities of what can physically be done, and what the budget contraints are. It's an interesting mix of the logic of science and the creativity of the artist."

**Career Options**

Architect
Art director
Commercial artist
Designer, industrial and fashion
Designer, interior
Horticulturist
Landscape architect
Mortgage banker, especially when one has obtained additional training or work experience in real estate.
Photographer
Property manager
Public administrator
Real estate sales broker
Regional planner
Urban planner

# ART HISTORY

| | | 1983 | 1985 | 1988 |
|---|---|---|---|---|
| **Enrollment** | BS or BA | 1,739 | 1,693 | 1,911 |
| **Boxscore** | Master's | 382 | 401 | 386 |
| | PhD | 112 | 105 | 97 |

**Overview**

A culture's nature is often best revealed by its art. Art historians apply that principle when comparing past eras in Western history or when relating Western forms of thought and feeling with those of other cultures.

That's the academic perspective on art history. For students, art history programs offer a means of immersing themselves in cultural and aesthetic issues. Some students want to pursue careers as curators or archivists at the many museums and galleries across the nation. Others, knowing that they have an eye for art and design, but lacking the interest in pursuing a career as an artist, use art history to hone their intellectual abilities in art for careers in media, advertising, publishing, fashion, or design. Bear in mind, though, that some art history programs require courses in studio art.

Yet another career path for art historians is art therapy, working with handicapped or disabled people. There is a trend toward providing additional training and certification for this specialty.

Many colleges provide art history training in conjunction with nearby galleries or museums. Many of these schools, and schools distant from such cultural settings, have art history departments which offer extensive internships in other parts of the country—or abroad. Thus, art history can be a ticket to travel and to familiarity with other cultures. A few schools combine art history and archaeology, so that one can study the art of the past or the present.

The general perception is that art history is significantly less difficult to study than most other majors. That can be a problem, as some businesspeople believe that it is too lightweight a factor for serious professionals. On the other hand, the extra time leaves students open to the many other opportunities college has to offer, ranging from internships to extracurricular activities.

**Concentrations**

Depending on the school, art history may be available as a BA degree or as a BFA (Bachelor in Fine Arts). Art history programs are dominated by survey courses that cover the eras of art (prehistoric, ancient, medieval, Renaissance, Baroque, and modern, plus the art of various non-Western cultures), followed by upper-level courses on specific periods or cultures. Concentrations include:

**Museum Studies,** focusing on the structure and operation of museums and other repositories of art, leading to curatorship or museum administration.
**History of Architecture,** which traces the traditions and influences

of architecture and can lead to teaching, criticism, or curatorial work.

**Art Therapy,** which teaches how to provide therapy for the very young, the aged, or the mentally ill. Usually advanced schooling and state licensing are required.

**Arts Administration,** preparing students to be administrators for schools, local and federal governments, and private organizations that deliver artistic experiences to students or the public.

**Course Sampler**

**ARTH 3851 Museum Method**
Basic problems of administration, cataloguing, and storage; field trips to local museums; readings and research on collections, historical backgrounds, and philosophies of museums.

*(University of Denver)*

**Art-Arch 455 Topics in Medieval Art and Architecture:   Art of the Medieval Courts**
From Charlemagne to Avignon and the Dukes of Berry and Burgundy. An investigation of art and secular leaders of the Middle Ages. Art as propaganda in the earlier Middle Ages; art as a reflection of the courtly circles of the later Middle Ages.

*(Washington University in St. Louis)*

**185. Contemporary Art:   1940–1980s**
Survey of contemporary developments in the arts from the events leading to Abstract Expressionism to the present, including photography, performance, and the more traditional arts of painting, sculpture, and architecture. Lecture course with field trips.

*(Santa Clara University)*

**Assessment**

"I chose art history for the wrong reason—because it was easy," says one 1980 graduate from Kenyon College. Even so, she says, "I gained psychological insights into people, maturity, and cultural and historical knowledge. And I improved my ability to write well and concisely."

After earning an MBA, she started a career as a business consultant involved in financial analysis, future cash flows, and business research. "Business school was much more vocationally-oriented than my undergraduate schooling. That's where I learned financial analysis and computer software. That has been a big help to me."

Art, replaced by art history, was the point of departure for Donald Anderley, associate director at a major museum on the West Coast. "I certainly wasn't planning at the outset to land up where I am today, but when I come to terms with the fact that I lacked the talent to be a professional artist, I still knew that I had a profound interest in art," he recalls.

Mr. Anderley won a position as a technical assistant for a slide library of art at the New York Public Library, and after several years' experience, studied library science at the graduate level. That, in turn, led to the museum directorship, where his days are spent as an administrator, coordinating the activities of researchers, visiting specialists, and staff personnel. The number of books and documents he is responsible for has grown twentyfold over the past 6 years. "There is no question that, at least for my branch of library science, a background in art and art history is essential. You have to have a knowledge of the subject in order to be a good curator or administrator."

Another art history graduate, Eugenie Vasser (Tulane, 1979), sees connections between what she studied and her current occupation as owner/operator of Flagons, a hot new bistro in New Orleans. While attending school, and for a time afterwards, she worked in a number of galleries in the city. That experience led to a position selling newspaper advertising, and then an advertising agency job, both of which made her familiar with the dynamics of retailing in New Orleans. "Art history teaches a certain level of worldliness or culture," is her assessment. "That helps with the running of the bistro—to know what sophisticated customers will expect in the way of service and cuisine. I also think that my art history background guided me in furnishing and decorating the bistro; the ambiance of a bistro is very important to its success."

**Career Options**

Advertising account executive
Art director
Association executive
Consumer-goods salesperson
Designer, industrial and fashion

Design, interior
Editor, book
Editor, magazine
Executive search consultant
Information specialist, particularly if academic training concentrated on library research.
Journalist
Librarian
Marketing manager
Photographer
Publicist
Travel planner
Vocational teacher

# BIOLOGICAL SCIENCES

### (Biochemistry, Botany, Microbiology, Physiology, Zoology)

| | | 1983 | 1985 | 1988 |
|---|---|---|---|---|
| **Enrollment** | BS or BA | 39,982 | 38,445 | 36,761 |
| **Boxscore** | Master's | 5,696 | 5,059 | 4,769 |
| | PhD | 3,341 | 3,432 | 3,598 |

**Overview**

Biology is the study of life. Since life appears in such a dizzying array of forms, biology has become specialized into dozens of categorics, from biochemistry to zoology. At the undergraduate level, and among working biologists, the cellular level of life dominates —microbiology. Microbiology offers a window to most of the world of biology, because many of the principles that control all forms of life can be bound among single-cell plants and animals; these cells are also fairly easy to study (they're small, reproduce rapidly, and eat inexpensive nutrients.)

Besides studying biology for its own sake, students enter biology programs to prepare for medical school. In fact, biology can also lay a foundation for many other health-care careers:   public health-care administration, veterinary science, nursing, physical therapy, agriculture, animal husbandry, and nutrition. The growing emphasis on environmental preservation is creating another career path for biologists: conservation, wildlife study, and occupational safety.

Besides health-care and the environment, there are several other general career areas for biologists. Many teach at the high school or college level. Also, the large industry that delivers health-care products—from pharmaceuticals to hospital supplies to instrumentation for scientific research—seeks biology graduates for manufacturing, marketing, and sales positions. The familiarity with the technical aspects of these products is an advantage for the biology graduate. Finally, a biologist's experience is setting up experiments, running instrumentation, and reporting results is obviously helpful in a wide range of research careers.

**Concentrations**

The most general distinctions in biology are among plant biology, animal biology, and human biology. There are dozens of specialties within these three groups. Many undergraduate programs provide one or two courses in each specialty, leaving the detailed coursework to the graduate schools. The most common specialties are:

**Molecular biology,** the study of the ways in which biologically derived molecules like DNA function and carry out specific tasks in organisms. Molecular biology is the central discipline of the booming industry of biotechnology (gene-splicing).

**Biochemistry,** the study of the chemical basis of life. Living cells have been likened to miniature chemical factories; biochemists study these chemical reactions.

**Genetics,** the study of how organisms reproduce and pass on hereditary information from one generation to the next. A subspecialty is **Cytogenetics,** which examines the detailed cellular changes during reproduction. Because of this emphasis on abnormalities in cellular growth and reproduction, cytogenetics is a key avenue of cancer research.

**Pathology,** the study of the genetic or environmental causes of diseases and other abnormalities in plants, animals, or humans.

**Botany,** the study of plants—their structure, interrelationships, diseases and applications.

**Entomology,** the study of insects.

**Ornithology,** the study of birds.

**Herpetology,** the study of reptiles.

**Paleontology,** the study of ancient life forms through analyzing fossil records.

**Microbiology,** the study of bacteria, germs and other single-celled life forms.

**Ichthyology,** the study of fish.

**Zoology,** the study of the higher life forms, except humans. Zoologists are often employed to administer zoos. A subspecialty of zoology concerned with apes and other human-like animals is **Primatology.**

**Mycology,** the study of fungi.

**Marine Biology,** the study of life forms and systems in aquatic environments. A subspecialty is **Limnology,** the biology of inland (fresh) waters.

**Ecology,** the study of systems of organisms and how they interact with their environment. Because of the growing concern over environmental quality, ecology is in the spotlight these days.

**Course Sampler**

**Biology 203 Comparative Anatomy**
We will compare the development and evolution of major anatomical features of vertebrates from fish to mammals, using preserved sharks, mud-puppies, and cats. The course will emphasize lab work, and students should provide their own dissecting equipment.

*(Bard College)*

**CLA BI 420 Principles of Biochemistry**
Survey of major topic areas of biochemistry. Protein structure determination, enzymology. Nucleic acid structure and synthesis; regulation of gene expression and protein biosynthesis. Bioenergetics, photosynthesis, and the metabolism of carbohydrates, lipids, and selected amino acids.

*(Boston University)*

**429 Marine Biology**
Biological processes in marine and estuarine habitats, and adaptations for life in sea; emphasis on environmental variables affecting distribution, abundance, and dynamics of marine organisms. Includes

12-day field trip to tropical marine environment during spring break and 5-day field trip to temperate marine environment late in [quarter].

*(Ohio University)*

## V23.0063 Introduction to Ecology

Basic ecological principles and concepts, including ecological relationship within ecosystems, energy flow, biogeochemical cycles, limiting factors, community ecology, population ecology, niche, climax, and major ecological habitats, are discussed. These topics are related to current environmental problems such as resource management, pollution, radiation, and human ecology.

*(New York University)*

**Assessment**

"I became interested in biological science as I felt that it was a science that could give me an insight into life and its meaning," recalls Michael Blotzer, an industrial hygienist who works for the US Department of Labor, Occupational Safety and Health Administration, in Augusta, ME. This federal agency is concerned with regulating and overseeing the safety of manufacturing and other types of work in which the risks of injury or death are high.

A 1973 BS graduate from Pennsylvania State University, Mr. Blotzer says that since he enjoyed biology as "knowledge for knowledge's sake," he continued his studies, earning a master's degree in molecular biology from Vanderbilt University in 1975. "Through my work I identify conditions that can hurt, maim, kill, or cause diseases in workers, and then work to get the conditions changed to minimize the hazard and protect the life and livelihood of the worker," he says, adding that "[my] academic training helps me to ask questions that cut to the heart of a problem."

A 1979 graduate of McGill University (Montreal) uses his training in physiology in an unusual way: he's an independent consultant to developers of medical monitoring equipment, helping develop the technology to provide more efficient patient monitoring through the use of sophisticated electronics. "My father was a doctor, but I was never that keen in following in his footsteps," he recalls. "I took lots of math courses as an undergraduate, as well as biology and physiology. For a master's degree, I continued my studies in physiology, and got very interested in using mathematical models to study the human mind."

As a result of this program, he became involved with several research projects using computers in conjunction with monitoring equipment. Today he works as a consultant in New York, where he is helping several medical laboratories with monitoring technology.

"To do this work, you need to have a good understanding of how the mind works, which physiology provided. Much of the neurophysiology I use now was self-taught, but that came after the basic training." In the future, he says, his work may take him more in the direction of electronic software development (such as interactive computer programs), where "the chance to be artistic as well as scientific" is available.

**Career Options**

**Business-to-business salesperson,** especially for medical, pharmaceutical or other health-care products for humans and for agriculture.

**Chemist,** especially dealing with biochemistry, occupational safety, or agriculture.

**College professor, science and technology**

**Chemical engineer,** in food, pharmaceutical, or cosmetic production management.

**Dentist,** following dental school.

**Earth (planetary) scientist**

**Ecologist**

**Food scientist/technologist**

**Horticulturist**

**Journalist**

**Life scientist**

**Medical technologist**

**Microbiologist**

**Optometrist,** following advanced schooling.

**Pharmacist**

**Physiologist**

**Physician (medical doctor)**

**Technical writer**

**Veterinarian**

# BUSINESS ADMINISTRATION

### (Banking and Finance, Business Economics, Labor Relations, Marketing, and others [not including Accounting])

|  | | 1983 | 1985 | 1988 |
|---|---|---|---|---|
| **Enrollment** | BS or BA | 174,393 | 178,508 | 192,590 |
| **Boxscore** | Master's | 62,199 | 64,254 | 66,329 |
|  | PhD | 743 | 805 | 1,051 |

**Overview**

The popularity of business administration among undergraduate and graduate students has soared in the past decade. The reason is readily apparent: a business administration degree offers direct preparation for a wide range of jobs in accounting, sales, marketing, management, production, customer service, and employee relations.

The rap against business administration is that it doesn't provide the same broad base of knowledge as most liberal arts degrees do. But just as many liberal arts students take some business courses to increase their attractiveness to employers, business administration students can hedge their bets by choosing a liberal arts minor or by taking a series of related liberal arts courses.

There are two general statements to make about business administration programs. First, practically all of them require at least a year's worth of accounting courses. There is often a separate track for an accounting degree (see ACCOUNTING).

Secondly, more programs are exposing their students to the business uses of computers. There are still plenty of experienced businesspeople who avoid computers like the plague, and will do so for the remainder of their careers. For new entrants to the job market, however, familiarity with computer technology and information systems is essential. Luckily, computers are getting not just more powerful, but also easier to use.

**Concentrations**     College and universities take many approaches to business administration. The most comprehensive programs have a School of Business, offering bachelor of business administration degrees with a wide range of specializations. Other schools offer a bachelor of arts or bachelor of science degree with a specialization in business administration. Some schools have separate programs for subjects like international business, hospital administration, public administration, marketing and advertising; others simply offer courses on those topics in the general business administration school.

At the graduate level, the options expand dramatically. Schools of business have been very aggressive in developing programs for very specific types of business activity. Thus, a close perusal of school catalogs will uncover programs in banking, finance, media management, entrepreneurship, direct marketing, manufacturing technology, information systems, agricultural management, and so on.

If there is an aspect of commerce or industry that can be identified, there is usually some school that offers a program concentrating on it. A close perusal of school catalogs will uncover programs like:

**Banking and finance**
**Media management**
**Entrepreneurship**
**Direct marketing**
**Manufacturing technology**
**Information systems**
**Hotel or travel management**

**Course Sampler**     FIN 335 Managerial Finance
Advanced-level exposure to capital budgeting decisions, cost of capital, working capital management, and mergers and acquisitions. Deals with current theory and practice of corporate finance.

*(Western Kentucky University)*

**Marketing 313 Channels of Distribution**
Studies the channels by which goods flow from the manufacturer to ultimate consumer; includes an examination of wholesalers, retailers, manufacturer's representatives, agents, etc. Evaluates the impact of

distribution policies on marketing mix, product design, pricing, and target segments.

*(Fashion Institute of Technology)*

## MGT 6325 Product Planning
Study of new-product development process. Use of market research data and marketing models for product design, test marketing, product positioning, market segmentation, market share estimation, and product portfolio management.

*(Georgia Institute of Technology)*

## BA 366 Organizational Behavior
An integrated and interdisciplinary study of behavioral science for management. The course attempts to integrate the psychological and sociological aspects of human behavior as they relate to management. Focus is on individual, group, and organizational behavior. Topics include communication, motivation, group dynamics, leadership, power, reward systems, organizational structure, and managing conflict and change.

*(Pepperdine University)*

**Assessment**

"I wasn't sure which way to go with my career, except that I knew I wanted to do something in business," says Scott Helland, a 1985 business-administration graduate of Kings College. "This was a good way to leave my options open."

Mr. Helland now works with a major Wall Street investment firm as a financial consultant, helping individuals select savings and investment plans. "I took courses in finance, economics, and general business management." His education gave him the knowledge necessary to pass the Series 7 examination required by the National Association of Securities Dealers of brokers and investment agents dealing in securities. "There was a lot of stock market terminology that I had been exposed to in college that made the examination fairly straightforward for me."

"Market research is the field that I'm most interested in," says Sarah Webber, a 1989 graduate of Salem State College with a degree in marketing. "I've worked all through school, and have come to know that I don't want to work for a big corporation, but I will enjoy the chance to specialize in marketing research." Currently working in administration for a hotel, Ms. Webber is about to take a new job at a research firm. "I took several courses in psychology as a student, and that made me think more about how consumer choices are made. Aside from that, the general courses in statistics, forecasting, and other business skills have been a help in my work."

For Patrick Murphy, a business administration graduate of Bryant College (1986), the use of computers is a key element of his career. He concentrated on Management of Information Systems (MIS), and now works for an aerospace manufacturer as a senior programmer and systems analyst. "At the time I started school, MIS was just beginning to be offered at colleges," he says. "I knew I had an interest in computers, but I also knew that I wanted a business background." As a continuation of his business training, he is on the verge of finishing up an MBA program at the University of Hartford.

His business training helps in many ways—for example, he utilizes it in his work as a member of a team that meets regularly to analyze production problems and recommend improvements. "While my work often involves sitting before a computer terminal writing code, this team assignment requires communication skills and a knowledge of organizational behavior," he says.

"My interests were in being employed after graduation, and in majoring in something relevant to business," says Kelly Starr, a 1988 labor relations graduate of Cornell University. She now works as a human-resources representative for a major oil company, handling employee relations and community relations for a division of the firm. "The courses I took in organization behavior, labor economics, and labor law are beneficial to the work I do now," she notes. "I can't say where my career is going to go from here, but it seems that industrial psychology continues to be an interesting topic for me," she says, adding that graduate school is a possibility.

**Career Options**    Accountant
Advertising account executive
Association executive
Bank administrator
Business administrator

Business-to-business salesperson
Consumer-goods salesperson
Direct marketer
Economist
Editor, magazine
Executive search consultant
Financial analyst
Financial planner
Franchise manager
Hotel manager
Information specialist
Insurance agent
Investor relations manager
Journalist
Lawyer, following law schooling.
Management consultant
Marketing manager
Mortgage banker
Purchasing agent
Real estate sales broker
Risk manager
Shipping manager
Social worker
Stockbroker

# CHEMICAL ENGINEERING

|  |  | 1983 | 1985 | 1988 |
|---|---|---|---|---|
| **Enrollment** | BS or BA | 7,185 | 7,146 | 3,926 |
| **Boxscore** | Master's | 1,368 | 1,544 | 1,103 |
|  | PhD | 319 | 418 | 579 |

**Overview**    All manufacturing can be divided into two parts:   either the components are individually assembled, or materials are processed continuously. The former, used in such industries as automobiles and electronics, is usually the province of the mechanical engineer; the latter, involving chemical reactions, mixing, separating or purifying, is that of the chemical engineer.

Chemical engineering grew out of technology developed by mechanical engineers a century ago. They recognized that the material changes raw materials underwent during processing required a background in chemistry to comprehend, and that this background also facilitated an understanding of how *processes* could be analyzed.

The teaching of modern chemical engineering combines the math and physics that most engineering students learn with a full plate of chemistry courses. Because much of chemical manufacturing is dependent upon derivatives of petroleum (a carbon-based material), chemical engineers are usually required to take organic chemistry. As upper-classmen, students choose either theoretical studies of how processes are analyzed, or courses in specific industrial applications of chemical engineering, including petroleum and petrochemical refining, food processing, and pharmaceuticals. The rapidly growing fields of biotechnology and environmental services are also drawing more chemical engineers. Several schools have encouraged this development by offering courses related to these industries.

In graduate school, the study of chemical reactions becomes more prominent; these students share many of the same concerns as graduate chemistry students. Frequently, however, the chemical engineering researcher is looking at problems and processes that can be found in industry (applied research), while chemists focus on pure research.

**Concentrations**

Being inherently specialized, most concentrations in chemical engineering are closely related. The most basic breakdown is between the general study of chemical processes and preparation for specific industries. The range includes:

**Polymer Engineering,** the study of plastics and similar materials that are created synthetically. Some universities make polymer engineering a part of an independent department of **Materials Engineering.**

**Biochemical Engineering** (a.k.a. **Bioprocess Engineering, Bio-**

resource Engineering), which focuses on the chemicals of life: pharmaceutical products, foods, wood, textiles, and agriculture.

**Process Control,** which is of special interest to chemical engineers, because the methods and technology for controlling continuous chemical-manufacturing processes differ significantly from assembly-line manufacturing.

**Environmental Engineering,** which is sometimes an independent department, and sometimes part of a civil engineering department. Because most environmental problems involve polluting chemicals, there is much that chemical engineering technology can do.

**Course Sampler**

**CHE 431. Polymer Chemistry and Reactions**
Synthesis and production of polymeric materials from monomers or by modification of natural polymers. Various polymerization reactions, their catalysis and their mechanisms and kinetics are considered, as well as industrial systems used for polymerization.

*(University of Maine)*

**ECHE 367. Process Control**
Feedback control of chemical processes. Topics include:   Mathematical modeling of the dynamics of typical heat and mass-transfer processes; linearization; dynamic behavior of linear processes; stability; Laplace transforms, block diagrams and transfer functions; steady-state and dynamic performance of PID controllers; tuning of PID controllers; Internal Model Controllers; analysis of control system performance via Root-Locus, frequency response diagrams. . . .

*(Case Western Reserve University)*

**CH E 478. Special Methods in Industrial Microbiology**
Selection and development of strains for industrial microbiological processes. Control and optimization of processes in the foodstuffs, pharmaceutical, and chemicals industries. Physicochemical and microbiological assay methods. Survey of industrially important microorganisms.

*(New Mexico State University)*

**Assessment**

Jayadev Chowdhury followed the study of chemical engineering in India with a master's degree in the same topic from Worcester Polytechnic Institute, from which he graduated in 1977. Now employed as an editor on an engineering journal, he had extensive experience as an industrial research engineer. His employer at the time manufactured equipment for petroleum production, so he developed chemical means of enhancing oil recovery and trouble-shooting oil well problems.

"The basic chemical engineering education in science and math helped me to pick up subjects that were not part of my training, such as geology or geochemistry," he says. "With chemical engineering, you can branch out to practically any other career path."

The many required papers and the thesis have also prepared him well for work as an editor, he says. While Mr. Chowdhury was working in industry, the writing skills were important for completing funding proposals, managing staff, targeting research topics, and justifying acquisitions for laboratory equipment.

William Buck, a 1979 chemical engineering graduate from Michigan State University, has had varied responsibilities in the chemical industry, which led up to his current assignment as operations supervisor at a petrochemicals plant, where he places special emphasis on workplace and environmental safety. Before that he was a process control engineer for another petrochemical manufacturer, where he managed computer systems and energy conservation projects. Before that, he worked as an environmental and production engineer at a Midwestern utility company.

In referring to his current focus on safety, Mr. Buck says that "my chemical engineering background provides an excellent foundation for understanding industrial hygiene, environmental and safety issues—all of which are bound by the common thread of productivity and quality." He adds that "as a supervisor in the chemical industry, one has to be very safety-conscious, in addition to working on productivity and quality issues."

**Career Options**

Aerospace engineer, especially with regard to advanced materials technology in aircraft.

Business-to-business salesperson

Chemical engineer, where the hot fields currently are process automation, quality control, and pollution control.

College professor, science and technology

Computer systems analyst, particularly for such technologies as factory process control.

Energy engineer
Food scientist/technologist
Industrial/manufacturing engineer
Lawyer, especially in patent law.
Metallurgical and materials engineer
Nuclear engineer
Petroleum engineer
Physician (medical doctor); at times, some medical schools look
    extremely favorably on candidates who have studied chemical
    engineering.
Safety engineer

# CHEMISTRY

|  |  | 1983 | 1985 | 1988 |
|---|---|---|---|---|
| Enrollment | BS or BA | 10,769 | 10,482 | 9,025 |
| Boxscore | Master's | 1,622 | 1,719 | 1,694 |
|  | PhD | 1,746 | 1,789 | 1,990 |

Overview

"Better living through chemistry" used to be the slogan of DuPont Company, the largest chemical company in the United States. While that tagline is more open to question in these days of atmospheric pollution, toxic waste dumps, and other environmental insults, on the whole, most people would agree that our lives are enriched by the many new materials and compounds that the chemical industry has produced. The problems that this onrush of technology has spawned will themselves be cured, or at least neutralized, by more chemistry professionals. So the chemistry profession has a bright outlook these days.

Chemistry, at its heart, is the study of how materials function and react with each other. Pure chemical research looks very much like physics, as scientists attempt to understand how atoms and molecules are controlled by subatomic forces. Applied chemistry looks like business administration, with the chemist as a sales or marketing executive concerned with building market share, distributing products, and determining pricing. Many chemists teach, and many do independent research on campus or at commercial laboratories.

Potential chemical manufacturing employers include the chemical industry, of course, but also all industries where materials undergo chemical change are potential chemical manufacturing employers, including metals refining, pharmaceuticals, food processing, synthetic fibers, plastics and rubber compounds, paints, fertilizers, paper, and wood products. Chemists are employed as researchers (in a role very similar to that of researchers in academia), quality control managers, production supervisors, and sales and marketing professionals.

Another growing career opportunity for chemists is in environmental protection and government regulation. Chemists have the tools to decipher the extremely complex interactions among chemicals and life forms of the environment.

Since chemistry, like biology, is one of the basic sciences of nature, many students also enter chemistry programs to prepare for careers in health-care and medicine.

**Concentrations**

**Organic Chemistry,** the study of carbon-based compounds, including all biological compounds as well as materials derived from petroleum.

**Inorganic Chemistry,** the study of minerals, metals, and certain specialized compounds.

**Physical Chemistry,** the study of the physical properties of materials rather than their reactive properties; this concentration is a good preparation for materials manufacturing and research.

**Biochemistry,** the study of the chemical basis of life (see BIOLOGY).

**Quantum Chemistry,** the study of the properties of matter below the atomic level. While most quantum chemists work in research, this field is also good preparation for working in the microelectronics industry.

**Analytical Chemistry,** the study of the techniques for measuring or identifying chemical species, rather than the chemicals themselves. Analytical chemists use such high-tech instruments as scanning electron microscopes, chromatographs, and spectrometers.

**Petroleum Chemistry,** study that prepares the chemist for working on the production and refining of petroleum and natural gas.

**Catalysis,** the study of the technique of speeding up a chemical reaction by adding compounds. Catalysis is vital to many forms of chemical manufacturing and has some applications in biochemistry.

**Nuclear Chemistry,** the study of radioactive materials used for power generation, weapons, and medical analysis.

**Forensic Chemistry,** the application of analytical techniques to criminal investigation.

## Course Sampler

**Chem 116. Introductory Quantitative Analysis Laboratory**
Introduction to chemical laboratory techniques. Topics:   volumetric, gravimetric, and spectrophotometric methods of quantitative analysis, and chemical equilibria.

*(Washington University in St. Louis)*

**141–142. Physical Chemistry**
Thermodynamics, properties and kinetic theory of gases, elementary wave mechanics, and the development of atomic structure and chemical bonding, homogeneous and heterogeneous chemical and physical equilibria, chemical kinetics, electrochemistry, elementary statistical thermodynamics.

*(Hofstra University)*

**370. Organic Synthetic Methods**
A continuation of the study of organic reactions with an emphasis on their synthetic utility. Functional group transformations will be emphasized rather than carbon-carbon bond-forming reactions. Examples from the modern literature which stress mildness of reaction conditions and control of stereochemistry and regiochemistry, as well as overall yield of product will be emphasized. Photochemical or electrochemical methods will be mentioned where applicable. The laboratory will expand upon the techniques gained in the first course in organic chemistry. Ability to plan efficient syntheses and a reliance on the literature will be required.

*(Allegheny College)*

## Assessment

Jonathan Crowther, a 1979 BA chemistry graduate from Drew University, has continued his interest in analytical chemistry through graduate school and into a research job in the pharmaceutical industry. He is group leader in the analytical branch; he supervises other chemists in the analysis of proteins and pharmaceutical compounds and other polymers. "I had great teachers, and the chance to work, as both a student and a student-employee, in very good, well-equipped laboratories," he recalls. He came to school with the belief that he would major "in some type of science," took chemistry, and kept going.

"Chemistry education tends to be a field where you get more and more specialized as your education continues," he notes. "As an undergraduate, you have the chance to learn about a wide range of chemical principles." His administrative work today requires much report-writing, and he values the writing-intensive liberal arts courses he took as an undergraduate.

Meanwhile, P. K. Ramani has turned almost completely away from the training in chemistry he received in 1980 at the University of Malaysia, but he nevertheless finds the experience a big help. Ramani works as a business manager for a cable television network, handling finance, marketing, and administration. "I wasn't a very good student," he admits, saying, "At first, I thought I might be going to medical school, but that interest didn't last." He continued his education by obtaining an MBA at the New York Institute of Technology in 1984, and began working in telecommunications.

Still, the scientific training has been useful in several ways. While working in telecommunications, he taught himself the technical details of the switching and cabling equipment. "I had a very limited knowledge of what to do, but I knew what books to read, and knew how to teach myself," he recalls. That experience, combined with the business training, prepared him well for being a marketing and financial manager for the cable television company.

Chemistry and the law make a good team, according to a 1977 chemistry graduate. She studied chemistry "because it was the one thing I couldn't do well" upon entering college; she needed the challenge to keep her interest up. She worked as a research and regulatory-affairs chemist for several years, attended law school at night, and is now a practicing lawyer. "Science teaches you to be very observant, and not to make fast prejudgments," she says. "And when I am analyzing the details of a case, I need the same observational skills in order to pick the case apart." In addition, her firm has handled a number of cases pertaining to environmental issues—a situation that calls for direct knowledge of chemistry.

**Career Options**

Business-to-business salesperson

Chemist; current hot fields are petrochemical research and production, advanced materials, and environmental remediation.

College professor, science and technology

Chemical engineer involved in chemical manufacturing.

Dentist, following dental schooling.

Ecologist, with regard to the interaction between chemicals and the environment.

Food scientist/technologist

Journalist

Lawyer, particularly for patent law.

Life scientist, with advanced training.

Petroleum engineer

Pharmacist, with additional training.

Physician (medical doctor); chemistry is one of the more popular preparations for medical school.

Risk manager

Safety engineer

Technical writer

---

# CIVIL ENGINEERING

| | | 1983 | 1985 | 1988 |
|---|---|---|---|---|
| **Enrollment** | BS or BA | 9,989 | 9,162 | 7,497 |
| **Boxscore** | Master's | 3,074 | 3,172 | 2,839 |
| | PhD | 340 | 377 | 481 |

**Overview**

Civil engineering is the oldest form of engineering study. It began when industrial nations first needed roads, canals, dams, bridges, factories, and office buildings. Then came railroads, airports, movie theaters—and someday, stations in space or settlements on the moon.

Today's civil engineers work with a diverse array of other professionals. Designs for large buildings are first generated by architects, but civil engineers are involved early in specifying the type and layout of the construction materials. Also, all public works, as well as most homes and office towers, must run a gauntlet of governmental reviews. The coordinating role played by the civil engineer makes communication skills an important part of civil engineering performance, and is one of the reasons that civil engineers are able to move smoothly into positions in real estate, the business world, and government.

Environmental engineering is a big part of the civil engineer's training, because the field has long been involved in public works such as water and sewage treatment systems. Civil engineers build treatment plants, water pipelines, and reservoirs, and construct and operate sewage works, landfills, and other disposal facilities. The new emphasis on guarding the environment will create many more opportunities for these engineers in the future.

**Concentrations**

The civil engineering curriculum begins with a set of math and science courses common to most engineering students. Courses follow on the properties of materials, then on the design and performance of assembled structures. Upper-class options prepare students for careers in:

**Architectural Engineering,** which concentrates on how large buildings can be designed and then constructed.

**Ocean Engineering,** which studies structures at the shore or in the ocean, such as oil-drilling rigs, piers and docks, and beach-front conservation systems.

**Sanitary Engineering** (a.k.a. **Environmental Engineering**), which focuses on water, sewage, garbage disposal, and land reclamation.

**Structural Engineering,** which applies the principles of building design to the building of bridges, vehicles (land, sea, and air), and tunnels.

**Transportation Engineering,** which focuses on the design of highways, rail lines, airports, and mass-transit systems.

**Construction Materials Engineering,** which specializes in materials science for developing better components for structures.

**Geotechnical Engineering,** which looks at what is *under* the buildings, highways, dams, and other structures. Geotechnical engineers have some of the same concerns as geologists. [See GEOLOGY].

**Course Sampler**

**CIE 445. Building Design**
The conceptual, preliminary, and final design of a building project. Economic, engineering, and socio-political constraints are considered. Owner, architect, engineer, and contractor relationships are explored. Course is professional in nature, utilizing the active involvement of practicing architects, engineers, planners, and contractors.

*(University of Maine)*

**ECIV 330. Soil Mechanics**
The physical, chemical, and mechanical properties of soils. Soil classification, capillarity, permeability, and flow nets. One dimensional consolidation, stress, and settlement analysis. Shear strength, stability of cuts, embankments, retaining walls, and footings. Standard laboratory tests performed for the determination of the physical and mechanical properties of soils.

*(Case Western Reserve University)*

**CE 335A. Structural Engineering Materials**
Mechanical behavior of materials: static tension, compression and bending, yield criteria, dynamic effects, creep, and fatigue. Structure of metal: atomic bonding, crystal structure, imperfections, dislocations, iron-carbon alloy system, T.T.T. relations, heat treatment of steel-alloy steels. Concrete: manufacture of cements, proportioning concrete mixes: concrete making, placing, curing; air entrainment; mechanical properties. Timber: structure, characteristics, and strength properties. composites: classification and mechanical properties.

*(Washington University in St. Louis)*

**Assessment**

For Valentine Lehr, a civil engineering degree from Manhattan College (1962) has opened the doors to a career in building and construction services. Following his undergraduate training, he began working at a firm that designed and produced electrical and mechanical utility systems for buildings, including heating, ventilating, and air conditioning (HVAC) equipment. Along the way, he earned a master's degree in civil engineering from the Brooklyn

Polytechnic Institute (now called New York Polytechnic). In 1969, he and several partners founded Val Lehr Associates, which has grown to a major engineering company providing HVAC consulting services for builders around the world.

"This type of work is more mechanical than civil engineering," he says. "Nevertheless, the transition from traditional civil engineering concepts to HVAC was made easy by the thorough grounding in engineering principles that a civil engineering degree has given me." As opposed to other engineering disciplines where he feels that the training is narrow, Mr. Lehr says that "civil and possibly mechanical engineering are the two disciplines that provide a broad foundation, and give the engineer a great deal of flexibility in what industries or types of businesses to find work."

Another civil engineer, a 1983 graduate of Rensselaer Polytechnic Institute used his undergraduate training as the springboard to a career on Wall Street. After earning his engineering degree, he followed up with an MBA, and then began working as a construction engineer at a major consulting firm, specializing in power plant and utility facilities design. "Over time, I found that I was much more interested in the business side of construction than in the engineering side. I made a conscious decision to pursue a career in finance, and wound up at a bank." This was followed by stints at two major Wall Street securities firms; now he is deeply involved in developing trading strategies for "fixed income" investments such as business loans.

"There is very little engineering knowledge involved in what I do now, but I would still study engineering if I had to repeat my education," he says. "Engineering taught me how to attack a problem where the means of solving it is unknown. Many investing situations are like that, and it takes persistence and confidence to work out a solution."

**Career Options**
Business-to-business salesperson, especially for materials and services commonly used in construction.

Civil engineer; the hot areas currently are public works and environmental projects.

Computer systems analyst, with a specialization in computer-aided drafting and design.

Corporate security specialist, concentrating on consulting services with firms that provide secured installations for government or for corporations.

**Cost estimator**

**Energy engineer** for energy management in buildings, as well as energy production at utilities and factories.

**Geologist**

**Hotel manager,** especially with regard to "facilities" management —making sure that the energy, electrical, and other utilities a hotel requires are functioning as designed.

**Insurance agent,** especially as preparation for upper-management in insurance companies, where investment in construction is important.

**Metallurgical and materials engineer,** concerned with the design and production of construction materials.

**Property manager**

**Purchasing agent**

**Urban planner,** with advanced schooling.

---

# CLASSICS

|  |  | 1983 | 1985 | 1988 |
|---|---|---|---|---|
| **Enrollment** | BS or BA | 594 | 509 | 524 |
| **Boxscore** | Master's | 150 | 143 | 125 |
|  | PhD | 42 | 44 | 53 |

**Overview**

What could be more remote from the workaday world than to study dead languages and to read books that discuss events of defunct cultures? That is the question confronting classics majors, and yet, as with all the liberal arts, the classics draws renewed interest from each generation of college students.

The heart of a classics program is to learn to read, write, and sometimes speak, Greek or Latin. Some programs require, and many students undertake to learn, both. There are also special courses in literature, history, religion, and philosophy.

There is probably no more rigorous way to learn the structure of Western languages than to learn Greek and Latin. Thus, classics graduates have a solid grounding in writing and related communication skills. Because of the intensity of logical construction to these languages, the classics are also a good preparation for graduate study in law and other highly analytical types of work. These languages also provide a solid preparation for research or practice in religion, since so many religious documents of value in Western cultures were written in Greek and Latin.

However, the dominant line of work for classics graduates is teaching. These languages are so valuable that they will always be taught in high schools and colleges (which cannot be said for all disciplines—for example, a branch of business might suddenly go out of fashion). Schools need a steady supply of new teachers, especially as the debate over educational quality rises.

**Concentrations**

Some schools do not require the knowledge of Greek or Latin in the original to complete the program. A few schools combine classics and modern Greek in the same program, or as a major/minor pair. (There is apparently no program that combines Latin with modern Italian.) Concentrations include:

**Latin and Greek,** which usually entails 2 years' worth of study in each language, or the demonstration of equivalent proficiency.

**Classical Literature,** focusing on the literary traditions of Greek, Roman, and other ancient Mediterranean civilizations.

**Classical Archaeology,** which emphasizes the artistic and cultural artifacts of the ancient Mediterranean civilizations. This is sometimes a cross-major with the departments of Anthropology and Archaeology (see ANTHROPOLOGY).

**Classical Civilization,** which studies Greek and Roman cultural, political, and religious institutions much as general humanities courses study modern cultures. The classical influence (i.e., revivals of ancient Greek and Roman thought) may be traced through medieval, Renaissance, early American, and 20th century culture.

**Course Sampler**

Ad7.0005 Intermediate Latin: Vergil
Writings of the greatest Roman poet, focusing on the most generally read portions of his most celebrated poem, the *Aeneid*. The meter of the

poem is studied, and the student learns to read Latin metrically to reflect the necessary sound for full appreciation of the writing. Readings in political and literary history illustrate the setting in the Augustan Age in which the *Aeneid* was written and enjoyed, the relationship of the poem to the other classical epics, and its influence on the poetry of later times.

*(New York University)*

### CLCV 201 Ancient Greece:   History and Civilization

A survey of ancient Greek culture and history from Minoan-Mycenean civilization through the ascendancy of Athens to the conquests of Alexander the Great. Attention is given to the social, political, and cultural influences of Greek civilization on Western society.

*(Denison University)*

### 322 Introduction to Greek New Testament

A study of the development of New Testament Greek, with readings in Mark and an introduction to textual criticism.

*(Concordia College)*

## Assessment

John Graebe, a 1985 classics graduate of Dartmouth University, went on to attend Harvard Law School, from which he graduated in 1988. For the next 2 years, he taught at a private boarding school in New England, and is about to take a clerkship to a federal judge. "I decided on the classics early on, and took 4 years of Latin and some Greek while attending high school," he says. "When I got to college, I decided that it was something I enjoyed, was good at, and would keep my interest up." He concentrated in Latin, taking courses on the writings of Plautus, Seneca, Vergil, and other famed Latin writers.

Did classics help him in law school? "Latin is a highly inflected language, and it sharpens your analytical skills to be able to pick it up and read it," Mr. Graebe believes. "It's like unraveling a puzzle." That close reading of texts is a requirement in law, where the implications of each sentence are carefully considered, and the writing style is precise. He did have a sampling of ancient law in one of his courses, but that had "very little" to do with modern American law. "Above all, the discipline to study and learn acquired in classics is a lasting influence."

Michael Hanas, a 1985 classics graduate of the College of the Holy Cross, teaches at the same school as Mr. Graebe. He stressed learning the languages while in college, with a view toward education as a career. At the academy where he works, Mr. Hanas is responsible for teaching history as well as languages. "I wish that I had had more history courses, because that is a gap in my education that I've had to fill since by studying the textbooks myself," he admits. In a way, his ability to teach himself is a testament to the value of his education. "My basic sales pitch to my students is that the study of ancient languages is inherently valuable because of the language skills it enhances. You also have a chance to study another culture deeply, to learn how people have lived in the past." When it comes to teaching American history, the classical tradition "provides insight into the development of the American system of government."

**Career Options**

Advertising account executive
College administrator
College professor, liberal arts
Copywriter
Editor, book
Foreign language teacher
Historian
Information specialist, if courses involved heavy amounts of library research.
Journalist
Lawyer
Librarian
Marketing researcher
Paralegal
Publicist
Teacher, K–12
Technical writer

# COMMUNICATIONS

### (Advertising Journalism, Mass Communications, Broadcasting, Public Relations)

| | | 1983 | 1985 | 1988 |
|---|---|---|---|---|
| **Enrollment** | BS or BA | 36,954 | 40,358 | 45,382 |
| **Boxscore** | Master's | 3,502 | 3,460 | 3,685 |
| | PhD | 205 | 228 | 232 |

**Overview**

Ours is the media age. Many of our celebrities are newscasters, journalists, and editors who tell us what is going on in the world and, in many subtle and not-so-subtle ways, try to influence the course of events.

As a result of this prominence, the study of journalism, in the broader context of mass communications, has grown to a fairly substantial size. The report card on the value of a communications or journalism degree, however, is mixed. Many professional journalists say that a solid liberal arts education is more valuable to a successful career than specalized training in communications, which often involves the details of writing, illustrating, and printing stories, or conducting filming sessions. If one intends to be, say, a sports reporter, then it is appropriate to study something like physical education; to be a science journalist, one should study physics or other science. Most agree, though, that a graduate-level degree in journalism or communications is a powerful boost to a career.

The communications field has grown so vast that there are many different ways to approach its study. The most traditional form of study is journalism, which is tied closely to the newspaper industry. Students usually enter journalism intending to be a newspaper reporter or publisher. It is also possible to study the technical details of newspaper production at some schools, although this is often conducted within a department of graphic design. Similarly, film, television, and video can be studied from the perspective of newswriting and research, or of operating film or telecommunications equipment.

While many students start a journalism program intending to be a newspaper reporter or broadcaster, relatively few wind up with those jobs. Many graduates head for careers in public relations, communications, or magazine or book publishing. We can all relate to what we read every day in the newspaper, or see on the evening news every night, but in reality, much more reporting and broadcasting goes on in education or training, media relations for large corporations, advertising, and public relations. These fields will continue to grow as the simple problem of getting information delivered to the right person (a customer, a stockholder, a student) grows more complex.

A noteworthy element of most college programs in communications is some type of on-campus enterprise where real journalism, broadcasting, or filming is done. There is almost always a campus newspaper, which requires reporters, production personnel, and salespeople; many larger campuses also have a radio station, and the largest ones have a television station and film laboratory. Working in one of these enterprises amounts to an internship.

**Concentrations**

Communications students divide sharply into two types: those interested in print media, and those interested in film or broadcast media. "You can see the difference physically," avers one journalism student. "The broadcast majors are the ones with blown-dry hair and megawatt smiles. The print majors look dumpy by comparison." However distinct the differences between the two types of programs are, writing skills are paramount to both. Those interested in the production aspects of communications—preparing page proofs, or editing and broadcasting film and video—need to develop technical competence. For the creative use of paper or film in painting, filmmaking, or art photography, see FINE ARTS. Concentrations include:

**Journalism,** which is targeted mainly for future reporters, and can also entail production work and the skills of editing or rewriting.
**Public Relations,** which combines writing and speaking skills.
**Advertising,** which usually emphasizes the copy-producing (writ-

ing) side of the business; graphics students enter a Fine Arts program, future account executives enter a Business Administration program in marketing.

**Broadcasting and Film,** which ranges from the details of reporting or storyboarding to production technology and the legal issues surrounding mass media.

**Organizational Communications,** the study of communications channels in groups such as corporations or communities.

**Speech and Rhetoric,** which teaches speech as a form of persuasion and as a preparation for broadcasting.

**Mass Communications,** which is sometimes the title of a general survey of all common types of media, including their organization and how they fit into American society.

**Course Sampler**

**223 Interpersonal Communication**
Introduction to theories and models of interpersonal communication, which enhances understanding and development of interpersonal relationships. Course content covers topics such as listening behavior, interpersonal processing, dyadic interaction, conflict management, intercultural, intimate, and nonverbal communication.

*(Tulane University)*

**SCTA 414 Organizational Communication**
A course especially appropriate to management-bound students. It deals with central and coordinating functions of communication and the pragmatics through which individuals interact with groups and others in the organizational context. It examines concepts including human relations, message transmission, management team building, and managing interpersonal conflicts. Emphasis upon a theoretical understanding of communication within organizations. The course includes assigned readings, reaction papers, experiential exercises, and group projects.

*(Concordia College)*

**ICMA 270 Documentary Sketchwork**
An introduction to placing media in the service of inquiry into human behavior, social critique, and political persuasion through the documentary form. In-class screening, readings, and exercises will be aimed at helping students develop the ability to record and structure documentary evidence into unified and meaningful statements.

*(Antioch College)*

### PUB 530 Sports Information Programs

Study of the role and function of the sports information director. Includes public relations techniques applied to sports information; press releases, publications programs, office and staff organization, time utilizations, news media, and formats.

*(Eastern Kentucky University)*

### COM CM 418 Writing for Broadcast Advertising

Techniques for creating television advertising that attracts attention and holds it. Students research a problem; analyze the target audience; create the advertising concept; write the commercials; prepare storyboards; and consider the problems of casting, directing, editing, and testing.

*(Boston University)*

**Assessment**

"When I came to college, I intended to study English and then become a reporter for the *New York Times*," says Colleen Connery, a 1983 communications graduate of Hartwick College. "I fell into a radio internship, where I worked as an announcer, advertising salesperson, technician, talk show host—you name it. That experience made me want to specialize there, and I was able to structure an independent-study program that took me in the direction of radio." Independent study was in order, she says, because an advisor suggested she take liberal arts courses like history while undertaking the course requirements for communications.

Since graduation, however, Ms. Connery has branched out. She worked for a public relations firm for several years, and now works as an employee communications editor for a division of a major manufacturing firm. "In this job, I write and produce newsletters and other literature, I travel, interview staff people in the firm, and I take photographs. The flexibility of my course of study allowed me to become familiar with all these communications responsibilities." She also cites courses in public speaking and journalism as helpful to her in her work today.

"I don't know why, but from the time I was 12, I wanted to be a reporter for a national newspaper," says Susan Monshaw, who graduated from Rutgers University in 1986. She did get to work at the *New York Times*, as a business staffer, and then moved to an engineering magazine. "The important thing for me in college was learning how to be a better writer," she says. "I was an A student in English in high school, but when my first term paper was written in college, it got a terrible grade—I had to learn how to do better." Overall, she says that she might reconsider her decision to major in journalism; she would definitely take journalism classes, but perhaps would take a major in which she learned more science, business, or statistics.

Another 1986 graduate of Rutgers has parlayed his studies into a career in national politics. Larry Guillemette, who now works as the director of educational programs for the Congressional Youth Leadership Council (a non-profit group that provides governmental experience to high school students), had worked as the press secretary for a Congressman. "Some of my professors thought that I had 'sold out to the other side' by taking that type of work, but in reality, a press secretary does many of the same things a reporter does: gathers information, gets out news, deals with the issues of the day."

Mr. Guillemette says that he used his journalistic skills "every day" while acting as a press secretary, especially in general writing and communicating. He also was glad he knew how to construct a story to get it published or aired. Even so, he feels that his journalism training was too narrow, concentrating too much on writing newspaper stories. "You need to be a good generalist to work in media in Washington," he says. "I would have liked fewer writing or newspaper courses, and more traditional liberal arts courses on history, political science, or economics."

| | |
|---|---|
| **Career Options** | Advertising account executive |
| | Association executive |
| | Business-to-business salesperson |
| | Consumer-goods salesperson |
| | Copywriter |
| | Corporate trainer |
| | Direct marketer |
| | Editor, book |
| | Editor, magazine |
| | Executive search consultant |
| | Experiential educator |
| | Film/video engineer, especially for communications majors who concentrate on the technology of communications. |

Human-resources manager
Investor relations manager
Journalist
Management consultant
Marketing researcher
Marketing manager
Media planner
Photographer
Public administrator
Publicist
Radio/television announcer
Telecommunications manager, assuming familiarity with communications technology is acquired through learning or experience.

---

# COMPUTER SCIENCE AND ENGINEERING

**(Programming, Systems Analysis, Information Science)**

|  |  | 1983 | 1985 | 1988 |
|---|---|---|---|---|
| **Enrollment** | BS or BA | 25,525 | 40,717 | 36,663 |
| **Boxscore** | Master's | 5,608 | 7,596 | 9,926 |
|  | PhD | 285 | 278 | 505 |

**Overview**　Computer science has boomed in the past two decades, both on college campuses and in the working world. With the advent of the personal computer (PC), computers are rapidly becoming a fixture in every office, like the typewriter or coffee machine. Colleges are eager to show off their computer centers, or to install networks of PCs throughout their dormitories and study centers.

Computer science traces its roots to the joint efforts of electrical engineers and mathematicians. The former developed the first circuit designs (hardware) that could carry out an operation, the latter wrote the instructions that told the computer what to do (software). As computer scientists needed to create and maintain increasing numbers of applications, computer engineers arose to write instructions for the internal running of the computer. This "program" could be written as a message stored in the computer's memory, or even as the actual circuit diagrams. (The term for such programs is "firmware.")

Computer applications continue to grow more diverse. There are programs for business, science, telecommunications, manufacturing, and finance; there are programs for PCs exclusively, and others for larger computers, including the supercomputer that handles huge batches of numbers in the blink of an eye. The variety of applications has led to other academic programs, such as information science, which focus on the practical uses rather than the computer's internal workings.

Thus, the student interested in working with computers can either choose from programs oriented to the uses or to the design and construction of the machines. Electrical engineering dominates in computer design and manufacture. Students interested exclusively in applications need to know very little about computer hardware; conversely, there are computer and electrical engineers who know very little about how the computers they design will be used.

**Concentrations**

**General Computer Science**, teaching the general principles of computer technology, applications, and programming.

**Computer Engineering**, focusing on computer hardware and methods of organizing the computer's internal structure and programs.

**Information Science**, dealing with specialized computer programs called database management systems, and the methods for organizing information.

**Course Sampler**

CS 280 Business Data Processing
Applications of programming skills to business data; program design and programming laboratory; business and financial reporting; data management; and a survey of data processing concepts and practices.

*(Illinois Wesleyan University)*

### CS 5722 Systems Programming I

Systems programs, which prepare programs for execution, are the primary subject of this course. The design and implementation of assemblers, macro-processors, and loaders are discussed in detail. An introduction to formal languages and grammars is given as a basis for a look at the elements of compilers and interpreters.

*(New York Institute of Technology)*

### ICS 2601–2602. Computer Organization and Programming I and II

Introduction to computer organization, machine assembly language programming, and assembly systems. Assembly language programming techniques.

Intermediate treatment of computer organization and machine programming. Input/output processing memory and processor structures, and interfacing. Basic computer logic design, gate minimization, cost evaluation, and combinatorial circuits.

*(Georgia Institute of Technology)*

**Assessment**

"I was undecided between math and computer science almost until my senior year, when I decided to graduate with a computer science degree," says Max Martinez, a 1985 graduate of Dartmouth University. Following graduation, he worked for 4 years as a systems analyst for an insurance company, while earning a master's degree in computer science from New York University. Now he is a programmer and software developer at a major architectural firm in Chicago, helping them develop and market a program that will allow architects to design on the computer.

"One of the unusual characteristics of my work is that I am working with architects-turned-programmers, who don't have the background in programming that I do," he says. "I'm glad that my undergraduate degree included basic liberal arts courses that help me communicate with them."

Mr. Martinez has a long list of languages that he can "speak" (program): C, Cobol, PL/1, Basic, Pascal, Lisp, Icon, SETL, Ada, and APL, among others. "Once you've learned one computer language, you don't have a hard time learning others," he says nonchalantly.

Computer graphics is the application that most excites Mr. Martinez. It was an important part of his graduate schooling, is the major element of his work now, and is the goal of his future career growth. "Ideally, I would like to move from this type of work to animation, such as is seen in the latest animated movies," he says. For such work, he believes that his strong concentration in math will be a help, since computer graphics requires complex mathematical techniques.

From the mid-1960s until 1983, Edward Rice worked on and learned about computing. His education culminated with a master's degree in computer science from the American University in 1983, and he has worked as a consultant, a software developer, an equipment technician—"practically everything that can be done with, or to, a computer," he says. Currently, he is working in a field quite removed from computing—a field he calls "citizen diplomacy," which involves setting up exchange programs between the United States and other countries. "I use computers as a tool every day, but at the moment only for things like cranking out mailing labels."

Overall, he advises choosing computer science programs carefully. "If you are interested in the theory of computing, fine—most schools teach that well. If you are interested in computer applications, choose the school and the courses carefully. You will always find that there is more going on in the outside world with computers than what you are taught in school."

**Career Options**
Artificial intelligence developer
College professor, science and technology
Computer engineer
Computer programmer
Computer service engineer
Computer systems analyst
Corporate security specialist
Demographer
Electrical engineer
Information specialist
Information broker
Industrial/manufacturing engineer
Management consultant
Operations/systems researcher
Statistician, with extra training in the mathematics of statistics.

**Technical writer,** primarily for software documentation.
**Telecommunications manager**

---

# ECONOMICS

|  | 1983 | 1985 | 1988 |
|---|---|---|---|
| **Enrollment** BS or BA | 20,517 | 20,711 | 22,950 |
| **Boxscore** Master's | 1,972 | 1,992 | 1,831 |
| PhD | 734 | 749 | 770 |

**Overview**

A 20th-century person is an economic person: a producer and consumer of goods and services, a source of wealth for society at large, and, if unable to provide adequate self-support, a responsibility for society. A couple of generations ago, economics was the battleground for shaping society, as the industrial nations of the world fought economic depression. In recent years, the attention of American college students has been riveted by the dramatic growth and dynamism of Wall Street and the financial services industries. Starting in 1990, a revolutionary change in the world economic order has occurred as the centralized economies have switched to American-style market economies. Yet there are still many theories and practices of economics around the world. There are also many aspects of the American economy that need modification and improvement. America must learn to function more efficiently as it establishes a new position in a new world order. Economics analyzes the ways our economy can be changed and improved, through learning how the various parts of American society affect each other, and studying the relationships between government, business, and the individual.

Economics is one of the most popular academic disciplines among college students. It offers the chance to learn skills highly valued in the business world—reading financial data, "running the numbers" on a budgetary statement, learning how to make a forecast. At the same time, it offers insights into social policies, politics, and international relations.

Many students take economics to prepare for a career in business; many go on to obtain an MBA.

**Concentrations**

**International Economics,** which studies other nations' economies, and how nations interact through trade, foreign aid, and investment.

**Applied Economics,** which uses economic tools to analyze specific situations of an individual, business, or government.

**Mathematical Economics and Econometrics,** which uses statistics and modeling theories to analyze national economies.

**Finance,** which pertains to investment and banking. Its study requires familiarization with the issue and sale of stocks, equities, and bonds.

**Course Sampler**

**ECON 303 Microeconomics**
Price system as allocative mechanism. Price and production policies of individual firms and consumers under alternative market conditions and analysis of these policies on social efficiency of resource allocation. Students expected to have understanding of elementary algebra and geometry.

*(Ohio University)*

**ECO 238 Money and Banking**
History of money and monetary standards; commercial banking in the United States; evolution and functions of the Federal Reserve system; the development of specialized banking institutions; the operation of credit and monetary controls; foreign exchange practices and problems; international financing institutions; contemporary issues in national and international finance.

*(Pace University)*

**Economics 242 Environmental Economics**
This course will analyze ecological issues and concerns from an economic perspective. Stress will be placed on the development of environmental economic theory and the analysis of orthodox and alternative solutions to ecological problems. Specific topics to be covered will include the interrelationship of the environment and the economy, pollution control strategies, public environmental policy,

energy needs and ecological problems, and the steady-state economy. Specific environmental economic issues will also be discussed.

*(Bard College)*

### ECON 400 Introduction to Econometrics

This course develops basic concepts of statistical theory and their applications to statistical inference. Parameter estimation techniques involved in postulated economic relationships between variables and the methods of testing propositions will be developed. The multiple regression model will be covered and students will be required to complete an individual course project involving the application of multiple regression.

*(Pepperdine University)*

**Assessment**

"Courses in accounting, finance, and the mathematics of finance are directly relevant to the work I do today," says Kevin Lonnie, a 1976 graduate of Princeton University. After completing college, he worked in banking and then earned an MBA degree from the Sloan School at the Massachusetts Institute of Technology. Now he is manager of financial planning at a medium-sized corporation.

Among other courses that have proven useful are microeconomics and statistics. As to *how* he learned his lessons, he cites the value of the long-term research papers that were required of him as both an undergraduate and a graduate student. "These were distasteful at the time because of all the work they required, but now I realize that they gave me good experience in applying knowledge as well as an understanding of the form and content of larger research work, which is useful in business." Over the length of his career, Mr. Lonnie foresees that his economics degree will provide a good background as well as many different career possibilities.

An economics graduate of Drew University, who also went on to get an MBA, is now Director of Equity Portfolio Management for the investment arm of a bank. He is directly responsible for over $1 billion in investment funds. "I was very naive about business and finance before college, and economics gave me the general knowledge necessary to make a career in business," he says. One part of this background that he finds useful today is an understanding of economic history—the economic theories of John Maynard Keynes and other major economists of the past. He also says a course in financial management gave him the analytical tools that he uses day to day: financial analysis, profit/loss estimates, and hurdle rates for investment returns. "Quantitative analysis and statistics are very important in the type of work that I do."

Portfolio management is the responsibility of Jonathan Nye, a 1979 economics graduate from Allegheny College. "My father ran a business providing services to the financial community, so I guess that I had it at the back of my mind to work in that field," he recalls. "Economics provided me with the training necessary to make good financial analyses—to determine cost/benefit ratios, and to see how macroeconomic forces affect the investments my firm makes."

| | |
|---|---|
| **Career Options** | **Actuary** |
| | **Bank administrator** |
| | **Business administrator** |
| | **Compensation analyst** |
| | **Cost estimator** |
| | **Demographer** |
| | **Economist;** the hot areas currently are international development and trade. |
| | **Financial analyst** |
| | **Investor relations manager** |
| | **Journalist,** especially for business reporting. |
| | **Management consultant** |
| | **Marketing researcher** |
| | **Public administrator** |
| | **Regional planner** |
| | **Statistician** |
| | **Underwriter** |

# EDUCATION

**(Elementary and Secondary Education, Physical Education, and Education Administration)**

| | | 1983 | 1985 | 1988 |
|---|---|---|---|---|
| **Enrollment** | BS or BA | 97,991 | 88,161 | 91,013 |
| **Boxscore** | Master's | 84,853 | 76,137 | 77,704 |
| | PhD | 7,551 | 7,151 | 6,544 |

**Overview**

Schools of education exist primarily to prepare teachers for elementary, primary, and secondary school, for special education, and for school administration. In most cases, college-level education is carried out by Phd graduates. The Education Departments usually have a complementary relationship to traditional liberal arts programs: a student majoring in education can take (in fact, is required to take) many liberal arts courses to complete a degree, while a liberal arts major can take education courses to obtain the necessary background for teacher certification. Generally speaking, an education major is for students who are sure that they want to be teachers or school administrators. Because many liberal arts colleges do not offer the education courses necessary for certification, some graduates of those schools take a master's degree or obtain intensive teacher training at another college.

The courses in a typical education department include social sciences such as psychology and sociology. These courses focus on developmental issues for early and later childhood. Because they often apply to adult learning as well, the training and experience of teaching can also be applied in vocational training and corporate training. Many former school teachers have moved into this more lucrative field. The experience of standing before a group of listeners can also be useful training for jobs in which presentation skills are important, such as sales, customer service, and the "facilitation" of meetings. Finally, students who major in special education are exposed to human-development issues that relate directly to social work and social services, such as the evaluation and therapy of the disadvantaged.

Teacher training has become controversial in recent years as the overall quality of American education has been questioned. Many practicing teachers themselves complain about the meaninglessness of the subjects they were required to learn to become teachers. More research is being done on the art of teaching and teacher preparation, and big changes may be coming for education departments.

To be certified, education students must spend time as student teachers or observers (which education departments often describes as "fieldwork"). Certification is granted by the state in which the teacher training is provided; however, many states have reciprocity agreements.

**Concentrations**

**Primary or Elementary Education**

**Secondary Education,** in which teachers specialize in subjects taught at the typical high school: English, math, sciences, languages, social studies, etc.

**Special Education,** in which students learn to address the needs of pupils with physical or mental handicaps.

**Education Administration,** which is concerned with the management of educational enterprises, including facilities, sports programs, staff administration, and the like.

**Physical Education**—in a word, gym. Physical education professionals have moved beyond the school setting, however, into such areas as health club management, health-care, and professional athletics.

**Course Sampler**

**SED CT 556 Classroom Evaluation**
Emphasizes principles and procedures of testing and evaluation that are of primary importance to educational practitioners. Includes diagnostic tests, construction of classroom tests, observation techniques, and performance measures; norm and criterion referenced assessment; uses of standardized tests; current issues and controversies.

*(Boston University)*

### 231d The Craft of Teaching

What knowledge is of most importance? How should such knowledge be organized and taught? How is student achievement measured and evaluated? The general principles of curriculum planning and instruction, including the use of media and materials. Emphasis is on the scientific basis of the art of teaching. Each student will design a curriculum unit in a commonly taught elementary or secondary school subject. Directed participant-observer exercises in area elementary and/or secondary schools.

*(Colby College)*

### Education 321 Teaching Reading in the Elementary School

This course examines basic skills of teaching reading to children grades K–6: developing sight vocabulary, word-attack skills, reading readiness, and basic strategies of approaching reading instruction, introducing basic comprehension concepts, organizing the reading instructional time, selecting reading materials, and evaluating students' reading progress.

*(Concordia College)*

**Assessment**

"After studying sociology and history at George Washington University, I decided that I was not interested in teaching," says Frank Taylor. Now president of a non-profit economic-development organization in Kentucky, he followed his undergraduate schooling with a Peace Corps assignment, and then with a doctorate in economics of education from Columbia University in the late 1960s. As part of his dissertation, he did fieldwork in Brazil, which led to an assignment in evaluation and program development for international aid efforts in that country.

"The common element in my work has been community and human-development," he says. "The study at the economics of education gave me an introduction both to education and to community development."

Martha Madsen, meanwhile, studied English and psychology at Colgate University (1986), then pursued an intensive 1-year master's degree in education from Harvard University. She now works as a high school teacher in Massachusetts. "I started college thinking that I liked English, but I found the curriculum too general. I became interested in psychology as a way to get involved in human services. Both my parents are teachers, and I suppose that did something to influence me. Graduate school was an interesting experience, because most of my classmates were already teachers. They brought a high level of enthusiasm and real-world experience to the classes.'' Having taught for several years now, she is not sure whether to continue in that profession, or to branch out into other work as an educator, perhaps in a museum setting.

For Mary Ellen Blatus, a degree in physical education opened doors to two related careers: police officer and police instructor. A 1986 graduate of Manhattan College, she has worked in the police department of a major Northeastern city, and, after she returns from maternity leave, is scheduled to be promoted to sergeant. She has already won an award for valor from her department. ''Most police officers, if they go to college, study criminal justice, and there's nothing bad about that. But I've felt that there are two parts to police work: knowing the law, and the physical aspect. Physical education prepared me for that part of the work.''

Although education courses were part of her curriculum at Manhattan College, Ms. Blatus says that she knew she wouldn't be a high school gym teacher after she graduated. ''The program I took stressed knowledge about one's body: good training, nutrition, physical limitations. That came in handy when I took on an assignment to be an instructor at the Police Academy.'' The education courses have also proved invaluable in street-cop work: ''You learn that you can talk your way out of many situations, to be tough, but not to be threatening. My physical education training gave me a lot of the confidence that's needed in those situations.''

**Career Options**

College administrator
College professor, liberal arts
Corporate trainer
Dancer/dance therapist
Elementary/high school administrator
Experiential educator
Foreign language teacher
Job counselor
Librarian

Public administrator, especially for education or training pro-
grams.
Teacher, K–12
Vocational (adult) teacher

# ELECTRICAL AND ELECTRONICS ENGINEERING

|  | | 1983 | 1985 | 1988 |
|---|---|---|---|---|
| **Enrollment** | BS or BA | 18,049 | 21,691 | 23,598 |
| **Boxscore** | Master's | 4,531 | 5,153 | 6,692 |
|  | PhD | 550 | 660 | 860 |

**Overview**

Electrical engineering is the dominant discipline in engineering, both on campus and in the engineering world. Just over one out of four engineering students is enrolled in this discipline. Why should it be so dominant? The answer lies in the ubiquity of electricity in modern society. Electricity not only provides power (from the utility, across the transmission wires, into your home), but it is the basic form of energy for long-distance communications and for controlling most types of complex machinery. Electricity is also essential to nearly all forms of computing.

The history of electrical engineering parallels the innovations in technology in the past century. The first "electricians" worked on power and electric lighting. Other parts of the electromagnetic spectrum soon gave rise to radio, and eventually television. The number of "radio engineers" grew extremely rapidly after World War II, and soon there was an agreement between the respective professional societies to merge the old profession of power engineering with the new one of communications and electronics. Since then, the electronics orientation of electrical engineering has come to dominate the entire profession. The commercially useful properties of small crystals and ceramics to modulate extremely low electrical currents gave rise to the now-mighty electronics industry.

**Concentrations**

The conventional training of electrical engineers stresses the general principles of electromagnetism, semiconductor technology, and power generation. In some undergraduate programs, and most graduate programs, the chance to specialize is readily available in such programs as:

**Power Engineering**, the study of power generation and utilization.

**Communications engineering**, which entails all aspects of wire-based, satellite, radio, and related means of rapidly transporting information.

**Control Engineering**, the application of electronics to control electrical machinery.

**Microelectronics engineering**, the study of integrated circuit design and manufacture, and computer components.

**Systems Engineering**, the general approach to combining power, control, and communications in commercially useful devices.

**Course Sampler**

**EE 6361 Integrated Circuits**
Design, fabrication, and application considerations of monolithic linear integrated circuits (ICs). Analysis of unconventional circuitry contained in typical ICs. Applications of available ICs.

*(Georgia Institute of Technology)*

**EE 321 Electromagnetics and Materials I**
Introductory treatment of static electrical and magnetic fields in free space, and stationary matter and physical properties of field, charges, and currents. Included are: electromagnetic field vectors and field equations, boundary conditions, Poison's equation, solutions of Laplace's equation for scalar electric and magnetic potentials, vector potential, polarization and magnetization of charges and currents, and unified macroscopic treatment of fields in matter. Electromagnetic energy.

*(Ohio University)*

**ENG SC 415 Communication Systems**
Signal analysis, transmission of signal and power density spectra: amplitude modulation, angle modulation, pulse modulation, and various forms of pulse-code modulation systems. Noise and noise calculation in the performance of various communication systems. Information transmission. Practical examples of communication systems.

*(Boston University)*

**Assessment**

"I like the feeling of being on the leading edge of electronic technology," says a 1983 graduate of Northwestern University in electrical engineering. She moved directly from school to the aerospace industry and is employed as an electronics specialist for a major airplane builder. She says that the typical range of courses on circuits, semiconductor devices, and electrical principles are invaluable to her work. Some of her hours are spent writing computer programs at as terminal, some in developing electronics packages for the "avionics" (aviation electronics) systems of jet fighters. "This work requires presentations before my team of co-workers, as well as general presentations to management. Communication skills are always important."

While she was a student, she was in a co-op program under which she alternated each semester between school and work at her current employer. "When I was tired of schoolwork, I would be working the next semester, and vice versa. I also learned many 'real-world' things that helped my schoolwork." She is undecided about her future, but sees that more engineering training will be necessary in systems theory and electronics before she can move into management.

**Career Options**

Aerospace engineer, with regard to "avionics"—the electronics of aircraft.
Artificial intelligence developer
Business-to-business salesperson
College professor, science and technology
Computer engineer
Computer service engineer
Computer systems analyst

**Electrical engineer;** the hot areas currently are microelectronics, computers, and power generation.
**Energy engineer**
**Film/video engineer**
**Industrial/manufacturing engineer**
**Lawyer,** especially patent law.
**Telecommunications manager**

---

# ENGLISH

## (English Literature)

| | | 1983 | 1985 | 1988 |
|---|---|---|---|---|
| **Enrollment** | BS or BA | 32,301 | 33,708 | 39,106 |
| **Boxscore** | Master's | 5,645 | 5,820 | 6,073 |
| | PhD | 1,137 | 1,196 | 1,127 |

**Overview**

English is one of the largest and most central liberal arts majors on the American campus. By studying literature and developing writing and speaking skills, English majors gain a strong expertise in communications. Communications skills can be applied in a broad range of jobs in which interacting with people is essential. Careers range from the obvious (sales, training, media) to the not-so-obvious (law, medicine, business management, and banking, to name a few).

Traditionally, the English department has been one of the largest on the college campus, and the number of students has held up in recent years. The 37,133 BA graduates in 1987 puts English (and the related majors that go under the title of Letters) at number 10 among college majors.

Most undergraduate English departments have not incorporated specific career tracks into their curricula. The major exception is the use of an English degree for teaching. An English degree can be used to teach at the grade school or high school level, and, with graduate schooling, at the university level. (Some extra training in teaching methods is usually required, especially for public-school teaching.) Teaching, in turn, opens many doors to the business world, ranging from sales or customer service to training, public relations, and advertising. Public relations and advertising are "teaching" tasks in the sense that their purpose is to communicate how a company's products or financial structure is worth the attention of customers.

**Concentrations**

**Composition, Grammar and Expository Writing,** the most basic concentration in English, lends itself readily to teaching.

**Literature,** which varies widely by school, region of the country, and the student's academic interests; might include courses in American literature, British literature, Western American literature and literary criticism.

**Technical Writing and Communications,** which involves preparing the student "to meet the demands of business, industry, and government . . . in the high technology field," according to the program description at New York Institute of Technology. Technical writing ranges from preparing the user's manuals for computer programs to communicating scientific and technical information via film, audiotape, or the printed page.

**Creative Writing,** which includes fiction, poetry, theater, and screenwriting, is sometimes in the English department, and sometimes in a separate creative writing major.

**Course Sampler**

**E Comp 211 Practice in Composition**
Study in fundamentals of rhetoric, consistency in grammatical structure, and varieties of usage with attention to audience adaptation and the writer's style. Frequent practice in writing, primarily exposition, although specific assignments will be determined by each class' needs.

*(Washington University in St. Louis)*

**English 209 Development of English Poetry**
The course will begin by a reading of the anonymous song lyrics of late Medieval England, and go on to concentrate on the major poets who wrote in the English Renaissance, roughly from 1500 to 1700. The vitality of poetry during this period comes in part from the creation of a

strong poetic tradition, flexible enough to accommodate changing forms and values. Yet within this tradition, poetic activity becomes the means to new modes of awareness, self-consciousness, and human relationship. Poets to be read include Skelton, Wyatt, Spenser, Sidney, Shakespeare, Donne. . . .

*(Bard College)*

### English 363 Modern American Literature

An examination of literary currents between the World Wars. Both the cosmopolite and national movements in poetry, fiction, and drama are included, with attention to "proletarian" literature and the continuing development of minority writings, particularly the Harlem Renaissance.

*(Illinois Wesleyan University)*

**Assessment**

"Learning how to write" and "learning how to think" are two of the main themes that graduates of English programs mention.

"Lots of writing back in college helps me with all the writing I do today," says Debbie Kosofsky, a 1979 graduate of Washington University (St. Louis). Ms. Kosofsky works as a television producer for a nationally broadcast show. She got her start at a television network by being willing to take a low-level job handling transportation arrangements for the guests on television talk shows. Over time, this exposure led to work in selecting guests and developing show themes. "Originally, I wanted to be a newspaper journalist, but I found in college that I really didn't like that type of work," she says. Besides the training in writing, the English program provided her with "a sense of literature, culture and history —all things that I need to do my work today."

Another English graduate who did turn his training into a career in newspapers is Richard Baudouin (Tulane, 1975), a Louisiana newspaper editor and television commentator. "I started college being interested in philosophy and anthropology, but a love of poetry, and the desire for a broad liberal arts education, brought me to English," he says. That schooling, combined with becoming the editor in chief of the school newspaper, led him into the journalism field. "A lot of kids study journalism in order to work on a newspaper," he observes. "That's fine, especially at the graduate level, but I think it leaves you too specialized when you graduate.

You need to learn about life, and about art and history and all the other traditional things while in college."

By a circuitous route, Charles Coombs (University of New Mexico, 1968, MA, 1971) transformed his English degree into a career in computer systems analysis and technical support. "I started college by spending 3 years flunking out of math and physics before I went into English," he wistfully remembers. While in school he began doing technical writing to support himself, took a few computer programming courses, and worked as a systems analyst. "It's hard for me to imagine a more appropriate major for a computer technician than English. I am able to write computer code because I understand how languages, including computer languages, work. I used that understanding to evolve a grammar for programming languages that went well beyond anything people were teaching in 'structured' programming classes, and made my work absolutely bulletproof." He stresses that even while concentrating on programming, the majority of his time was taken up with writing business plans, negotiating, and speaking—in English, not in a computer language. "They don't teach you that stuff in computer school."

A more literary use of an English degree is illustrated by the career history of Martha Millard (Drew University, 1980), owner of her own book agency. Ms. Millard represents several major fiction and non-fiction writers, acting as their agent when dealing with publishers. "I had a vague intention of being a journalist before college," she recalls. "During and after school, that feeling got sharpened into a desire to work in publishing, which I did for a couple of years after graduation." Not finding that her career interests matched the publishing world's, she switched to agency work.

"Both as an agent and as an editor, I use my English literature background to analyze a piece of writing. Publishing revolves around determining what books will sell, and the more you develop a taste and judgment for literature, the more successful you can be. I get great satisfaction out of working with writers who I think make a difference in American culture."

Many students take English to prepare for law school, and that route has been successfully traveled by Sara Pearl, an attorney. She complemented a 1980 degree in English from Colgate University with a law degree, and now works for a New York advertising agency, handling their contracts and litigation activities. "Nothing *specific* to my English degree is used in my work now," she says, "but the general skills I use routinely: reading critically, writing cogently." She adds that "I felt at Colgate that I was enrolled in one of the university's best majors," taught by top-notch professors who were engaging, interesting teachers. "Reading is a pleasure and an avocation that lasts far beyond one's college years."

**Career Options**

Association executive
College professor, liberal arts
Consumer-goods salesperson
Copywriter
Editor, book
Editor, magazine
Elementary/high school administrator, with educational credentials.
Human-resources manager
Information specialist
Journalist
Lawyer
Librarian
Marketing manager
Paralegal
Publicist
Radio/television announcer

# GEOLOGY

**(Geological Engineering, Mining Engineering, Geophysics)**

| | | 1983 | 1985 | 1988 |
|---|---|---|---|---|
| **Enrollment** | BS or BA | 6,102 | 6,308 | 2,552 |
| **Boxscore** | Master's | 1,552 | 1,692 | 1,530 |
| | PhD | 295 | 289 | 350 |

**Overview**

Before recorded history, there is history to be found in rocks. This history seems remote (to say the least—it goes back over 4 billion years), yet it is very important to our lives today. Consider the effects of the 1989 San Francisco earthquake.

Aside from earthquake damage control, geologists' skills are vital to the search for minerals and petroleum, the construction of mines and tunnels, and the assessment of stone as a construction or foundation material. Finally, through their knowledge of how the earth and water interact, geologists are becoming critically important to environmental work, from the siting of new factories to the cleanup of toxic waste dumps.

Because geology is rarely taught in high school, many college geology departments expend considerable effort in their introductory courses to attract students to the field. Geology programs study everything from the ancient life recorded in fossils (paleontology) to the tectonic plates on which entire continents sit (and which are causing all the earthquake problems along the San Andreas Fault in California).

Both during study and as a career, geology offers an interesting mix of travel and office work. Many school programs include field trips or internships in geologically interesting regions, like the Rocky Mountains. Working geologists can spend the better part of their workday out of doors—running an oil rig, taking mineral samples as part of a geological survey—in some of the most exotic parts of the world. Conversely, many geologists do pioneering work by sitting at a desk in front of a computer screen.

**Concentrations**

**Hydrogeology,** the study of the effects of fresh or salt water on the rock formations of the earth's crust.

**Petrology or Mineralogy,** the analysis and classification of rocks.

**Petroleum geology,** which concentrates on crude oil in the ground.

**Geological and Mining Engineering,** which applies geological principles to the construction and operation of mines.

**Geophysics,** the study of the fundamental forces affecting the earth's matter.

**Paleontology,** the study of the fossil record of prehistoric forms of life, has much in common with paleobiology (see BIOLOGY).

**Course Sampler**

**GEOL 360 Structural Geology**
Principles of rock deformation and interpretation of folding and faulting and related topics. Field-oriented structural problems, structural maps, and use of stereographic projections.

*(Ohio University)*

**GEOL 2010 Landform Analysis: Geomorphology**
Identification, description, and analysis of landforms created by earth processes such as fluvial, glacial, eolian, coastal, karst, and tectonics. Includes laboratory.

*(University of Denver)*

**EPSC 321 Stratigraphy and Sedimentation**
Introduction to origin of sedimentary rocks, stressing physical and chemical processes involved in producing, transporting, and accumulating sediment. Transformation of sediment to sedimentary rock. Stratigraphic classification, correlations, and analysis of lithologic patterns.

*(Washington University in St. Louis)*

**Assessment**

The petroleum industry has been the career path of Susanne Shelley, a 1986 graduate of Colgate University in geology. She followed her baccalaureate with a master's degree in geology from the University of South Carolina, then was hired by an oil company to work as a petroleum geologist. "It's my responsibility to analyze subsurface geological data [seismic lines and well logs], while working with economists, geophysicists and production engineers to make recommendations to management on whether or not to develop a potential oil or gas reservoir."

Of her undergraduate training, Ms. Shelley says that a "strong, integrated framework" of geology courses has proven to be a help in her daily work. "From mineralogy and petrology, through structural geology, paleontology, and geophysics—an understanding of those are required to analyze the complexities of subsurface puzzles." She says that the highlight of her undergraduate years was a 2-month school-sponsored field trip during the summer between her junior and senior year, when she and some classmates traveled throughout New England, doing mapping and geological studies. "We camped, worked, and played together, getting to know the professors on a first-name basis."

For Keith Johns, a 1986 geology graduate of Allegheny College, geology has been the ticket to a career in environmental consulting. He works for a small environmental firm in the Washington, DC area, where he does studies to define the extent of pollution in groundwater formations around the country. Mr. Johns also attended the University of South Carolina for a master's degree in geology, graduating in 1988. At South Carolina, he specialized in a branch of geology known as sedimentology, the study of soils. This, combined with hydrogeological studies during his undergraduate years, gave him the tools to do the test work for his employer.

An example of how his training benefits him occurs during the analysis of core samples brought up by a well. "We use electronic instruments in the well to "log" it—to show the types of geologic formations in the area. Then I look at the type of soil that is in the formation, and do some chemical analyses to determine the extent of contamination." It helps a lot if a geologist enjoys the outdoors: "I've done fieldwork in rain, in hot summers, and in cold winters."

"Environmental work has proven to be very satisfying to me," he says, noting that a career in environmental law might lie in the future. "It's a good feeling to work on something that will have an impact on the future condition of the planet."

**Career Options**   **Civil engineer,** in the sense that geologists are involved with construction-site preparation and large-scale construction (i.e., water reservoirs).
**Earth (planetary) scientist**
**Geologist;** the hot areas currently are environmental projects and water resource planning.
**Petroleum engineer**

# HISTORY

### (American Studies, American Civilization)

| | | 1983 | 1985 | 1988 |
|---|---|---|---|---|
| Enrollment | BS or BA | 16,465 | 16,048 | 18,194 |
| Boxscore | Master's | 2,040 | 1,921 | 2,092 |
| | PhD | 575 | 468 | 519 |

**Overview**

History is one of the great traditions of liberal arts, and acting as its repository has been one of the main functions of universities over the centuries. History has been, and continues to be, one of the most popular college majors. Yet there are few places in our society, aside from college campuses or high schools, where history is "done":  state historical offices, a few dozen local historical societies, large organizations with staff historians, a handful of national magazines, and the work of some freelance biographers and history writers. Historical researchers or writers are usually affiliated with a university or teach. In the index of professions most commonly used by the US Bureau of Labor Statistics, there is no listing for "historian."

History majors therefore have to overcome a gap between school and career. Luckily, a great number of the previous generation also studied history in college, and understand the value of a history degree in the business or commercial world.

How do you make the transition from study to employment? The keys are your understanding of social traditions and trends, and your communication skills. There are few ways to gain a better understanding of a culture than through studying its history, but it is up to you to apply that understanding to the contemporary situation. That understanding begins with a heavy dose of reading (essentially, library research), and writing. Research and writing are vital tools in any career.

At the graduate level more than the undergraduate, there is a trend toward using hard data in historical research. Students study old records (of births, deaths, number of homes, numbers of employees, earnings, and the like) to determine what *really* went on in the past. Such study builds skills in statistical analysis.

**Concentrations**

Most students are interested in American history. World history is often taught by regions (Asian Studies, African Studies). It is possible, however, to study non-US history at many universities. The range of concentrations include:

**American History**
**Modern European History**
**Ancient or Medieval History**
**Pre-Law,** a program that includes courses preparing the student for law school admission.
**Historiography,** the "history of history," often taught at the graduate level; concentrates on how historical study has changed over time.

**Course Sampler**

**433 American Diplomatic History**
American foreign relations from the late 19th century to the present; emphasis on development of major trends such as isolationism, imperialism, and internationalism.

*(Eastern Kentucky University)*

**266 A History of the American South**
This course will cover selected topics in Southern history from the establishment of the Southern colonies in the 17th century to the civil rights struggle of the 1960s. It will explore the basic economic, social, and political facets of Southern history, as well as such specific issues as race relations and the Southern literary imagination. Throughout the course, an attempt will be made to define the factors that made the South such a distinctive and important region in American history.

*(Denison University)*

**Seminar: Women in Medieval and Renaissance Europe**
Examines the role and status of women in medieval and Renaissance Europe, exploring theological and medical attitudes toward women, as well as economic and social determinants for women's lives. Topics

include the development of the institution of marriage; the ideal of romantic love; women's religious experience; and women's economic, literary, and artistic contributions to society. Balances between studying women as a group in history and examining individual women, when possible through their own words.

*(New York University)*

### HIST 2152 Russia from Alexander I to Lenin

The tsarist empire in the Napoleonic period in the forefront of European reaction; the emancipation of serfs and other reforms; economic and educational trends in the late 19th century; revolutionary movements; World War I and the revolution of 1917.

*(University of Denver)*

**Assessment**

"My studies in college have little direct impact on my career," says Don Pettit, an advertising manager for a major cosmetics company and a 1977 graduate of Princeton University. "However, history has contributed to a general framework of knowledge and understanding of people that allows me to do a better job of understanding consumers."

In developing products and marketing plans, Mr. Pettit depends on his sense of American society today. He feels the best way to sharpen that sense is to look at the past. History also offered him the "ability to teach myself."

Another history major working in marketing and advertising, Beth Graebe (Holy Cross, 1988), is employed in the financial services field. She markets her company's retirement-investment plans and mutual funds. "I took history because I loved it," she remembers. Today, the courses that I took give me a sense of what is best to do in advertising." The reason for this is that she took courses in modern social history—the patterns of living and working of common people, rather than in "big events" like wars. One course looked at American society from the perspective of young people who became adults during each decade of the 20th century. Each decade studied had advertising campaigns as a window.

"I enjoyed how history is taught—we had small groups that would discuss the topics we were studying, so my speaking skills were improved. And of course, the research and writing requirements taught me organization and communication skills,'' she adds.

The love of the subject, rather than any specific career goal, brought Tricia Freedman to history at Bucknell University, from which she graduated in 1989. "I tried some other courses to test this interest, but I found myself completely bored by things like economics," she says, "so I stuck with what I loved."

Ms. Freedman now works as an assistant account executive at a public relations firm that works with universities. "This work combines my skills in public relations with my interest in higher education." She may continue schooling in education administration in the near future. The history studies taught her research, organization, and writing skills, all of which she uses regularly in her office.

**Career Options**

Advertising account executive
Association executive
Business administrator
College administrator
College professor, liberal arts
Consumer-goods salesperson
Copywriter
Editor, book
Editor, magazine
Historian
Human-resources manager
Information specialist, especially if education required substantial library research.
Journalist
Lawyer
Marketing manager
Paralegal
Political Scientist
Public administrator, with additional training in public administration.
Teacher, K–12
Travel planner

# HOME ECONOMICS

**(Human Ecology, Family and Consumer Sciences, Food Science)**

| | | 1983 | 1985 | 1988 |
|---|---|---|---|---|
| **Enrollment** | BS or BA | 16,705 | 15,555 | 14,285 |
| **Boxscore** | Master's | 2,406 | 2,383 | 2,059 |
| | PhD | 255 | 276 | 309 |

**Overview**

Home economics evolved in collegiate education years ago as one of the primary degrees pursued by women; the assumption was that a college education could help ladies when they became homemakers and mothers. With the rising number of women becoming professionals in careers of all kinds, this assumption has become quaint, to say the least. Home economics education has not stood still however; today it is involved in consumer affairs policy and legal issues, in nutrition and family social services, and in the marketing of consumer goods. Home economics remains one of the larger academic programs on college campuses. It is still most popular with women.

**Concentrations**

Some home economics programs concentrate on scientific or technical issues, such as nutrition or clothing manufacture, and some concentrate on aesthetic themes, such as interior design, consumer goods selection, or fashion. The approaches and subject matter vary greatly among schools. Key areas include:

**Food Science and Nutrition,** which prepares students to be dieticians, nutritional experts, or institutional food managers. The training can also be applied in consumer goods marketing and product development.

**Family and Community Services,** which emphasizes training in social services for community health, education, or well-being.

**Homemaking, Fashion, and Interior Design,** which overlap in some schools with programs in commercial art or design. Some schools offer concentrations on the technology and methods of marketing and manufacturing textiles and other consumer goods; some offer training in fashion selection and design.

**Home Economics Education,** which combines teacher preparation (usually for teaching in high school) with homemaking issues.

**Course Sampler**

**FCS 161 Individual and Family Environments:   The Individual**
Focuses on the individual within the family as he or she relates to the environment (food, shelter, and resources). The individual's growth and development across the life cycle is examined from professional perspectives of dietetics, education, food management, housing and interior design, individual and family studies, and retailing.

*(Miami University)*

**HEC 2202 Nutrition and Man**
A study of the nutrients required by humans for normal physiological function with emphasis on nutrient requirements, sources, digestion, absorption, metabolism, and functions. Consideration of contemporary nutritional issues to include:   overweight, malnutrition; health; natural and organic foodstuffs; athletics' diets; and nutrient requirements throughout life. Emphasis on nutrition consumerism.

*(Appalachian State University)*

**TCF 313 Apparel Design Analysis**
Visual analysis of apparel and the human form through identification and application of the elements and principles of design. Consideration of clothing as an aesthetic expression and of individual physical and social clothing needs throughout the life cycle.

*(Eastern Kentucky University)*

**Assessment**

"Home economics doesn't have much to do with my career now, but it did help me get my start," says a 1971 graduate of Baylor University in Texas. She went on several years later to obtain a law degree, and has worked since as a corporate counselor and as a law school administrator.

After her undergraduate schooling, she worked for several years as a demonstrator of electrical appliances and other home appliances, under the sponsorship of a local utility company. Such promotional activities have given way, in many parts of the country, to customer-service representation. "This type of work used to be fairly straightforward," she says. "But today, the job entails answering questions about rate structures, energy efficiency and the like. That type of work has become more complex."

Being a "foodie"—one who is interested in all aspects of preparing or working with food—has produced a career as a food stylist, a recipe writer, and a published author for Carol Gelles, a 1977 master's graduate from New York University. With her degree in home economics, and with training in education that she is undertaking currently, the next step will be to teach home economics at the junior high level. "Home economics education in schools has changed dramatically from what it was a generation ago, when girls gathered in a kitchen to learn how to bake, or sat around a table learning how to sew. Today, it is a course in life skills. It offers a tremendous opportunity to open up the minds of young people," she says. "I've worked in the glamour parts of the home economics profession; now I will be getting back down to earth."

Getting to "earth" follows a number of years spent as a freelance food stylist, who as, Ms. Gelles explains, is as the professional concerned with getting food to look just right in preparation for filming a commercial or movie. "This is a kind of profession where much of the learning is by experience on the job," she says. "I began by working with an established food stylist, then branched out on my own."

A home economics background, as regards food, teaches the student how to follow a recipe exactly, says Ms. Gelles. That discipline proved valuable in making preparations for, and conducting, food styling sessions while expensive film crews waiting for a cake to rise or for a table arrangement to be completed.

In recent years, Ms. Gelles has turned her talents to cookbook writing; she published "The Complete Whole Grain Cookbook" (Donald I. Fine, Inc.) a couple of years ago and is currently working on another book.

Another home economist, Dolores Custer, has worked as a food stylist, teacher (at both culinary schools and at colleges, and recipe writer (for magazines). "When I was considering how to turn my love of food into a career, I had two choices," says the 1979 graduate of New York University. "Either I could go to culinary school to become a chef, or I could go the home economics route. Home economics offered a larger number of career options, although it has the drawback of requiring courses in textiles or family life which weren't important to me." The most important aspect of home economics that Ms. Custer sees is that it is not solely for teaching teenagers in school; there are many other professional avenues open to the trained home economist.

**Career Options**

Association executive
Business administrator
Consumer-goods salesperson
Corporate trainer
Designer, industrial and fashion
Designer, interior
Dietician/nutritionist
Editor, magazine
Experiential educator
Financial planner
Franchise manager
Home economist
Hotel manager
Human resources manager
Marketing researcher
Teacher, K–12
Travel planner
Vocational (adult) teacher

# INDUSTRIAL ENGINEERING

(Manufacturing Engineering, Operations Research)

| | | 1983 | 1985 | 1988 |
|---|---|---|---|---|
| **Enrollment** | BS or BA | 3,748 | 3,914 | 4,082 |
| **Boxscore** | Master's | 1,432 | 1,462 | 1,815 |
| | PhD | 118 | 139 | 162 |

**Overview**

Once mechanical, electrical, and chemical engineers have devised the machines and procedures for a new manufacturing process, the industrial engineer steps in to organize a factory to make it. Industrial engineers don't usually specialize in one type of technology, but rather in the *systems* that make manufacturing work. These systems include the obvious (assembly lines, packaging machinery, and so forth) and the not so obvious (the workforce, quality measurement and control, financial controls to monitor the profitability of the operation).

This engineering specialty is in the spotlight today, as United States manufacturers hustle to modernize their factories to keep up with foreign competition. Where the US once dominated the world in manufacturing excellence, it now finds itself in a dogfight to compete for international markets.

Basic industrial engineering grew out of a philosophy called "scientific management" shortly after the turn of the century, when the assembly line became dominant in manufacturing. Today's industrial engineers study how workers work, how assembly lines are designed, and how quality and productivity are measured. The computer has become a basic tool for the industrial engineer.

**Concentrations**

**Industrial Engineering,** which studies theoretical as well as practical applications of manufacturing technology.

**Manufacturing Engineering or Engineering Technology,** which concentrates on practical, real-world applications.

**Operations research,** which pertains most directly to transportation and scheduling problems, and has obvious relevance to factory management.

**Systems Engineering,** which is a general term for large engineering problems; some schools make systems engineering part of the electrical engineering discipline rather than industrial engineering.

**Course Sampler**

**IE 7052 Facilities Design and Materials Handling**
The main objective of the facilities layout function is to increase operational efficiency of the plant through effective integration of manufacturing equipment, materials handling systems, plant facilities,

and labor requirements. This course will provide a thorough analysis of the various quantitative and computerized models that have been developed to cope with the increasing complexity of layout problems.

*(New York Institute of Technology)*

### ISE 435 Quality Control and Reliability

Application of statistics to the control of quality and reliability in products and services. Design of acceptance sampling and process control systems, including attention to inspection and test methods. Design and implementation of quality assurance programs, including non-statistical dimensions of quality systems.

*(Ohio University)*

### MY 310 Industrial Safety

A study of industrial safety including topics of accident causation and analysis, common industrial accidents, personal protective equipment, housekeeping procedures, materials handling and storage, machine safety and guarding, and health standards common to industry. Compliance with current state and federal safety laws and regulations as they relate to industry will also be covered. Field trips utilized when appropriate.

*(Hofstra University)*

**Assessment**

"Doing industrial engineering is my way of making a difference in the world," says David Briskman, a 1987 BS graduate from Cornell University with a degree in operations research/industrial engineering. He followed up his baccalaureate with a master's from the same school. Now he works as a systems analyst at a large food-processing company in the Northeast. "My job title sounds like a computer job, and I've got a computer on my desk, but what I do is definitely engineering."

Mr. Briskman develops methods of improving the productivity and efficiency of manufacturing and distribution processes. One term for this is "manufacturing resource planning" or MRP. By devising a better MRP system, he can reduce manufacturing costs and improve profitability. "I could have had more lucrative job offers if I hadn't gone into manufacturing, but I take all the talk about lower quality and efficiency of American manufacturing seriously. I want to do something about it."

Of the courses in undergraduate and graduate school, Mr. Briskman remembers best a class project involving a mock manufacturing problem. His team acted as an actual product design group, and had to propose a new product, a means of manufacturing and distributing it, and a budget. "This was interesting because there is no pat answer to any of the issues," he recalls. "I learned about real-world problems, and how to present my case convincingly."

"I sampled most of the engineering programs as an under-classman," says Todd Whitlow, a classmate of Mr. Briskman's at Cornell. "I wound up in industrial engineering/operations research because that gives me a chance to work on large scale manufacturing problems," he says.

Mr. Whitlow works at a small computer-software company, developing programs that help run manufacturing processes. "In my undergraduate classes, I was exposed both to computer technology and to economics and production issues," he says. "This makes for interesting problems to work on."

**Career Options**

Business-to-business salesperson

Designer, industrial and fashion

Human-resources manager

Industrial/manufacturing engineer; hot areas currently are quality control and factory automation.

Management consultant, especially with regard to manufacturing technology.

Mechanical Engineer

Operations/systems researcher

Purchasing agent

Safety engineer

Shipping manager

# MATHEMATICS

### (Statistics, Actuarial Science)

**Enrollment Boxscore**

|  | 1983 | 1985 | 1988 |
|---|---|---|---|
| BS or BA | 12,453 | 15,727 | 15,888 |
| Master's | 2,837 | 3,184 | 3,422 |
| PhD | 698 | 285 | 752 |

**Overview**

Mathematics is another science that has been strongly influenced by computer technology, generally to its benefit. It is certainly true that many math majors can now find ready employment in industries that make computers, write software for computers, or use computers heavily.

A big distinction between the math that we remember from high school (or try hard to forget) and the math taught in college is evidenced by the decreased importance of the manipulation of numbers and the increased importance of the understanding and manipulation of symbols. Math becomes training in analytical thinking, and in abstracting essential principles from the mix of events that make up the everyday world. Thus, math has applications to complex areas of economic activity, such as business management and consulting, finance, and government policy.

In fact, for a short period of time before the stock market crash of 1987, mathematicians were "in" on Wall Street. So-called "rocket scientists" were academically trained mathematicians who used powerful computers to devise techniques for trading securities that could lock in profits. The research into mathematical trading strategies hasn't disappeared in the aftermath of the crash, but investment houses now approach new types of trading more cautiously.

For mathematical research in the sciences, a doctoral degree is obligatory. Outside of science and academia, however, there are numerous opportunities for mathematical research with a lesser degree, especially where computer technology is concerned.

**Concentrations**

Most undergraduate programs in math follow a fairly standard set of courses exposing the student to the liveliest realms of math. Some schools, observing that not all or even most of their students are headed for doctorate degrees and academia, have developed tracks for applied math, in which math tools can be applied to scientific, engineering, or policy-making problems. Concentrations include:

**Statistics,** the branch of math dealing with trends and probabilities. A hot specialty within statistics is biostatistics, which deals with health-related research and public policy.

**Actuarial Science,** which emphasizes the mathematical needs of the insurance industry.

**Mathematical Physics,** which combines math and the fundamental study of matter and energy.

**Operations Research,** which uses math tools to solve scheduling or distribution problems common in transportation, logistics, and telecommunications.

**Course Sampler**

**MA 243 Numerical Methods**
The mathematics of computation, algorithms, error estimation, and programming. Equation solutions, polynomial interpolation, linear equations, numerical integration, differential equations. Problems will be solved on the IBM PC.

*(Bucknell University)*

**MTH 4130 Mathematics of Statistics**
This course is an introduction to the inferential aspects of mathematical statistics. Topics to be included are:   Bayes estimators, maximum likelihood estimators, sufficient statistics, sampling distributions of estimators such as the Chi-square distribution and the t-distribution, confidence intervals, unbiased estimators, testing hypotheses, Neyman-Pearson lemma, the t-test, the F-distribution, introduction to linear models.

*(Baruch College, City University of New York)*

**MATH 4125 Introduction to Probability**
Introduction to probability theory with applications, discrete and non-discrete distributions, moments, laws of large numbers, central limit theorem with applications.

*(Georgia Institute of Technology)*

**Assessment**

"At the time I went to my college, I was leaning toward working with computers, but I wasn't sure enough to choose that, so I majored in math instead of computer science," recalls William Benjamin, who now works as a database administrator at a major commercial bank. The 1982 graduate of Hartwick College is now employed in maintaining a highly complex computer system that keeps tabs on customer accounts, helps run automatic-teller machines, and compiles financial results for the bank's many operations. He also writes new programming code that enhances the database performance.

"I suppose about 10–15% of my time is spent on what you might call mathematical questions, as opposed to pure computer programming—but that 10–15% is a big help," he observes. He feels his math background provides a deeper understanding of the bank's complex database program than a pure computer-science background would. Linear algebra, another part of his math education, is also a help.

Janet Bernhard, a 1982 graduate of Lafayette College, has applied her background in math in the business world. Until she had a baby, she worked full-time as the financial-services manager at a paper products manufacturer in New Jersey. She has since been working part-time and expects to go back into financial management in the near future.

"I had an aptitude for math, and I figured that I should make the most of that when I went to college," she says. At the time she went to college, there were relatively few personal computers available, so she had little exposure to computer programming. Since then, however, she has helped specify and install a computer network at her company's offices. "A math background applies to business in this way: you have good discipline, you are comfortable with the logic of problem-solving, and you can break down a problem into its elements and solve them," she says.

**Career Options**

Actuary

**Artificial intelligence developer,** assuming one's math interests are heavily oriented toward computers.

**College professor,** science and technology

**Computer engineer**

**Computer systems analyst**

Demographer
Financial analyst
Marketing researcher
Mathematician; hot areas currently are computer modeling and
    communications theory.
Operations/systems researcher
Physicist
Risk Manager
Statistician
Teacher, K–12
Underwriter

# MECHANICAL ENGINEERING

| | | 1983 | 1985 | 1988 |
|---|---|---|---|---|
| **Enrollment** | BS or BA | 15,675 | 16,794 | 14,918 |
| **Boxscore** | Master's | 2,511 | 3,053 | 3,330 |
| | PhD | 299 | 309 | 596 |

**Overview**

Mechanical engineering is the study of matter in motion—vehicles, machines, processes. That simple concept is applied to a wide array of industries and services:  transportation, aerospace, power generation, factory automation, and others. It's the second-largest engineering profession (behind electrical) and perhaps the most broadly distributed in commerce and industry.

The teaching of mechanical engineering reflects its roots in the search to understand energy and power production over a century ago. As steam power arose, mechanical engineering became concerned with developing engines and pressure vessels that could provide power to ships, trains, and vehicles. As electricity became commercially feasible, mechanical engineers became involved in hydropower, coal- or oil-fired furnaces, and nuclear power. While aerospace engineers and scientists worry about wing and fuselage designs for aircraft, mechanical engineers worry about the jet turbines that power the craft.

There are academic programs that include all of these applications of mechanical engineering expertise. In addition, colleges are aggressively upgrading their research and training in manufacturing and automation, even as industry seeks to upgrade its performance. Robotics, automated machinery, and combined design/production systems are now popping up in course work, especially at the graduate level.

**Concentrations**

With such a broad array of applications, it is possible for the mechanical engineer to specialize in many different programs. The biggest division is between those who are interested in power generation (by auto engines, jet turbines, utility plants, and related devices), and those who are interested in mechanical design (the components of machines, appliances, computers, and so forth). Concentrations include:

**Basic Engineering,** which covers hydraulics, heat transfer, tribology (the study of lubrication) and fundamental mechanical principles.

**Manufacturing and Automation,** which includes control systems, factory production, and industrial processes.

**Transportation,** which includes rail and air travel, shipping, and the systems that provide mobility.

**Energy Resources and Conversion,** which studies power generation, conservation, and alternative systems like solar or wind energy.

**Systems and Design,** which attempts to integrate technological components into efficient groups such as computer networks, production lines, or military equipment.

**Course Sampler**

ME 321 Energetics for Mechanical Engineers
Thermodynamic cycle analysis; vapor power, internal combustion, gas trubine, and refrigeration. Maxwell relations and generalized property relationships for non-ideal gases. Mixtures of ideal gases, psychrometics, ideal solutions. Combustion processes, first and second law applications to reacting systems. Chemical equilibrium. Compressible flow in nozzles and diffusers.

*(Washington University in St. Louis)*

### ME 4445 Automatic Control

Analysis and modeling of linear systems and compensation of feedback controlled systems using classical methods. Hydraulic, pneumatic, thermal, electrical, nuclear, chemical, and biomechanical examples.

*(Georgia Institute of Technology)*

### MECH 141 Introduction to Linear Systems

Study of fundamental characteristics of linear systems via analysis of simple electrical and mechanical models. Forced and natural response. Introduction to Laplace transforms and their use in mechanical vibrations, circuit analysis, and electromechanical systems such as AC/DC motors. Laboratory.

*(Santa Clara University)*

**Assessment**

"I'm a production engineer for office-automation products," says Robin Westfield, a 1988 mechanical engineering graduate of Cornell University. At a manufacturing plant in the Northeast, she spends part of her time at a desk, working with a computer to devise improvements in factory-floor layout for new production runs. The rest of her time is on the factory floor, trying to apply statistical principles to the efficiency and productivity of the factory. "Mechanical engineering is a good generic background to have in manufacturing," she says. "You get trained in all the important basics—chemistry, physics, heat transfer, mechanistics, and statistics. I don't use the knowledge of these subjects on a daily basis, but they come in handy frequently."

Ms. Westfield's short-term goal, she says, is to gain experience in production. Over the long term, she expects to move into mechanical design—developing the office machines her company sells, but not being so heavily involved in their actual production. Management may be the ultimate goal.

**Career Options**

**Aerospace engineer,** especially with regard to the power systems and structural design of aircraft.
**Business-to-business salesperson**
**Computer engineer**
**Designer, industrial**
**Energy engineer**

Industrial/manufacturing engineer
Mechanical engineer; hot areas currently are in materials technology and manufacturing quality control.
Metallurgical and materials engineer
Nuclear engineer, especially for power plants.
Petroleum engineer
Purchasing agent

---

# MODERN LANGUAGES

**(French, German, Italian, Spanish, Japanese, Chinese, etc.)**

| | | 1983 | 1985 | 1988 |
|---|---|---|---|---|
| **Enrollment** | BS or BA | 9,533 | 9,828 | 9,907 |
| **Boxscore** | Master's | 1,731 | 1,695 | 1,828 |
| | PhD | 485 | 436 | 411 |

**Overview**

College students are often required to study a foreign language; it is considered the mark of an educated person to be able to speak more than one tongue. Many valuable skills are obtained by majoring in a modern foreign language, which nearly 10,000 students do annually. The US Department of Education monitors the teaching of 18 distinct languages; others are lumped into the "foreign languages, other" category.

To speak another language fluently usually entails immersion in the culture of the people as well as learning their grammar. Thus, studying a language opens a door to other cultures, and may be the key to understanding that other culture. For decades, America has been castigated for having too few people that are fluent in the languages of foreign trading partners or supposed enemy states. American manufacturers who want to pursue international markets more aggressively need a better understanding of their overseas customers. Thus foreign language skills are a premium job qualification in today's business world.

Of course, there have always been a number of professions or businesses where language skills have been valued:   international banking and finance, import/export, and travel and tourism. Government service and teaching are other obvious career routes.

It used to be true that the study of a foreign language, especially German, was important for those pursuing careers in scientific research. This is less true today, because so much of the world's technical literature is now published in English. Nevertheless, many graduate schools of science still require at least a reading knowledge of other languages. Also, these days a scientist who can read or speak Japanese or Russian has a powerful career advantage.

Learning a language has other career benefits, too. First, it hones writing and speaking skills in your native tongue. The knowledge of other cultures is useful in therapy or counseling occupations, where it helps with treatment, diagnosis, or care. Lastly, a broader cultural background helps you relate to the outlooks or motivations of other people, which is useful in personal-service careers.

Another advantage of modern-language programs is an opportunity to study abroad. Many colleges and universities have set up their programs to reflect the ethnic heritage of the surrounding region; thus, one finds many Spanish language and literature programs in the Southeast and Southwest, Slavic languages and literatures in the Midwest, Asian studies on the Eastern and Western Coasts, and so on.

**Concentrations**

Obviously, each language is its own concentration. The majority of students study European Romance languages—French, Italian, or Spanish. German, Russian, Japanese, Chinese, and Arabic have waxed and waned in popularity, corresponding to world events.

Depending on the school and the intentions of the faculty, language programs can have specific objectives:

**Language and Literature,** which starts with learning the language, then uses it to study the literature of a country or culture.
**Language and Civilization,** which concentrates on political and social issues; many schools have specific programs in international relations, others combine these public-affairs or governmental concerns with the study of a language.

Linguistics, the study of the theory of language, which often entails acquiring skills in at least one foreign language.

Foreign Language Teaching, which adds courses in education to prepare students for certification as high school language teachers.

**Course Sampler**

**German 301 Advanced German:   The German-Speaking World**
for students who have completed German 101–102 and German 201–202. Other students with an advanced level of competence will be admitted with permission of the instructor. The course will correspond to an exploratory journey through the German-speaking world. Documentation taken from the press as well as literature and film will take us from West Germany to various German-speaking areas. Conducted in German. Intensive practice in all four language skills—listening, speaking, reading, writing. Review of grammar tailored to student's needs.

*(Bard College)*

**Spanish 175 Spanish Applied Linguistics I**
Introduction to the study of applied linguistics. Detailed scientific analysis of the phonology of modern Spanish. Contrastive analysis of Spanish and English sound systems. Required of all majors and prospective teachers of Spanish.

*(Santa Clara University)*

**Russian 270 Through the Soviet Media**
Readings and discussions of articles on current events from the Party newspaper *Pravda*. Individual readings on selected topics for term project. In Russian for students with advanced skills.

*(Bucknell University)*

**ITAL 13 Summer Workshop in Italian Language and Civilization**
Given in conjunction with the Hofstra Summer Program in Italy. Conversational topics will be supplied by daily contact with Italian life and newspapers. Designed to train students in understanding contemporary Italian usage.

*(Hofstra University)*

**Assessment**

"I chose a double major in French and German to get a well-rounded, broad-based education, and because I enjoy learning," recalls Hugh Moran, an independent financial consultant in California. Mr. Moran, a 1976 graduate from the University of California (Los Angeles), went on to earn an MBA in international finance, partly at a German university. After several years in Switzerland, Norway and Germany, he returned to the United States, worked for a major accounting firm, and then went out on his own.

"There were a few chances while I was with the accounting firm to go to Europe, but mostly I went for personal vacations," he says. "Today I have an international mix of clients—my biggest client is from Brazil, and I have clients from Norway as well." The language training has helped him understand people from other cultures. The transition from undergraduate school was a little bumpy, because he didn't have the usual mix of business and economics courses that many people bring to an MBA program, but Mr. Moran says that he wound up scoring extremely well in his accounting courses.

Kris Morris, a 1976 graduate of Occidental College in German, now works as an executive search consultant for the firm Cowen, Morris, and Berger, where she is a partner. The firm is retained by corporations and arts organizations to recruit experienced, high-level executives for new openings. Her first work experience, in the alumni relations office of her alma mater, exposed her to human-resource issues.

"Studying a foreign language allowed me to feel at home with other cultures. In my line of work, there are levels of communication between people—including unsaid things. When I am meeting with people to discuss new positions, or meeting with candidates for those positions, I need to be able to assess the dynamics of an organization, and to gain a clear understanding of the people I am interviewing," she says.

On occasion, she is able to use her knowledge of German when dealing with international assignments, or with people in education and the arts. Aside from specific knowledge, she says that her college experience increased her capacity for critical thinking and helps her analyze situations.

Analysis is also the key word for Carol Ehnis, a New York clinical neuropsychologist who studied French and Spanish at Antioch College (1965). "I practice an unusual form of evaluation and counseling for those, especially children, with learning disabilities and attentional disorders. These problems are sometimes indicated by speaking difficulties, but many children with such difficulties simply have bilingual adjustment problems, not a neurological disorder. As I studied foreign languages as an undergraduate, I am better able to make this distinction.''

Ms. Ehnis continued her studies at the City University of New York, and New York University, where she graduated in 1977. She says that she made a conscious decision not to major in psychology as an undergraduate, because she felt that she would be taking many of the same courses as a psychology graduate student. While in graduate school, she took many courses in physiology, which helped her understand more about the biological basis for many learning disorders. Knowing Spanish has its practical side as well; she counsels many Spanish-speaking people in her New York practice.

**Career Options**

Bank administrator
Business-to-business salesperson
College professor, liberal arts
Editor, book
Editor, magazine
Executive search consultant
Foreign language teacher, in schools or in private training.
Hotel manager
Journalist
Marketing manager
Teacher, K–12
Travel planner

# PERFORMING ARTS

### (Theater, Music, Dance)

| | | 1983 | 1985 | 1988 |
|---|---|---|---|---|
| **Enrollment** | BS or BA | 13,866 | 13,340 | 11,901 |
| **Boxscore** | Master's | 4,810 | 4,944 | 4,434 |
| | PhD | 522 | 521 | 584 |

**Overview**

You can train for a career in the performing arts without attending college, but like students of the Visual Arts (see *Visual Arts*) Performing Arts majors learn skills that can help in many lines of work.

These other skills may be even more valuable for Performing Arts graduates than Visual Arts graduates, because they face not only intense competition for assignments, but also the difficulty of finding a place to practice and perform while they hone their skills. Many artists need only an easel and a supply of paints and brushes, but actors, directors, and playwrights need a stage, and dancers and musicians need a place both to practice and to perform. While studying at college, performing artists have ready access to these essential facilities.

Depending on the specific major and the college, academia represents a significant opportunity for career networking among performing artists. Most teachers have professional experience, and the best schools have widespread alumni networks that can provide entree to arts careers.

Many performing artists, knowing the difficulties that they will face after graduation in lining up work, attend college to acquire skills that will produce a job with adequate income to support themselves while they are getting established. Teaching, marketing, and administration are among the careers that can be started by a degree in performing arts. Alternatively, many performing artists prefer to take relatively menial jobs (word processing, typing, waiting tables) while waiting for their big break. This is especially true of artists who spend a considerable part of regular working hours in practice, and actors who must be free to attend open casting calls.

**Concentrations**

**Music,** including music education, music therapy, instrumental music, voice, composition.

**Dance,** including dance therapy, choreography, modern dance, folk dance, ballet.

**Theater,** including acting, stage direction, stagecraft (set design, lighting design), playwrighting; some schools combine theater and film in the Visual Arts department.

**Course Sampler**

**Music 140–150 Keyboard Harmony I and II**
A concentrated course for applied piano majors involving keyboard playing of chorales (three parts), figured bass (of given progressions as well as progressions composed at the keyboard by the students) and score reading of chamber and orchestral music by Mozart and Haydn. . . . [Music 150] includes keyboard transpositions of songs (down and up, whole step, half step, etc.), improvisations (in styles of Bach, Haydn, Mozart, Schubert), chorale playing (four or more parts, and analysis of their harmonic progressions at sight), score reading (chamber and orchestral scores of Beethoven), and figured bass (progressions composed by the student using modulatory concepts).

*(Allegheny College)*

**29 Rehearsal and Performance**
Active participation in the preparation and performance of departmental productions as actors, stage managers, assistant stage managers, assistants to the director. Major design/technical assignments.

*(Santa Clara University)*

**329 Advanced Directing**
A course in directing for advanced students of theater art. Projects are concerned with the interpretation of text and integration with the aspects of theater art. Topics of study include tryout and rehearsal methods, as well as practice in translating textural analysis into principles of staging. The final course project for each director is the public performance of a complete one-act play.

*(Concordia College)*

**Dance 203 Composition I**
Finding personal movement and transforming it into dance; class projects that introduce the formal elements of composition. Extensive improvisation accompanies formal education.

*(Washington University in St. Louis)*

**MUS 138, 338 Jazz Ensemble**
A select instrumental ensemble which emphasizes the performance of big band literature in a wide diversity of styles, as well as the study of improvisation. A variety of performance experiences are provided and may include concerts, jazz festivals, and a studio recording session.

Outstanding professional guest artists are featured in many concerts. Auditions are held at the beginning of each semester.

*(Pepperdine University)*

**Assessment**

For May Wu, an MFA (Master of Fine Arts) in theater from the Yale School of Drama (1986) has been the ticket to a career in film and video for one of the major cable television networks. Her undergraduate work at the New College of the University of South Florida pointed her in the direction of theater. At the school, she combined training in public policy with a heavy dose of work at nearby theaters. Now she works as a programmer, selecting arts and comedy programs for the cable network and reviewing scripts and promos to find new talent.

"New College stresses independent, self-directed study," she notes. "I didn't start out being interested in theater, but through the exposure I got while in school, that became my career direction." Ms. Wu, whose ultimate goal is to produce dramatic works, cites her exposure to arts administration as the first step toward her programming/production work. "I did a senior thesis on arts administration, and then went to drama school.

"To do any sort of work in drama or the arts, you need to have a background in *everything*," she says. "Opera, music theory, art history, film criticism—all these things help me assess new projects."

John Rustin, a playwright in the Los Angeles area, studied theater arts at both the bachelor and master's level (Occidental College, BA, 1978, MA, 1980). He has had three of his plays published, and two produced, since graduation, in collaboration with another playwright, Frank Semerano. Nevertheless, to keep a steady income, he works as a word processor at the Jet Propulsion Laboratory managed by the University of California.

Studying under Omar Paxson, then a professor of theater arts there, Mr. Rustin was exposed to all aspects of theater: writing, directing, acting, and stagecraft. While in theory one can work at being a playwrite nearly anywhere and at any time, Mr. Rustin sees distinct advantages to attending college. "To learn how to write, a playwrite needs to see his work produced on stage. Only then does he see what works, how the words, actions, and setting interrelate, and how a character expresses himself. Experience in acting itself also enhances that," he says. All these things were available to him at Occidental; "it would be tough to get access to these things outside of college."

Being a playwright leads to a variety of work possibilities, most obviously screenwriting. Mr. Rustin is trying his hand at that, even as he reassesses his continued interest in theater. "I've been modestly successful—many playwrights never get to see their work produced—and I feel good about that." He sees future possibilities in commissioned pieces, as a form of entertainment or training for organizations' meetings, conferences, or celebrations.

Julie Schwarz-Evans, a conductor, performer, and music instructor at Alfred University (New York), combined academic study with private instruction en route to earning a bachelor of music in violin performance at Boston University (1982) and a master's from the University of Michigan. In addition to teaching at Alfred, she provides private instruction and conducts the University Orchestra.

"The lessons of my private violin instructors, and my experiences playing in the University Symphony Orchestra, directly relate to my current teaching/performing responsibilities," she says. I learned specifics about technique and experienced first-hand the great orchestral works." She adds that her curriculum added writing, and that communications skills are very important to her work. Musically, the chance to work in a group setting clarified her "sense of direction" in music.

Ms. Schwarz-Evans' husband, Thomas Evans, is an assistant professor at Alfred University. His studies began at Clarion State University (Clarion, PA), from which he graduated in 1976. That was followed by a master's degree at Boston University (1981), and a DMA (Doctor of Musical Arts), specializing in trombone performance, from the University of Michigan (1987). While he also teaches and performs, he stresses his work as a music conductor and teacher. "The courses that best helped me prepare for my profession were the conducting classes, various ensemble experiences, and of course, the hours spent practicing on my instrument." As preparation for teaching, he was obliged to take education courses, but "ironically, these were the courses that helped me the least."

To decide on becoming a musician, according to Mr. Evans, "is not difficult; you usually have a calling." The uncertainties of finding employment, though, complicate the decision. Looking back on college, he says that "there were times when it seemed as if college was getting in the way of my education. For example, there were far too many times when I could not attend musical performances because I had to spend my evenings working on class assignments. Attending these performances, in most cases, would have been more of an education than writing a paper on behavior modification." Still, he "absolutely" would pursue a college education again the same way if he had it to do over.

**Career Options**

Art director
Camera operator/cinematographer
College professor, liberal arts
Dancer/dance therapist
Designer, interior
Designer, industrial and fashion
Editor, book
Editor, magazine
Executive search consultant
Experiential educator
Film/video engineer, especially for those who acquire training in film technology.
Human-resources manager
Marketing manager
Media planner
Photographer
Publicist
Radio/television announcer
Teacher, K–12
Temporary worker; this tends to be the usual form of employment for performing artists until they get established.
Travel Planner

# PHILOSOPHY AND RELIGION

|  |  | 1983 | 1985 | 1988 |
|---|---|---|---|---|
| **Enrollment** | BS or BA | 6,483 | 6,400 | 5,959 |
| **Boxscore** | Master's | 1,091 | 1,167 | 1,098 |
|  | PhD | 404 | 468 | 405 |

**Overview**

Philosophy and religion were the capstones of education until this century. Many of the oldest schools in the country were originally founded as schools of religion. Also 150 years ago, all science was "natural philosophy," treated simply as an offshoot of philosophy itself.

That was then, and this is now. Today philosophy has lost much of its connection with science (except for a recent form of study known as "history and philosophy of science"). Religion, of course, is very much a part of the American scene, but the specific programs leading to a divinity degree and the practice of religion are beyond the scope of this book.

It is possible at more than a few schools to study philosophy and religion, which come together naturally in the subject of ethics. Ethics—determining what is morally good—has received new emphasis as more issues of moral behavior are debated in science, business, and government.

There are some indications that philosophy and science are returning to a common ground. This connection is being forged by the ubiquitous computer, according to David Soles, a professor of philosophy at Wichita State University. "The study of philosophy is relevant to new computer technology and the subject of artificial intelligence," he says. "Not all data or information is numerical; computers are being designed now to work with symbols, rather than simply equations and numbers, and much of philosophy is the study of symbols and their logical manipulation." In fact, he says, certain philosophy departments are leaders in developing artificial-intelligence technology.

Beyond computer technology, philosophy is broadly applicable to professions where incisive, analytical thinking is necessary, including law, government, finance, and management consulting. It is also telling that while universities offer a wide variety of programs, nearly all have a department of philosophy, even if they have only a handful of majors. The study of philosophy is one of the most ancient forms of learning, yet can be one of the most modern as well.

**Concentrations**

It is next to impossible to study philosophy without also studying the history of philosophy. Many who concentrate on the latter go on to be teachers of philosophy at colleges and universities. Concentrations include:

**Philosophy and Mathematics,** with a special emphasis on a system of analysis known as symbolic logic. This combination makes a powerful preparation for applying logical principles to problems in computer science.

**Philosophy and Religion,** which are considered a single entity at some schools. At various times in history, the "theory" of a religion was the same as a "theory" of philosophy; generally this is not true these days. However, a philosophical background can lead to a deeper understanding of religious belief.

**History of Philosophy,** which is often the basic program for philosophy majors. As in the academic study of literature, the body of knowledge of philosophy demands continual reinterpretation as social values change.

**Philosophy of Science,** which deals with reconciling humanistic philosophical beliefs with the new technology and discoveries that stream out of science laboratories.

**Eastern Philosophy,** which attempts to draw lessons of value to Western ways of thinking out of Confucianism, Buddhism, Zen, and other Eastern traditions.

**Course Sampler**

Philosophy 121 Ethical Theory
This seminar explores the possibility of the justification of human action and the making of ethical judgments. There are some who claim, in effect, that there are no justified moral claims. We will study their

arguments. There are others who try to show the way out of that sort of skepticism, and we will use what they have to say to develop some answers of our own. We will deal with problems of ethical relativity, morality, and international affairs. The course will also confront the problem of articulating our personal philosophies of life, their justification, and their relationship to morality. Through the eyes of some recent literature, the ancient question, "What is the best way to live?" is considered. Marxist and Existentialist ethics will be emphasized during a portion of the course. There will also be a special section on the relationship between morality and art.

*(Denison University)*

### CLA PH 107 Logic and Language
Critical study of the norms of linguistic usage and argumentation. Analysis of meaning, definition, vagueness, ambiguity, analogy, and metaphor. Introduction to deductive and inductive arguments and the informal fallacies.

*(Boston University)*

### Philosophy 617 Mental Representation
A survey and evaluation of major theories of mental representation drawing on recent work in philosophy of mind, cognitive psychology, linguistics, semantics, and artificial intelligence. Major topics: linguistic representation, the language of thought, propositional attitudes, mental imagery, and innate representations.

*(Tulane University)*

### 358 Existentialism
Existential thought from Kierkegaard to Camus, stressing such themes as freedom, existence, despair, authenticity, alienation, death, and revolt against system.

*(Ohio University)*

**Assessment**     Jennifer Duffy, a 1986 philosophy and religion graduate of Colgate University, now works as a program officer at the Center for Japanese Economy and business at Columbia University, where she is also studying for a master's in international affairs. Her work involves the administration responsibilities of the program, much as a college administrator operates. In the interim, she was an English teacher in Japan.

"Philosophy teaches you the basics of Western culture and how to think analytically," she says. The underlying themes of Western values became especially important to her as she encountered Japanese students, who would question her endlessly about history and family values in the United States.

For the long term, she expects to become a journalist and writer, possibly involved with international affairs. "Philosophy taught me how to write, how to think, and how to analyze what I am learning," she concludes.

**Career Options**

**Artificial intelligence developer**
**College administrator**
**College professor, liberal arts**
**Computer programmer**
**Computer systems analyst**
**Editor,** book
**Editor,** magazine
**Experiential educator**
**Foreign language teacher**
**Human-resources manager**
**Job Counselor**
**Journalist**
**Lawyer**
**Librarian**
**Marketing researcher**
**Psychologist,** assuming that graduate schooling in this subject is obtained.
**Technical writer**
**Vocational (adult) teacher**

# PHYSICS

**(Mathematical Physics, Astronomy, Astrophysics)**

|  |  | 1983 | 1985 | 1988 |
|---|---|---|---|---|
| **Enrollment** | BS or BA | 3,888 | 4,208 | 4,222 |
| **Boxscore** | Master's | 1,436 | 1,614 | 1,761 |
|  | PhD | 950 | 1,010 | 1,189 |

**Overview**

For most of this century, physics has had an almost magical image. It is the science of the basis of matter and energy. The magic was in theories like "The Big Bang" that deals with the beginning of the universe, and the idea that time can move faster or slower, as you choose. The bright image was tarnished somewhat with the invention of nuclear weapons. But it has been re-polished by the development of the microprocessor chip (the brain of any computer) and new superconducting materials that offer the promise of saving energy. Physics is exciting again.

These events are the backdrop for the study of physics; not many people earn a living by trying to alter the pace of time. The undergraduate study in physics introduces the general methods of physics research—laboratory experimentation, mathematical analysis—and their applications in some of the key employment areas—materials and microelectronics, telecommunications, aerospace.

There are said to be "experimentalists" who are excellent at devising instruments to conduct studies, and "theoreticians" who work at a desk with a piece of paper, a pencil, and their minds. Most pure research in physics is conducted by PhD-level students, who can find themselves working long hours as operators of complex electronic machinery (as, for example, at the particle-acceleration machines of the United States National Laboratories). Both undergraduate and graduate students with instrumentation experience can develop careers in industry running similar devices to do research, or, in some cases, manufacturing.

Astronomy is usually lumped together with physics simply because most of its research deals with matter and energy. A good astronomer knows physics well. Some teachings of astronomy come back to physics itself, in the form of a new understanding of subatomic matter.

**Concentrations**

**Experimental Physics,** which specializes in new types of sensors and instruments for analyzing the physical world.

**Mathematical Physics,** which is theoretical research.

**Solid-State Physics,** which focuses on crystals, semiconductors, and all the materials that go into microelectronics.

**Optics,** the study of light, which is particularly active lately with advances in lasers and fiber-optic communications.

**Astrophysics,** which is the study of matter and energy in stars and planetary systems.

**Geophysics,** which concentrates on the forces that affect the earth, such as earthquakes and volcanoes.

**Engineering Physics,** which is another term for applied physics, and refers to the use of physics to solve technical problems in manufacturing or similar mechanical systems.

**Course Sampler**

**Phys 4015 Physics for Telecommunications**
A basic course in the physics of communications systems. Topics include electricity and magnetism, optics, frequency band width relationships. This course will include an introduction to signal propagation in different media as well as amplification and signal correction as applied to electrical and optical systems.

*(New York Institute of Technology)*

**Physics 4 Electronic Circuits for Scientists I**
Linear electric circuits. Phasor analysis, transients, and Fourier series. Network theorems, Junction diodes, bipolar junction transistors, and field-effect transistors. Voltage amplifiers. Laboratory.

*(Santa Clara University)*

**CLA PY 408 Intermediate Mechanics**
Dynamics of particles and rigid bodies. Newtonian mechanics.
Oscillatory motion and motion under a central force. Lagrange's and
Hamilton's equations. Poisson brackets. Rigid-body motion.
Introduction to relativistic mechanics.

*(Boston University)*

**Assessment**

"Physics gives a broad understanding of the world and the universe we live in," offers David Dwyne, a 1983 physics graduate from the University of California at Berkeley. Mr. Dwyne works as a network manager for a group of computers. The management involves maintaining the software and hardware that interconnects the computers, and overseeing the types of activities that the network supports. "I use my physics-derived problem-solving abilities practically every day in my work," he says. "The computer skills I learned as a student are directly related to my work now."

"I went into physics because, after studying electrical engineering as an undergraduate, I wanted to know where the equations I was using came from," recalls Thomas Lettieri, a physicist at the National Institute of Standards and Technology (formerly, the National Bureau of Standards). "Enginers use equations, but often don't even know where they come from."

To fill this perceived gap in his academic training, Mr. Lettieri went on the University of Rochester's optics section ( a part of the physics department), where he earned a PhD in 1978. At NIST, where he joined after graduation, Mr. Lettieri is involved with developing methods to measure the size or texture of materials with extremely precise lasers and other instruments. He was also involved, several years ago, with studying small plastic beads that were formed in the microgravity environment of the US Space Shuttle; these beads, in turn, could be used as a visual check of the accuracy of many types of lab instrumentation.

"Today, I split my time between running experiments on the instruments we have here, and sitting in front of a computer keyboard to file reports and keep up with the flow of paper," he says. "When the instruments are up and running, the tendency is to use them as long as possible. Later, when experiments are complete, or the machine stops working, the time comes to sit down and make sense of what has been discovered.

**Career Options**

Aerospace engineer, in the sense that research is performed on new materials and propulsion technologies.

College professor, science and technology

Computer engineer, especially for those who concentrate on computer programming during their education.

Earth (planetary) scientist

Electrical engineer, especially for those who study solid-state physics.

Energy engineer

Geologist

Mathematician

Metallurgical and materials engineer

Nuclear engineer

Physicist, who is generally employed in research and development.

Technical writer

---

# POLITICAL SCIENCE

### (Political Studies, International Relations)

| | 1983 | 1985 | 1988 |
|---|---|---|---|
| **Enrollment** BS or BA | 28,493 | 29,107 | 31,255 |
| **Boxscore** Master's | 2,966 | 2,850 | 2,790 |
| PhD | 479 | 506 | 454 |

**Overview**

Political science is the study of governments and governing processes—laws, economic systems, rules of behavior. Over the years it has proven to be one of the most popular social sciences. Some graduates go on to law school, but for the many that do not, there are job opportunities in government (at federal, state, and local levels), in political lobbying, in non-profit social-welfare activities, and in research and consulting. Political scientists like to point out that the root of the word "idiot" is a Greek term describing someone with no interest in the affairs of state.

Teaching in a practical manner how the US government works is the most apparent goal of academic programs in political science. A second goal is to compare alternative systems of government and teach the evolution of government theory.

A recommended part of most political science programs is an internship with political parties or government agencies, locally or in Washington. Political science majors also do fieldwork (taking surveys, amassing data) much like other social scientists.

Even so, there are few jobs (relative to the number of graduates) that directly employ the training of political science students. Indirectly—via a knowledge of how the American political system works—political science graduates find jobs in consulting, corporate government-affairs offices, and a wide range of social-service occupations. An academic training that provides skills in handling data via computer, research, and communication of results stands many graduates in good stead as they approach the job market.

For those who concentrate in international politics, the arena of international affairs and business beckons. Generally, companies don't hire baccalaureate college graduates and immediately send them overseas or into their international business departments, but with experience (and perhaps advanced training), that opportunity becomes more likely.

**Concentrations**

**American Politics,** a more detailed look at political parties, governance and legislative and economic issues.

**Comparative Politics,** which examines political systems in relation to each other. An older concentration, **Comparative Legislation,** looked specifically at laws.

**International Politics,** while also comparing various systems, also covers inter-governmental relations.

**Political Theory,** a theoretical examination of government.

**Course Sampler**

**Political Studies 213 Latin American Politics**
This is an introductory course to Latin American politics. The purpose is to acquaint students with the diversity of socio-political and economic situations in Latin America. The course will examine the historical formation of the state in the region and different situations of dependence:   national control of export systems (Argentina, Brazil),

and enclave economies (Chile, Venezuela, Mexico, Peru, Bolivia). Particular attention will be paid to the role of the middle classes in the process of modernization. Competing theories of Latin American under-development (modernization, dependency, corporatism, bureaucratic-authoritarianism) will be analyzed. The second portion of the course will be devoted to examining party systems and political institutions in selected countries: Mexico, the Southern cone (Argentina, Brazil, Chile, Uruguay), the "stable" democracies (Venezuela, Colombia, Costa Rica), and Central American political regimes: El Salvador, Guatemala, and Nicaragua.

*(Bard College)*

### POL105–106 I & II Survey of Political Economy

This course will introduce students to the major economic ideas and theories at work in the world today as well as the form and function of world economic systems and the nature of the global economy. Students will review the role of government in the promotion and protection of particular political and economic systems and interests. Students will read from the works of John Stuart Mill, Adam Smith, David Ricardo, Parson Malthus, Karl Marx, J. M. Keynes, Friedrich von Hayek, Ludwig von Meises, David Gordon, Milton Friedman, and others. Topics covered will include fiscal and monetary policy, theories of price, inflation, labor, unemployment, taxation, national debt, trade, and the rise of multi-national corporations. Particular focus will be given to the US political economy, its institutional structure, and banking system.

*(Pace University)*

### Political Science 306 American Judicial Process

The structure and practices of national and state judicial institutions. Emphasis on the decision-making process of the United States Supreme Court, courts as policy-makers, personnel procedures in the judiciary, judicial compliance and impact, and judicial politics.

*(Illinois Wesleyan University)*

**Assessment**

For William Samuelson, political science offered an introduction to the business world; he has risen rapidly, and become an assistant vice president at a New England bank. The 1982 political-science graduate of Hartwick College says that he was considering law school when entering college, but decided against it. "The

professors I had in political science were a factor in my decision—
they were some of the best teachers I ever had," he remembers.

Mr. Samuelson felt the learning he was acquiring in the Political
Science department was more topical than that in history or economics, stating, "public affairs has been an ongoing interest of
mine." Specific job skills learned? "As much as anything, political
science required me to do a lot of writing, and writing and analysis
takes up a lot of my time in my current job."

At the bank, Mr. Samuelson is a lending officer; part of his
responsibility is to present the loan application of a client before a
bank management committee, which rules on the application.
Solid preparation is key to successfully performing his job. "In
several of my classes at school, we were required to do a lot of
reading of legal briefs, and then make a presentation in class. That
taught me to be organized, and to do a lot of analytical thinking.
Both of those qualities are important in the presentations I make
before the bank committee now."

Susan Pasko, now an executive search consultant in New York,
began her college career at Lafayette College thinking that she
would be a journalist. She worked on the school newspaper, but
decided early on that her interests were more in the area of
human-resource management. After completing her degree in
American Civilization in 1984, she worked in employee relations
for a variety of businesses and consulting firms. Now she is research manager at the search firm, where she guides a staff of
researchers that identify job candidates for positions that the firm
is hired to fill.

"My undergraduate studies were multi-disciplinary, involving
international affairs, history, economics, and sociology, among
others," she says. "I would say that the main thing I learned from
my studies that helps me in my work is how to do research—how
to use library materials, databases, indexes, and the like. For my
senior project, I was involved in a multi-disciplinary team project
looking at social issues. That taught me the dynamics of group
decision-making, which relates very directly to the corporate
world."

Political science as an undergraduate student, and urban planning as a graduate student, has been the key to a career in social
services planning for Michele Mindlin-Wallace. After earning her
bachelor's degree in 1970 at the State University of New York

(Binghamton), she earned her master's degree in 1972 at Hunter College. "I've always had a fundamental interest in government and the political process," she says. "If I were going to college today, I might go to law school, but as a woman at that time, law school seemed less accessible."

Her work experience started in social services research and administration, and she has had experience with health-services administration. Currently, she is a grants administrator for a drug-abuse research organization.

"The courses I've had in urban law have been the most benefi-cial," she notes. "When a new law is written, its ramifications must be studied carefully; usually, the law has a potential impact on the programs I'm involved in." Overall, she says, urban plan-ning is not the "natural entree" to social services administration; public administration or social work tend to be more common. But, she says, "my background gives me a better sense of the whole picture—the systemics of a social problem. Social workers tend to look at problems in terms of individual needs and abilities, and the public administrator tends to have a financial orientation."

**Career Options**

**Advertising account executive**
**Association executive,** especially for lobbying organizations.
**Bank administrator**
**Business administrator,** usually with graduate schooling in busi-ness administration.
**Consumer-goods salesperson**
**Editor,** book or magazine
**Elementary/high school administrator**
**Executive search consultant**
**Financial planner**
**Human-resources manager**
**Insurance agent**
**Investor relations manager**
**Journalist**
**Lawyer**
**Management consultant**
**Marketing manager**
**Paralegal**
**Political scientist;** hot employment areas currently are in business consulting and non-profit foundations.

Public administrator
Publicist
Regional planner
Real estate sales broker
Stockbroker

---

# PSYCHOLOGY

|  | | 1983 | 1985 | 1988 |
|---|---|---|---|---|
| **Enrollment** | BS or BA | 40,364 | 39,811 | 44,961 |
| **Boxscore** | Master's | 8,378 | 8,408 | 7,862 |
|  | PhD | 3,108 | 2,908 | 2,988 |

**Overview**

Thousands of students choose to major in psychology, and a wide range of specializations are available. Psychology makes an excellent preparation for graduate study in business, law, medicine, and other professions. It also offers substantial career opportunities within itself, for counselors, clinicians, teachers, and personnel administrators.

Without question, another of the reasons for the popularity of psychology is that it offers profound opportunities to learn about yourself. This appeals to college students who are learning how to be adults, finding their place in the world, and above all, discovering who they are. Perhaps more than any other major, psychology offers the chance to learn about yourself while learning the skills to start your career.

Traditional psychology involves the application of scientific investigation to the behavior of humans and other higher forms of life. College students are introduced to this perspective by the classic laboratory experiments with pigeons or mice. Most psychology students later do survey studies of people to research such topics as learning, attention, and reactions to motivational factors.

Outside the laboratory, the large body of knowledge that already exists in psychology is applied to groups, organizations, and social institutions. In its broadest application, psychology interacts with anthropology, economics, and sociology to gain understanding of humans and their social structures.

**Concentrations**

**General Psychology,** which samples the various specialties in the field without any particular emphasis; includes courses in experimental psychology, which teaches how humans (and other higher forms of life) interact with their environment.

**Applied Psychology,** which applies the basic techniques and perspectives of psychology to social, business, and personal issues in fields such as advertising, motivation, training, or education.

**Industrial/Organizational Psychology,** which covers the special conditions in manufacturing plants and offices; many graduates are employed in corporate human-resource management.

**Clinical Psychology,** which prepares students to be consulting psychologists who help people with handicaps or personality disorders; usually an advanced degree and state certification are required.

**Human Factors Engineering,** a new field which deals with the interfacing of people with machines, computers, and other complex equipment.

**Child (Developmental) Psychology,** which concentrates on the special conditions of youth and maturation; advanced study and licensing are usually required of a child psychologist.

**Biological Psychology (Psychobiology),** which analyzes the physiological roots of many aspects of human nature in physiological conditions, and their effects on health and well-being.

**Psychotherapy,** which studies human nature in order to provide therapy to cure or relieve personality problems. Advanced study is nearly always required.

**Social Psychology,** which studies the interaction between the individuals and groups, emphasizing how social structures can harm or benefit the individual.

**Course Sampler**

PSYC 351 Industrial/Organizational Psychology
This course is concerned with the application of psychological principles to personnel policies, working conditions, production efficiency, and decision-making in various kinds of industrial and non-industrial

organizations. The topics dealt with include employee selection and training, attitude and performance assessment, working conditions and efficiency, employee counseling, leadership development, and organizational climate.

*(Pepperdine University)*

### Psych 301 Experimental Psychology
Training in the logic and techniques of psychological research intended to provide students with experience in design and interpretation of psychological research. Emphasis on experimental control, library research, quantitative treatment of data, and clarity of scientific writing.

*(Washington University in St. Louis)*

### 408 Intimate Relationships
Social psychological barriers to interpersonal intimacy as well as the dynamics of long-term personal relationships are considered. Topics include: shyness, loneliness, romantic attraction, self-disclosure, envy and jealousy, intimate communication, sex roles and reciprocity in close relationships, sexual behavior that affects and is affected by such relationships, and relationship termination. Marriage and the family are considered as frequent institutional contexts but will not be the primary focus.

*(Tulane University)*

### 274 Applied Psychology
A survey of non-clinical applications of psychology, including as possibilities such content areas as consumer behavior, advertising, the impact of mass media on behavior, forensic, environmental, and medical psychology.

*(Colby College)*

**Assessment**

"I was one of those weird people who knows exactly what they want to do for a career when they enter college," recalls Vicki Lynn with a smile. "I wanted to be a school counselor." To reach that goal, she majored in psychology at Syracuse University, graduating in 1976. She followed undergraduate studies with a master's degree from Pennsylvania State University in counseling education. For the past 11 years, she has been a career counselor at Rensselaer Polytechnic Institute, and is now director of the Career Development Center there.

"What I remember most distinctly about my undergraduate studies was the basic foundation courses—the theories of development, abnormal psychology, and the like." She tested her interest in school counseling by taking internships in social-service organizations, which enriched her understanding of psychology while confirming that she wanted to be a counselor.

Lisa Wolk, a 1986 psychology graduate of Colgate University, says that her undergraduate studies helped her decide on her current career as a kindergarten teacher in Dover, Massachusetts. "Psychology showed me the basic driving forces of individuals— how they are motivated, why they behave the way they do," she says. "I also had courses in cross-cultural development, which showed me how certain developmental aspects are innate, regardless of your upbringing."

Finally, "The program at Colgate was heavily oriented toward experimental psychology, so there were courses in statistics and biology to take." She relates that being comfortable with statistics was very helpful in graduate school in Elementary Education courses, which she completed at Smith College.

**Career Options**

Advertising account executive
Art director
Business-to-business salesperson
Business administrator, with graduate schooling.
College administrator
Compensation analyst
Computer programmer, if one's studies were computer-intensive.
Consumer-goods salesperson
Corporate trainer
Direct marketer
Elementary/high school administrator
Executive search consultant
Health-service administrator
Human-resources manager
Insurance agent
Job counselor
Journalist

Lawyer

Management consultant

Marketing researcher

Marketing manager

Psychologist, especially in the clinical treatment of the elderly, the
disabled, and children.

Social worker

Stockbroker

Teacher, K–12

Vocational (adult) teacher

---

# SOCIOLOGY

### Social Work, General Social Sciences

|  |  | 1983 | 1985 | 1988 |
|---|---|---|---|---|
| **Enrollment** | BS or BA | 28,062 | 24,299 | 26,233 |
| **Boxscore** | Master's | 10,751 | 10,442 | 10,773 |
|  | PhD | 755 | 764 | 707 |

**Overview**

Sociology and social work together are among the most popular
undergraduate college majors. Generally, the social work program
is geared directly for work in social services, such as public agencies, charities and health-care. Sociology, on the other hand, is
oriented around the study of individuals and their relationships
with groups and with society at large. Except for the academic
study of sociology, a degree in this program provides few career
opportunities where sociological science is applied directly (there
are, however, a great number of occupations where it is applied
indirectly).

Sociology and anthropology (see ANTHROPOLOGY) are very
similar in orientation, and at many schools, the departments are
combined. The distinction—a fine one—between them is usually
that sociology deals with modern society and with social institu-

tions. Anthropology is oriented toward ancient or primitive societies, and seeks to understand basic human activities and the relationship between the individual and the environment.

The Enrollment Boxscore above masks a dramatic difference in the degree pattern between sociology and social work. Relatively few sociology undergraduates go on to graduate school in sociology; in social work, there are more masters graduates than baccalaureates in certain years (an indication that in addition to many social work undergraduates continuing their schooling, undergraduates from other programs also enter the masters program). The masters in social work (MSW) degree is a common requirement for many jobs in public agencies.

The courses in social work departments provide an introduction to the basic techniques of interviewing and surveying, and then fill in the background of how public agencies function. A great variety of social services are offered by public and private agencies in the United States, and the types of recipients also vary: children, the poor, the disabled or handicapped, the unemployed. Fieldwork as a practicing social worker is obligatory in many programs; this feature is so formalized that in some cases, the student is required to purchase professional liability insurance before beginning the fieldwork.

Usually the coursework in sociology covers the basic theories and lessons, and then focuses closely on issues or problems of the day. For example, many departments offer courses on the sociology of the workplace, or on broadbased social issues such as racism, education, or health-care delivery. Many programs offer courses that compare today's social patterns with those of the past —for example, urban living at the turn of the century compared with suburban living today. Other programs attempt cross-cultural analysis—comparing the patterns of social organization of other countries or cultures with the American pattern. The goals are to determine what makes sense; how problems are handled; how opportunities are created.

Like certain other liberal arts, sociology has become "scientific" in recent years; an essential part of sociological research is gathering and then analyzing data such as income, schooling, working habits, health-care, or nutritional trends. Much of this type of work relates very directly to marketing research in the business world. Learning to use a computer is also becoming a standard element of sociological training.

Finally, since the aim of much sociological research is to develop ways for us all to live better with each other, there is a strong element of social service and welfare in sociology. Many people who go on to careers in community service or non-profit organizations started by studying sociology.

**Concentrations**

Social work programs assume that the student is preparing for a career as a social worker; the decision then is what type of social work to become engaged in.

Basic sociology involves the study of the underlying theories of social structure and behavior as they have evolved over the past half-century. Sociology concentrations reflect the social controversies of the moment; to use a 1960s word, sociology is nearly always "relevant."

Current programs include:

**Social services for children,** involving health-care, education, and social adaptation of the young.

**Social services for the sick and handicapped**

**Social services for counseling,** which runs the gamut from job counseling to dealing with governmental agencies.

**Women's studies,** often an independent academic department that seeks to analyze the role of women in society; strongly emphasizes past traditions and how they are changing.

**Ethnic studies (including African-American, Hispanic, and Asian),** which also sometimes exists as an independent academic department, begins with a grounding in basic sociological theory, then examines special issues pertaining to the ethnic group.

**Society and law,** which concentrates on the legal and political systems that formalize the relationships most of us have with each other; many students go on to law school.

**Course Sampler**

**SOC 220 Introduction to the Family**
Primary emphasis on American family and how it has been changing. Among specific topics explored are interaction within family, family in relation to other institutions, mate-selection, marriage and its alternatives, family disorganization, and future of the American family.

*(Ohio University)*

**CLA SOC 209 Crime and Delinquency**
Analysis of criminal and delinquent behavior. Evaluation of current
theories and research into causes and sociological implications of these
behavior patterns. Examination of criminal justice systems including
police, courts, and corrections.

*(Boston University)*

**SOC 304 Developmental Sociology and Social Policy**
This course considers theories of regional, national, and international
development. It generally compares/contrasts structural-functional and
structural-critical explanations of social change. It specifically covers
modernization theories, theories of imperialism, and theories of
dependency. The course materials include research studies on Southeast
Asia, Africa, and Latin America, which entails considerations of social
policy, especially the status of women and minorities.

*(Antioch College)*

**Assessment**

"I am most interested in the interface between corporate America
and community services," says Kathleen Flynn (BA sociology,
Colgate University, 1986). She exercises that curiosity by working
as a senior agency relations manager at the United Way of Buffalo
and Erie County in New York State. As part of her responsibilities,
she meets with corporate executives to coordinate fundraising and
corporate contributions to United Way. Another part of her job is
to review funding allocations and activities with the member agencies of United Way—a large group of charities and community-
service organizations.

Traditionally, United Way functions by coordinating donations
and distributing them to member agencies. Ms. Flynn says that her
studies at Colgate helped her learn what services communities and
individuals need. "It was an awakening for me," she says. "I was
always interested in some type of work for social change, and the
study of sociology opened my eyes to how social strategies could
be carried out."

Another lesson learned was the "nature of business"—how
businesses grow, how marketing is done, how they interrelate
with the communities where they are headquartered, or where
factories are. Ms. Flynn says that this business training helps her
to understand how to appeal to the interests of businesses when

seeking support for United Way. Also, United Way itself uses sophisticated marketing techniques for its fundraising. "In high school, I had some sense of social responsibility; in college, I came out with a commitment to social work."

Social work is also the guiding force in the career of Kate Early (BA sociology, Hartwick College, 1983), an Assistant Attorney General for the State of Oregon. Ms. Early's focus is on helping make government work better to serve its citizens. In particular, she is currently involved in a federally sponsored study of how child support is determined in family courts, and is seeking to make this support more fairly allocated. During undergraduate school, when she was an intern at a legal-services clinic, she first realized that a law degree could be a powerful tool in social work. She earned her law degree from American University (Washington, D.C.).

Was sociology a good preparation? Definitely; she says: "First, it's important to get all the concepts of sociology down pat to do effective social work," she notes. "Then, sociology enhanced my ability to see all sides of an issue, to empathize with people, and to understand why they are the way they are." That has proven to be invaluable in her work, which is often with people in anguishing circumstances—for example, in a divorce process, under arrest, or in an abusive situation. "The sociology degree left a few gaps in my education as I entered law school," she observes. "I wished that I had taken a few more courses in history or political science—which I could have done, but I wasn't interested at the time." Still, the lack "did not prevent me from doing very well in law school."

| **Career Options** | Advertising account executive |
| | Art director |
| | Business-to-business salesperson |
| | College administrator |
| | Compensation analyst |
| | Consumer-goods salesperson |
| | Corporate trainer |
| | Demographer |
| | Editor, magazine |
| | Elementary/high school administrator |

Executive search consultant
Health-service administrator
Hotel manager
Human-resources manager
Job counselor
Journalist
Lawyer
Marketing researcher
Media planner
Public administrator
Social worker
Urban planner
Vocational (adult) teacher

# VISUAL ARTS

### (Studio Art, Commercial Art, Graphics, Film, and Photography)

|  |  | 1983 | 1985 | 1988 |
|---|---|---|---|---|
| **Enrollment** | BS or BA | 22,684 | 22,505 | 19,823 |
| **Boxscore** | Master's | 3,038 | 2,995 | 2,180 |
|  | PhD | 46 | 60 | 42 |

**Overview**

Both the teaching and the generation of art are centered around campuses, at which artists in residence try to guide students who are fulfilling the requirements of a college degree while practicing their art. The "academization" of art is controversial in the art world. Some argue that artists not attending college produce a "purer" art, and many self-taught artists pride themselves on their lack of academic influence.

However, while it is true that art cannot usually be taught, it certainly can be learned. College students can choose from a wide range of programs, with a large or small degree of regimentation. By attending college, the artist gains skills in research, history, and culture that can help develop a vision of art.

College also offers many opportunities to learn a marketable skill, related to work in art, that could provide an adequate living while developing talents and gaining clients. For example, painters can learn skills appropriate to magazine or book illustration, which can provide a well-paying job while providing practice of fine arts skills.

Another feature of studying fine arts in college is, bluntly put, the chance to make professional contacts. Like a few other professions, artists make their way in the world on the basis of getting to know the right people. The networking that can go on among classmates, teachers, and supporters of the arts is a definite plus for the college student.

At most schools, slightly more than half of the 4-year course load is in arts courses. The remainder is in courses that teach proficiency in writing, as well as in "distribution requirements" for courses in different programs.

**Concentrations**

Schools arrange their visual-arts programs in many diverse ways. Many combine fine arts and art history in the same department; the artists are required to take several history courses, and the art history students are required to take a few drawing or composition classes. Here are some of the specific visual arts programs.

**Art,** including art education, art therapy, ceramics, sculpture, printmaking, painting.

**Graphic (Media) Arts,** including advertising, commercial art, graphic design, art direction, cartooning, computer graphics.

**Photography**

**Film and Video,** including cinematography, film editing, film history and criticism, film production.

**Course Sampler**

**F-208 Drawing Workshop**
In this course the student continues to develop competence in conventional and unconventional drawing techniques. Value studies and volumetric analysis, contour drawing, calligraphy and collage are explored and compared. A variety of dry and aqueous media are employed. Emphasis is also placed on developing the students' awareness of the formal significance of these techniques in relation to

both current and historical art models. Drawing is examined in its relationship to painting and sculpture and to design, planning, and performance notation.

*(School of Visual Arts [New York City])*

### 193. Computer Design Workshop

An interdisciplinary workshop in which engineering, art, and communications students learn to use graphics computers and software. Students work in teams to explore solutions to important social problems, use the computer to illustrate solutions, and complete formal presentations of their findings.

*(Santa Clara University)*

### ARTD 2345 Graphic Design 4:  Symbol Design

Introduction to the skills, concepts, and communication processes associated with designing symbols for public understanding, with focus on the invention and designing of abstract and concrete symbols from animate and inanimate objects. Studio projects are based on theoretic and real situations and relate to brochures, product, letterhead, containers, and poster design.

*(University of Denver)*

### Art 135 Printmaking I

An introduction to printmaking media. Coursework is structured around a sequence of problems introducing the following techniques: collagraphy, woodcut, lineo-cut, and intaglio (engraving, drypoint, and etching). The student will also be introduced to the history of prints and artists that lend influence.

*(Illinois Wesleyan University)*

**Assessment**

"I knew from an early age that I wanted to be in a creative field, and along the way I became pretty sure that that field would be advertising," reminisces Dexter Fedor, a 1979 graduate of Washington University in St. Louis, with dual degrees in fine arts (graphics) and business administration. Now senior vice president and creative director of the Bloom Agency in Dallas, Mr. Fedor has had several recent coups, including the wildly successful "California Raisins" advertising campaign of the late 1980s.

"I learned a lot about design and graphics at school," he says. "The program there has a very classical approach, teaching basics in drawing, color, design, and structure." He says that he could have gone through a program in advertising specifically, but he favors the "broad base" that fine arts has given him. His successes, however, have pushed him rapidly from the beginning of his career, when his work was "90% creative, 10% administrative," to his current managerial level, where the proportions are reversed. "I still work with creative ideas, trying to do some of it myself, and trying to direct others."

A 1989 BFA graduate of the Massachusetts College of Art, Jeff Venier is another artist who always knew what he wanted to do: graphic design. He now works at a trade publisher in the Boston area. "One of the things I liked at the college was the variety of courses that were required, including performing arts, photography, and sculpture—it was a little bit of everything, which has expanded my range of knowledge," he says. Admission to the school is very competitive, requiring the submission of a portfolio. In his working career, Mr. Venier has continued the expansion of his knowledge by becoming adept at computer-based design and publishing systems, all through on-the-job training.

Offering a longer career perspective on art, Robert Torpor says that "education about myself" was one of the main things he learned at Syracuse University, where he studied fine arts, graduating in 1958. He went on to earn a master's degree in art history (University of Rochester), and over time, developed a specialty in marketing and advertising for higher education. Author of numerous books, he is now owner of Torpor & Associates, a marketing communications firm.

"Being able to think creatively, and to use words to describe abstract ideas, are some of the best things I learned in college," he recalls. "Learning how to use a library was another. The most important thing I have learned in the past 15 years has been how to use a computer for fun and for work. That has allowed me to do more, and to communicate better." He describes himself as a heavy user of new communications technologies, such as computer-based networks. "Without the skills I learned in college there is no way I could have been as successful as I have been."

**Career Options**

Art director
Camera operator/cinematographer
Commercial artist

**Computer programmer,** with regard to computer-generated graphics and desktop publishing.
**Designer, industrial and fashion**
**Designer, interior**
**Experiential educator**
**Film/video engineer**
**Photographer**
**Publicist**

# PART II

# THE

---

# CAREERS

# CAREERS BY THE NUMBERS

In this section, you will find descriptions of the jobs for which a college degree, or equivalent in advanced training, is necessary or advisable. The list tends to favor entry-level positions over those usually assigned to experienced businesspeople or professionals. In America, as the saying goes, anyone can be President, but you probably aren't reading this book to find out how.

The general introduction at the beginning of the book will help start you thinking about the job market. Once you have identified an area, or group of related professions, that might be your ambition, you will have questions that this section can help you answer:

- What are the day-to-day activities in a particular profession?
- What skills are needed to excel in that line of work?
- What are the near-term prospects for expanding opportunities and career growth?
- What does this profession pay?

The job descriptions that follow will provide answers to these questions. Following each job's descriptive title is a list that identifies typical undergraduate academic programs that people in these professions have attended. This list is of an advisory nature only; many occupations are open to any type of college graduate —if not initially, certainly once appropriate experience has been obtained.

Each entry ends with addresses of organizations that can give additional information about that career.

Another good source of career information is the US Bureau of Labor Statistics (BLS), a part of the US Department of Labor. Their Dictionary of Occupational Titles (DOT) is an exhaustive list of trades, professions, and occupations. For the college graduate, however, the DOT is not much help. It is very good at telling you what you need to do in order to be an auto mechanic, as opposed to an airplane mechanic, but it is much less helpful in distinguishing between a groundwater geologist (a hot field at the moment) and a mining geologist (a rather grim field currently).

This is not a knock against BLS; as you will see, many of the listings that follow depend on BLS data. The DOT's shortcomings reflect the difficulties in describing just what people do for a living, and how they studied for it in high school or in college.

Another invaluable project of BLS is the forecast of future job demands, which makes up a part of the biennial *Occupational Outlook Handbook* (an excellent publication), and a related publication, *Occupational Projections and Training Data*, which lists all the numerical facts concerning projections and educational requirements for employment. From this mass of data, we have selected the following tables. They'll help you compare the various careers that may interest you. Included are tables of the Fastest-Growing Professions (ranked by growth rate and then alphabetically), the Top Professions for Women, Top Professions for African-Americans, Top Professions for Hispanics, and College-Educated Workers, 1988.

Every two years, the BLS uses surveys of current employment to determine how many workers, in various specialties, are needed for a certain employment sector. Then it runs econometric models of future growth of the US economy. Assuming that the number of workers necessary today for a given volume of output will be roughly comparable to those of tomorrow, the BLS estimates future professional growth. Three estimates are made: for low, moderate, or high levels of economic growth. Throughout this book, the moderate case is used.

The first two tables here (pp. 142–147) show the most recent projections, made in the fall of 1989, by growth rate and also, for your convenience, alphabetically. The master list from BLS includes nearly all types of jobs with at least 25,000 workers. We have selected those professions in which college graduates are likely to be employed. The final table, College-Educated Workers, 1988, shows the rough percentages of degreed graduates in these employment sectors; what is important to note here is that, while only a portion of the occupations in the first two tables *require* a college degree, most of them have college graduates as participants. I have excluded most types of employment where few workers are college graduates, or where a college degree would be only marginally beneficial.

The table called Top Professions for Women (pp. 146–147) lists the professions in which the proportion of women exceeds their average representation in the total workforce (in 1988, the overall average was 45.2%). College-educated women have made great strides into the professional ranks; these data show how far they had come by 1988. I am emphatically *not* listing these professions in the belief that these are where women "belong"; rather, I want to show the professions in which artificial barriers to women have fallen fastest. The projected growth rates for the professions are also listed, the same ones as found in the first table.

Similarly, the remaining tables (pp. 147–148) list the top 25 professions where African-Americans and Hispanics have made the greatest entree. The percentages indicate which fields have the fewest barriers to entry for minority college students.

The last table (p. 149) suggests how important a college degree is to groups of professions. Published BLS data does not provide more detail than these groups, so the list of job titles is not identical to those in the preceding tables. Still, there are some nuggets of information to be obtained from this data. For example, over four times as many people in financial and business services sales have a college degree, as do people in retail sales. Another nugget is that over one out of two "health assessment and treatment" workers (nurses, etc.) have a college degree; that's higher than the number of managerial executives, and not far from the number of math and computer scientists so endowed. Keep in mind, though, that these percentages reflect what has already happened rather than what will happen. Some of the people that make up this base of data graduated from high school or college 30 or more years ago. They entered a job market very different from today's.

A careful reader of the entries in the following pages will note that not all of the professions have BLS growth data. There are a variety of reasons for this. Generally, BLS does not publish data on professions with fewer than 25,000 practitioners, believing that the data and projections will not be statistically reliable. Another reason may be that the profession has only recently appeared, and the machinery of the BLS surveying and data-forecasting system has not yet caught up with the profession. Where available, I have

"The Careers" continued on p. 149

### OCCUPATIONAL PROJECTION, 1988–2000
### BY GROWTH RATE

| OCCUPATION | 1988* | 2000* | % change |
|---|---|---|---|
| paralegal personnel | 83 | 145 | 75 |
| nuclear medicine and radiologic technologist | 132 | 218 | 66 |
| medical record technician | 47 | 75 | 60 |
| physical therapist | 68 | 107 | 57 |
| operations and systems researcher | 55 | 85 | 55 |
| securities and financial services sales worker | 200 | 309 | 55 |
| travel agent | 142 | 219 | 54 |
| computer systems analyst | 403 | 617 | 53 |
| occupational therapist | 33 | 48 | 49 |
| computer programmer | 519 | 769 | 48 |
| respiratory therapist | 56 | 79 | 41 |
| electrical/electronic engineer | 439 | 615 | 40 |
| employment interviewer, employment service | 81 | 113 | 40 |
| registered nurse | 1577 | 2190 | 39 |
| electrical and electronic technologist | 341 | 471 | 38 |
| recreational therapist | 26 | 35 | 37 |
| management analyst | 130 | 176 | 35 |
| engineering or science manager | 258 | 341 | 32 |
| mathematical scientist, actuary, statistician | 46 | 61 | 32 |
| aircraft pilot/flight engineer | 83 | 108 | 31 |
| lawyer | 582 | 763 | 31 |
| producer, director, actor | 80 | 104 | 30 |
| computer and peripheral equipment operator | 316 | 408 | 29 |
| food service and lodging manager | 560 | 721 | 29 |
| social worker | 385 | 495 | 29 |
| underwriter | 103 | 134 | 29 |
| designer | 309 | 395 | 28 |
| dietician, nutritionist | 40 | 51 | 28 |
| physician/surgeon | 535 | 684 | 28 |
| speech pathologist/audiologist | 53 | 68 | 28 |
| artist, commercial artist | 216 | 274 | 27 |
| cook (restaurant) | 572 | 728 | 27 |
| economist | 36 | 45 | 27 |
| educational counselor | 124 | 157 | 27 |
| pharmacist | 162 | 206 | 27 |
| psychologist | 104 | 132 | 27 |
| biological scientist | 57 | 72 | 26 |
| marketing, advertising and PR manager | 406 | 511 | 26 |
| veterinarian and veterinary inspector | 46 | 57 | 26 |
| architect | 86 | 107 | 25 |
| editor, writer (inc. technical) | 219 | 274 | 25 |
| claims examiner, property and casualty insurance | 30 | 37 | 23 |
| accountant/auditor | 963 | 1174 | 22 |

## OCCUPATIONAL PROJECTION, 1988–2000
### BY GROWTH RATE (*CONTINUED*)

| OCCUPATION | 1988* | 2000* | % change |
|---|---|---|---|
| farm managers | 131 | 160 | 22 |
| landscape architect | 19 | 25 | 22 |
| loan officer, counselor | 172 | 209 | 22 |
| personnel, training and labor relations manager | 171 | 208 | 22 |
| agricultural and food scientist | 25 | 30 | 21 |
| personnel, training, labor relations specialist | 252 | 305 | 21 |
| mechanical engineer | 225 | 269 | 20 |
| clinical laboratory technologist | 242 | 288 | 19 |
| education administrator | 320 | 382 | 19 |
| financial manager | 673 | 802 | 19 |
| photographer, camera operator | 105 | 125 | 19 |
| property and real estate manager | 225 | 267 | 19 |
| radio and TV announcer | 57 | 67 | 19 |
| recreation worker | 186 | 221 | 19 |
| science and math technician | 232 | 275 | 19 |
| teacher, secondary school | 1164 | 1388 | 19 |
| industrial engineer | 132 | 155 | 18 |
| chemist | 80 | 93 | 17 |
| civil engineer | 186 | 219 | 17 |
| real estate sales worker | 422 | 493 | 17 |
| teacher, preschool/elementary | 1597 | 1876 | 17 |
| chemical engineer | 49 | 57 | 16 |
| geologist, oceanographer | 42 | 49 | 16 |
| optometrist | 37 | 43 | 16 |
| reporter, correspondent | 70 | 82 | 16 |
| TOTAL, ALL OCCUPATIONS IN BLS | 118104 | 136211 | 15 |
| cost estimator | 169 | 194 | 15 |
| public relations specialist | 91 | 105 | 15 |
| urban and regional planner | 20 | 23 | 15 |
| construction and building inspector | 56 | 64 | 14 |
| dispatchers (trucking and other) | 202 | 217 | 14 |
| inspector/compliance officer, except construction | 130 | 148 | 14 |
| insurance sales worker | 423 | 481 | 14 |
| purchasing manager | 252 | 289 | 14 |
| aeronautical/astronautical engineer | 78 | 88 | 13 |
| dentist | 167 | 189 | 13 |
| metallurgist and material engineer | 19 | 22 | 13 |
| physicist and astronomer | 18 | 21 | 13 |
| adult, vocational teacher | 467 | 523 | 12 |
| librarian, curator | 159 | 176 | 11 |
| police and detective supervisor | 88 | 97 | 10 |
| musician | 229 | 251 | 9 |
| police detective and investigator | 61 | 66 | 9 |

## OCCUPATIONAL PROJECTION, 1988–2000
### BY GROWTH RATE (CONTINUED)

| OCCUPATION | 1988* | 2000* | % change |
|---|---|---|---|
| forester and conservation scientist | 27 | 30 | 8 |
| wholesale, retail buyer, except farm products | 207 | 220 | 6 |
| college and university faculty | 846 | 869 | 3 |
| public administration Ch. Exec., legislative, general | 69 | 71 | 3 |

\* Employment, 1,000's
SOURCE:   Selected data from BLS

## OCCUPATIONAL PROJECTION, 1988–2000
### ALPHABETICALLY

| OCCUPATION | 1988* | 2000* | % change |
|---|---|---|---|
| accountant/auditor | 963 | 1174 | 22 |
| adult, vocational teacher | 467 | 523 | 12 |
| aeronautical/astronautical engineer | 78 | 88 | 13 |
| agricultural and food scientist | 25 | 30 | 21 |
| aircraft pilot/flight engineer | 83 | 108 | 31 |
| architect | 86 | 107 | 25 |
| artist, commercial artist | 216 | 274 | 27 |
| biological scientist | 57 | 72 | 26 |
| chemical engineer | 49 | 57 | 16 |
| chemist | 80 | 93 | 17 |
| civil engineer | 186 | 219 | 17 |
| claims examiner, property and casualty insurance | 30 | 37 | 23 |
| clinical laboratory technologist | 242 | 288 | 19 |
| college and university faculty | 846 | 869 | 3 |
| computer and peripheral equipment operator | 316 | 408 | 29 |
| computer programmer | 519 | 769 | 48 |
| computer systems analyst | 403 | 617 | 53 |
| construction and building inspector | 56 | 64 | 14 |
| cook (restaurant) | 572 | 728 | 27 |
| cost estimator | 169 | 194 | 15 |
| dentist | 167 | 189 | 13 |
| designer | 309 | 395 | 28 |
| dietician, nutritionist | 40 | 51 | 28 |
| dispatchers (trucking and other) | 202 | 217 | 14 |
| economist | 36 | 45 | 27 |
| editor, writer (inc. technical) | 219 | 274 | 25 |
| education administrator | 320 | 382 | 19 |
| educational counselor | 124 | 157 | 27 |

## OCCUPATIONAL PROJECTION, 1988–2000
### ALPHABETICALLY (CONTINUED)

| OCCUPATION | 1988* | 2000* | % change |
| --- | --- | --- | --- |
| electrical and electronic technologist | 341 | 471 | 38 |
| electrical/electronic engineer | 439 | 615 | 40 |
| employment interviewer, employment service | 81 | 113 | 40 |
| engineering or science manager | 258 | 341 | 32 |
| farm managers | 131 | 160 | 22 |
| financial manager | 673 | 802 | 19 |
| food service and lodging manager | 560 | 721 | 29 |
| forester and conservation scientist | 27 | 30 | 8 |
| geologist, oceanographer | 42 | 49 | 16 |
| industrial engineer | 132 | 155 | 18 |
| inspector/compliance officer, except construction | 130 | 148 | 14 |
| insurance sales worker | 423 | 481 | 14 |
| landscape architect | 19 | 25 | 22 |
| lawyer | 582 | 763 | 31 |
| librarian, curator | 159 | 176 | 11 |
| loan officer, counselor | 172 | 209 | 22 |
| management analyst | 130 | 176 | 35 |
| marketing, advertising and PR manager | 406 | 511 | 26 |
| mathematical scientist, actuary, statistician | 46 | 61 | 32 |
| mechanical engineer | 225 | 269 | 20 |
| medical record technician | 47 | 75 | 60 |
| metallurgist and material engineer | 19 | 22 | 13 |
| musician | 229 | 251 | 9 |
| nuclear medicine and radiologic technologist | 132 | 218 | 66 |
| occupational therapist | 33 | 48 | 49 |
| operations and systems researcher | 55 | 85 | 55 |
| optometrist | 37 | 43 | 16 |
| paralegal personnel | 83 | 145 | 75 |
| personnel, training and labor relations manager | 171 | 208 | 22 |
| personnel, training, labor relations specialist | 252 | 305 | 21 |
| pharmacist | 162 | 206 | 27 |
| photographer, camera operator | 105 | 125 | 19 |
| physical therapist | 68 | 107 | 57 |
| physician/surgeon | 535 | 684 | 28 |
| physicist and astronomer | 18 | 21 | 13 |
| police and detective supervisor | 88 | 97 | 10 |
| police detective and investigator | 61 | 66 | 9 |
| producer, director, actor | 80 | 104 | 30 |
| property and real estate manager | 225 | 267 | 19 |
| psychologist | 104 | 132 | 27 |
| public administration Ch. Exec., legislative, general | 69 | 71 | 3 |
| public relations specialist | 91 | 105 | 15 |
| purchasing manager | 252 | 289 | 14 |

## OCCUPATIONAL PROJECTION, 1988–2000
### ALPHABETICALLY (CONTINUED)

| OCCUPATION | 1988* | 2000* | % change |
|---|---|---|---|
| radio and TV announcer | 57 | 67 | 19 |
| real estate sales worker | 422 | 493 | 17 |
| recreation worker | 186 | 221 | 19 |
| recreational therapist | 26 | 35 | 37 |
| registered nurse | 1577 | 2190 | 39 |
| reporter, correspondent | 70 | 82 | 16 |
| respiratory therapist | 56 | 79 | 41 |
| science and math technician | 232 | 275 | 19 |
| securities and financial services sales worker | 200 | 309 | 55 |
| social worker | 385 | 495 | 29 |
| speech pathologist/audiologist | 53 | 68 | 28 |
| teacher, preschool/elementary | 1597 | 1876 | 17 |
| teacher, secondary school | 1164 | 1388 | 19 |
| travel agent | 142 | 219 | 54 |
| underwriter | 103 | 134 | 29 |
| urban and regional planner | 20 | 23 | 15 |
| veterinarian and veterinary inspector | 46 | 57 | 26 |
| wholesale, retail buyer, except farm products | 207 | 220 | 6 |
| TOTAL, ALL OCCUPATIONS IN BLS | 118104 | 136211 | 15 |

* Employment, 1,000's
SOURCE: Selected data from BLS

## TOP PROFESSIONS FOR WOMEN

| OCCUPATION | 1988* | 2000* | % change | % female |
|---|---|---|---|---|
| medical record technician | 47 | 75 | 60 | 99.2 |
| registered nurse | 1577 | 2190 | 39 | 94.2 |
| dietician, nutritionist | 40 | 51 | 28 | 90.8 |
| speech pathologist/audiologist | 53 | 68 | 28 | 88.6 |
| teacher, preschool/elementary | 1597 | 1876 | 17 | 87.6 |
| librarian, curator | 159 | 176 | 11 | 87.3 |
| physical therapist | 68 | 107 | 57 | 77.3 |
| nuclear medicine and radiologic technologist | 132 | 218 | 66 | 75.8 |
| paralegal personnel | 83 | 145 | 75 | 75.7 |
| clinical laboratory technologist | 242 | 288 | 19 | 74.4 |
| recreation worker | 186 | 221 | 19 | 74.4 |
| social worker | 385 | 495 | 29 | 68.1 |
| computer and peripheral equipment operator | 316 | 408 | 29 | 64.3 |
| adult, vocational teacher | 467 | 523 | 12 | 63.6 |
| educational counselor | 124 | 157 | 27 | 60.4 |

## TOP PROFESSIONS FOR WOMEN (CONTINUED)

| OCCUPATION | 1988* | 2000* | % change | % female |
|---|---|---|---|---|
| personnel, training, labor relations specialist | 252 | 305 | 21 | 59.6 |
| public relations specialist | 91 | 105 | 15 | 57.1 |
| psychologist | 104 | 132 | 27 | 54 |
| education administrator | 320 | 382 | 19 | 53.4 |
| personnel, training and labor relations manager | 171 | 208 | 22 | 52.6 |
| teacher, secondary school | 1164 | 1388 | 19 | 52.6 |
| respiratory therapist | 56 | 79 | 41 | 52.5 |
| designer | 309 | 395 | 28 | 51.5 |
| dispatchers (trucking and other) | 202 | 217 | 14 | 51.5 |
| real estate sales worker | 422 | 493 | 17 | 51 |
| artist, commercial artist | 216 | 274 | 27 | 50.7 |
| cook (restaurant) | 572 | 728 | 27 | 49.4 |
| reporter, correspondent | 70 | 82 | 16 | 49.2 |
| editor, writer (inc. technical) | 219 | 274 | 25 | 49 |
| accountant/auditor | 963 | 1174 | 15 | 48.6 |
| TOTAL, ALL OCCUPATIONS IN BLS | 118104 | 136211 | 15 | 45.2 |

* Employment, 1,000's
SOURCE:   Selected data from BLS

## TOP PROFESSIONS FOR AFRICAN-AMERICANS

| OCCUPATION | 1988* | 2000* | % change | % Af.-Am. |
|---|---|---|---|---|
| cook (restaurant) | 572 | 728 | 27 | 18.2 |
| social worker | 385 | 495 | 29 | 17.6 |
| dietician, nutritionist | 40 | 51 | 28 | 17.1 |
| clinical laboratory technologist | 242 | 288 | 19 | 14.7 |
| computer and peripheral equipment operator | 316 | 408 | 29 | 14.2 |
| inspector/compliance officer, except construction | 130 | 148 | 14 | 13.3 |
| respiratory therapist | 56 | 79 | 41 | 12.5 |
| educational counselor | 124 | 157 | 27 | 12 |
| teacher, preschool/elementary | 1597 | 1876 | 17 | 11.3 |
| TOTAL, ALL OCCUPATIONS IN BLS | 118104 | 136211 | 15 | 10.2 |
| nuclear medicine and radiologic technologist | 132 | 218 | 66 | 10.1 |
| education administrator | 320 | 382 | 19 | 9.9 |
| recreation worker | 186 | 221 | 19 | 9.8 |
| radio and TV announcer | 57 | 67 | 19 | 9.7 |
| dispatchers (trucking and other) | 202 | 217 | 14 | 9.6 |
| personnel, training, labor relations specialist | 252 | 305 | 21 | 8.8 |
| electrical and electronic technologist | 341 | 471 | 38 | 7.7 |
| psychologist | 104 | 132 | 27 | 7.7 |
| teacher, secondary school | 1164 | 1388 | 19 | 7.7 |

## TOP PROFESSIONS FOR AFRICAN-AMERICANS (*CONTINUED*)

| OCCUPATION | 1988* | 2000* | % change | % Af.-Am. |
|---|---|---|---|---|
| librarian, curator | 159 | 176 | 11 | 7.6 |
| accountant/auditor | 963 | 1174 | 22 | 7.5 |
| science and math technician | 232 | 275 | 19 | 7.5 |
| producer, director, actor | 80 | 104 | 30 | 7.2 |
| registered nurse | 1577 | 2190 | 39 | 7.2 |
| musician | 229 | 251 | 9 | 7 |
| paralegal personnel | 83 | 145 | 75 | 7 |

* Employment, 1,000's
SOURCE: Selected data from BLS

## TOP PROFESSIONS FOR HISPANIC-AMERICANS

| OCCUPATION | 1988* | 2000* | % change | % Hisp. |
|---|---|---|---|---|
| cook (restaurant) | 572 | 728 | 27 | 14.2 |
| photographer, camera operator | 105 | 125 | 19 | 7.6 |
| TOTAL, ALL OCCUPATIONS IN BLS | 118104 | 136211 | 15 | 7.3 |
| inspector/compliance officer, except construction | 130 | 148 | 14 | 6.9 |
| educational counselor | 124 | 157 | 27 | 6.2 |
| computer and peripheral equipment operator | 316 | 408 | 29 | 6.1 |
| electrical and electronic technologist | 341 | 471 | 38 | 6.1 |
| physical therapist | 68 | 107 | 57 | 6.1 |
| architect | 86 | 107 | 25 | 5.8 |
| physician/surgeon | 535 | 684 | 28 | 5.4 |
| dietician, nutritionist | 40 | 51 | 28 | 5.3 |
| musician | 229 | 251 | 9 | 5.3 |
| property and real estate manager | 225 | 267 | 19 | 5.3 |
| chemist | 80 | 93 | 17 | 5.2 |
| paralegal personnel | 83 | 145 | 75 | 5 |
| operations and systems researcher | 55 | 85 | 55 | 4.9 |
| science and math technician | 232 | 275 | 19 | 4.9 |
| social worker | 385 | 495 | 29 | 4.8 |
| personnel, training, labor relations specialist | 252 | 305 | 21 | 4.5 |
| dispatchers (trucking and other) | 202 | 217 | 14 | 4.4 |
| designer | 309 | 395 | 28 | 4.3 |
| nuclear medicine and radiologic technologist | 132 | 218 | 66 | 4.3 |
| adult, vocational teacher | 467 | 523 | 12 | 4.2 |
| clinical laboratory technologist | 242 | 288 | 19 | 4.1 |
| education administrator | 320 | 382 | 19 | 4 |
| teacher, preschool/elementary | 1597 | 1876 | 17 | 3.9 |

* Employment, 1,000's
SOURCE: Selected data from BLS

## COLLEGE-EDUCATED WORKERS, 1988

| OCCUPATION | total emplymt. | 4 years' college or more | % |
|---|---|---|---|
| Managerial & Professional Specialty | 29007 | 17306 | 59.7 |
| Executive, Administrative & Managerial | 13928 | 6157 | 44.2 |
| Public Administrators & Officials | 552 | 252 | 45.7 |
| Management-related occupations (accountants, analysts, cost estimators, etc.) | 3732 | 1871 | 50.1 |
| Engineers | 1823 | 1370 | 75.2 |
| Mathematical & Computer Scientists | 730 | 467 | 64.0 |
| Natural Scientists (Chemists, Physicists, etc.) | 390 | 343 | 87.9 |
| Health Diagnosing Occupations (doctors, dentists, optometrists, etc.) | 779 | 724 | 92.9 |
| Health Assessment and Treatment (nurses, etc.) | 2152 | 1206 | 56.0 |
| Teachers, College and University | 772 | 667 | 86.4 |
| Teachers, except College | 3981 | 3345 | 84.0 |
| Lawyers and Judges | 762 | 721 | 94.6 |
| Technical, Sales & Admin. Support | 35267 | 6501 | 18.4 |
| Technicians | 3506 | 1129 | 32.2 |
| Health Technologists | 1176 | 258 | 21.9 |
| Engineering & Sci. Technicians | 1187 | 257 | 21.7 |
| Sales Occupations | 13509 | 3110 | 23.0 |
| Supervisors & Proprietors | 3770 | 895 | 23.7 |
| Sales Reps., Finance & Bus. Svs. | 2312 | 1022 | 44.2 |
| Sales Reps., except Retail | 1553 | 602 | 38.8 |
| Sales Reps., Retail | 5810 | 577 | 9.9 |
| Admin. Support Supervisors | 758 | 185 | 24.4 |
| Computer Equipment Operators | 865 | 138 | 16.0 |
| Protective Service | 1823 | 291 | 16.0 |
| Food Service | 5088 | 223 | 4.4 |
| Health Service | 1943 | 91 | 4.7 |
| Farm Operators and Managers | 1221 | 143 | 11.7 |
| TOTAL, Civilian over 16 yrs. | 112565 | 26291 | 23.4 |

SOURCE: BLS

included growth trends as demonstrated by the increase in membership in a professional society; some professional societies also conduct their own studies to uncover growth areas.

An important proviso of these projections is that even a profession with zero growth will have openings due to retirements or career changes. In fact, a profession with a 10% "exit rate" will have a nearly 100% turnover during a decade.

How good are the BLS projections? On the whole, the estimate for total employment in the future tends to be pretty good. For specific occupations, the trend is usually correct (i.e., whether a profession will grow or shrink), although the numerical estimates are often off the mark.

The dynamic American job market is a glory to behold. Economists have dubbed our economy the "Great American Job Machine" because it generates so many new jobs and offers so many potential careers. Jump in!

---

# ACCOUNTANT

### Accounting, Business Administration

Accounting is one of the key professions in the business world. There are over 1 million accountants, and their numbers are expected to rise 22% during the next decade, somewhat above average of all professions.

The basic work of accounting is to keep the books on a business, totalling revenues and expenses, and writing a balance sheet. This service is provided by law for publicly traded corporations, which must have independent certification of the financial results they announce, and as a service for many individuals, whose investments, tax obligations, and earnings are aided by having an accountant's judgment.

The largest public accounting firms, which had been known as the Big Eight (now the "Big Seven" following the merger of two of them), are Arthur Andersen, Peat Marwick Main, Coopers & Lybrand, Touche Ross, Price Waterhouse, Deloitte Haskins & Sells, and Ernst & Young. These firms have offices across the country and abroad, and employ thousands of accountants to manage the books of hundreds of firms.

The common belief is that most or even all accountants are certified, but such is not the case: only about one out of three is. Certification is necessary for various types of business or governmental accounting, but is not essential for most other types. Still, obtaining the Certified Public Accountant (CPA) designation is a definite career boost. The American Institute of Certified Public Accountants gives a nationally standard examination, which is usually taken during the senior year in college. Several years' work experience must follow before full certification is granted.

Starting salaries for accountants are between $21,000 and $24,000. The large public accounting firms offer substantially higher salaries, and those who make the long haul to partnership status can earn well above $50,000 annually.

A large profession can be expected to have a variety of specializations, and this is indeed the case in accounting. One key specialty is tax accounting, which involves financial reviewing with an eye toward minimizing tax bills. Keeping up with US Internal Revenue Service rules, and those of states and localities, is enough work to keep thousands of accountants occupied full-time.

Another specialty is governmental and non-profit accounting, which involves financial management and the keeping of special financial records that such entities must have.

Many public accountants that work as sole practitioners also provide financial planning services (see **Financial Planner**), which entails a more active management of financial resources. To perform this work, the accountant must keep apprised of investment vehicles, their performance, and their tax advantages.

Because the large public accounting firms work closely with the upper-management of corporations, they often provide business advice beyond the accounting area. A current major growth area is helping companies integrate computers into business management and even factory-floor automation. One quarter of the major accounting firms' annual revenues now comes from this source.

**American Institute of Certified Public Accountants**
1211 Avenue of the Americas
New York, NY   10036
(212) 575-6200

# ACTUARY

### Accounting, Economics, Mathematics

An insurance company determines how much an insurance policy should cost by predicting what is likely to happen to our homes, business, property—indeed our very lives. Making these predictions is the responsibility of the actuary.

We hear about actuaries most often in relation to life insurance: the "actuarial tables" predict how long we are likely to live, based on location, lifestyle, and health. Actuaries also analyze many other types of insured risks, including shipping and other types of transportation, the effects of weather, and the liabilities of professionals such as doctors and lawyers.

Another aspect of actuarial work involves helping clients understand their exposure to risk. For instance, an actuary would explain to the owners of a railroad that if a train carrying a cargo of goods were to derail, the railroad would have to be able to satisfy the claims of the owners of the goods being shipped, fix any damage caused to nearby property, and perhaps even satisfy claims made for personal injury or loss of life.

Actuaries spend a lot of time going over industry statistics, studying health-care trends, and reviewing the implications of court decisions. All these sources provide data that must be analyzed by statistical techniques. The actuaries' conclusions then become the foundation for underwriters' work in writing insurance policies.

Training in math and economics is the best preparation for actuarial work. Degrees in statistics, math, and finance are common. Median salaries for experienced actuaries are around $40,000 to $50,000; the salary can be increased by obtaining certification.

There are about 16,000 actuaries working currently, most at the major insurance companies. A substantial number also work for state or federal government, where analysis of social trends is used to justify budgets for education, health-care and other social services. The health-care industry, including hospitals and medical organizations, also employ some actuaries to provide data on health-care trends.

Insurance is becoming a more important part of the American economy, partly due to rising costs, and partly due to the expansion of insured activities. For example, professional liability insurance, once common for doctors, is now becoming common for lawyers, engineers, and business executives as well. The Bureau of Labor Statistics projects that the number of actuary positions will rise by around 50% over this decade, propelled by a greater need for analysis in medical and insurance businesses.

**Society of Actuaries**
475 North Martingale Road
Schaumburg, IL   60173
(708) 773-3010

---

# ADVERTISING ACCOUNT EXECUTIVE

### English, History, Political Science, Psychology, Sociology, and most other liberal arts programs

The "account exec" is the key operative at advertising agencies. He or she is the primary intermediary between the advertising specialists (copywriters, art directors, media planners) and the marketing and sales staff of the client company or organization (the latter includes non-profit groups, government agencies, political parties, and others, many of whom spend hundreds of millions of dollars on advertising).

The account executive combines two critical skills:  selling (to convince the client to adopt an agency and its ad campaign), and marketing (to relate to the needs of the client). There is the constant pressure of serving two parties, since the account executives are responsible for helping their employers to earn a profit, while they are also responsible for helping the client improve its sales.

There is a certain degree of trafficking between the agency side and the client side, with marketers becoming account executives and vice versa. Also, a considerable number of companies have "in-house" advertising agencies—a department with all of the characteristics of a regular agency, but with only one client. Here, the account executive serves the marketing managers of other divisions of the same firm.

When everything works well, the advertising campaign is a thing of beauty. Having spent time with the client's market research people, the account executive goes to the agency creative staff for ideas on a campaign. A variety of ideas and means of execution are tried out (often through testing with actual customers), and media choices are made. The new product and campaign are "rolled out" at an expense of as much as $100 million, and all the participants hold their breath, hoping for a favorable result.

There is little in the way of direct training for account management work, aside from familiarity with advertising techniques, marketing, and selling. Some major agencies favor candidates with MBAs. Many account executives tend to be itinerant workers, staying at one agency or in one city for a time, then moving to another. The job itself adds to this instability, since an agency's main recourse when a major client drops the firm is to cut staff back.

The Bureau of Labor Statistics does not publish data on advertising workers specifically, except for the general category of "marketing, advertising, and public relations managers." This group is projected to grow by 26%, to 511,000, by the year 2000. The tradition among advertising agencies is to start executives at low salaries ($20,000 or less), moving them up rapidly as their responsibilities increase.

While television advertising is the most glamorous aspect of advertising agency work, it is currently not the fastest-growing one. There is a far-reaching trend away from advertising per se and toward other marketing methods such as promotion, discounting, and direct mail (see **Direct Marketer**) because of the high cost of advertising and the diminishing returns from investing in it, especially in major consumer markets. Agencies, and their account executives, have responded by diversifying into these alternative methods.

**American Association of Advertising Agencies**
666 3rd Avenue
New York, NY   10017
(212) 682-2500

# AEROSPACE ENGINEER

**Chemical engineering, Electrical and electronics engineering, Mechanical engineering**
**(Many schools offer degrees in aerospace engineering as well.)**

Space—the final frontier! The wings of man! To soar with the eagles! Somehow, when it comes to flying, people suddenly begin to dream. The ones who make those dreams practical are aerospace engineers.

Aerospace (and the closely related aeronautical) engineering is an invention of the 20th century; only kites and balloons were put into the air before the year 1900. The profession enjoyed a boom during the early 1980s, as the Space Shuttle program of NASA cranked up, and as larger defense budgets increased demand for engineering talent. As the decade wound down, both of these situations reversed. The tragic explosion of the space shuttle *Challenger* in 1986 delayed further launches for almost 3 years, and when they restarted, a much more conservative schedule was adopted. In addition, the high level of defense spending is expected to drop in the absence of a near-term military threat to the United States.

There are bright spots for the career, however. Commercial aviation construction is at historically high levels; the backlog at Boeing Co., the world leader, is worth over $60 billion. Although the plans are still being debated, the White House hasn't given up on a space station—a permanent, manned, orbiting platform—in the late 1990s. The most successful aspect of the space business remains communications satellites, and this area will continue to grow in the near future.

Aerospace engineering traditionally is organized around the various elements of an aircraft:   propulsion, structures, control, and guidance. Many electrical engineers join hands with aerospace engineers to work on the microelectronic gear that guides a modern jet; a Boeing 747, for example, carries over a ton of electronics on board. Propulsion systems include the jet turbines, as well as the high-strength materials that go into the turbine. Some aspects of aerospace structural work carry over into other structures, including buildings and other modes of transportation.

Over this decade, the Bureau of Labor Statistics projects a growth of 13%, to 88,000 engineers. The "low growth" scenario, which assumes a reduced level of defense spending and lower economic growth, projects a 3% increase, to 80,000 engineers. Student enrollments have been climbing upward, reaching 2,949 graduates in 1988, so there may be an oversupply if enrollments continue to grow. Currently, starting salaries are around $29,000 for graduates.

**American Institute of Aeronautics and Astronautics**
370 L'Enfant Promenade, SW
Washington, DC   20024
(202) 646-7400

---

# ARCHITECT
## Architecture and Urban Design

Building a home, school, or office building is a complex task that requires several sets of professionals. The first to get involved are usually architects, who develop the details of the purpose the structure is to serve, and then produce a design.

The traditional pattern of architectural work has been for a real estate developer or homeowner to commission the architect to do a design. The professional architect—half artist, half businessperson—would conceive a design and after spending hours at a drafting table, draw various renderings of the structure and specify plans for its construction. These drawings would then be passed on to a construction firm, whose engineers would work out the details of the structure, then oversee its construction.

Changing business patterns, and the impact of such tools as computers, are changing this picture. For one thing, less time is being spent at the drafting table, and more time in front of a computer screen. Recently developed computer programs allow the architect to draw via computer, and to flesh out construction details even while the design is being conceived. Another trend is that the business demands on architects now nearly rival the artistic, design-oriented demands. Architects are spending more time marketing the services of their firms (or themselves), and are paying closer attention to the economic needs of their clients. It is not enough to conceive a brilliant design; the design must also serve the business or budgetary needs of the client. Many architecture firms today are organized as a "design/build" firm, rather than as designers alone.

According to surveys by the American Institute of Architecture (AIA), the great majority of architectural firms are sole practices or small firms (fewer than 20 employees), but the majority of AIA architects—about 60%—work at larger firms.

The outlook for the profession is good, although business conditions at the moment make getting into the field difficult. The Bureau of Labor Statistics projects that the number of architects will rise by 25% over this decade, from 86,000 to about 107,000. This increase is projected to occur even though the field grew dramatically during the 1980s; AIA has recorded almost a 60% growth in membership during the past 10 years. The 1980s were characterized by rapid expansion in commercial construction. At the outset of the 1990s, business indicators showed a leveling off of construction budgets, and overcapacity in office space, hotel rooms, and other types of buildings. Many architects today are specializing in luxury-home construction, which is still going strong.

Salaries for architects are low in the beginning but can rise dramatically with experience and the development of a strong practice. AIA data show that the median salary for architect interns (the entry level for the profession) was $23,000 in 1988; the median for principals/partners was over $62,000.

The educational requirements for becoming a licensed architect are rigid. Most students enter a 5-year program that leads to a "first-professional" degree (bachelor's in architecture). In the sixth year, a master's degree can be earned. Alternatively, students can take any of a number of liberal arts degrees for 4 years, then attend graduate school for 3 to 4 years to earn a master's degree. Following graduation, the architect works as an intern for several years and prepares for a tough, 4-day examination sponsored by state licensing boards.

**American Institute of Architecture Students**
c/o American Institute of Architects
1735 New York Avenue, NW
Washington, DC   20006
(202) 626-7472

---

# ART DIRECTOR

### Architecture and Urban Design, Art History, Performing Arts, Psychology, Sociology, Visual Arts

Art directors are the third element in the triad that creates an advertising campaign (the others are the **Account Executive** and **Copywriter**). The art director pulls together the words of the copywriter and the messages that the advertiser wants to convey to create a visual message that communicates and persuades.

As advertising began with such mass media as newspapers, catalogs, and magazines, the roles of writer and art director became set by the medium of the printed page. Today, with television, video, film, and other advertising media, the creative process and the visual tools have changed. Nevertheless, most advertising art directors have a background in images for the printed page; some supplement this with training in film and cinematography.

Art directors are trained in some type of visual art, including commercial art (see **Commercial Artist**), but they must use visual images to persuade or sell. In the debate over artistically innovative advertising versus advertising that successfully sells a product, almost inevitably the latter is the favorite.

When major advertising agencies had their offices on Madison Avenue in New York, creative directors were famous for marching up and down the avenue, trying to attract the attention of agency personnel directors. Now, the more customary procedure is to show a portfolio of student projects from one of the many college programs in commercial art or advertising.

Art-direction jobs are available at places other than agencies. Many larger corporations have an in-house staff for marketing communications. Many publishers have advertising-like functions associated with book promotion. Finally, there are businesses that provide "visuals" (i.e., the illustrative material that accompanies a script) for films, documentaries, television, and publishing; they tend to be in major metropolitan areas.

The best art directors in advertising are also savvy marketers, and if marketing expertise is proven through successful campaigns, the director moves up in the agency's management. The next step up is the position of creative director, who oversees the work of both copywriters and art directors. Sometimes top creative directors and account executives start their own firms.

The Bureau of Labor Statistics projects a 26% growth rate for the general class of "marketing, advertising and public relations managers" and 27% for artists and commercial artists, so it seems clear that art direction will enjoy strong demand over this decade.

Art Directors Club
250 Park Avenue South
New York, NY   10003
(212) 674-0500

# ARTIFICIAL INTELLIGENCE DEVELOPER

**Computer science and engineering, Electrical and electronic engineering, Mathematics, Philosophy and Religion**

"Artificial intelligence" is the general term for advanced computer-programming techniques that allow a computer to simulate thought. Many people still don't believe that artificial intelligence (AI) exists—they quickly get into an argument over the nature of the mind and the nature of computers. Putting aside the philosophical debate, and simply looking at the products and activities that are generally categorized as AI, one can say not only that it exists, but that the use of it is growing by 50% per year. Several thousand (no one is sure exactly how many computer programmers, computer engineers, and industrial psychologists are already employed in the field, and with such explosive growth, the numbers are bound to increase.

According to the Department of Commerce, industry estimates of the size of the market for AI products range up to $700 million. An early wave of hardware products (and companies) utilizing AI has subsided, leaving mostly software firms and consulting services that use standard AI programs customized for specific applications.

The AI application that is on the most solid footing right now is expert systems. With an expert system, the knowledge and rules of thumb that experienced professionals use to run machinery, estimate tasks or projects, or predict future performance are organized into a database of rules and control points. A standard computer, running this expert system program, can then serve as a fairly good replacement or supplement for the original expert.

Building an expert system requires in-depth knowledge of how the program works, combined with the ability to extract useful information from the expert professionals. People who are trained to do this—they sometimes go by the title of "knowledge engineer"—are in especially high demand.

Other AI applications receiving research attention include programs for translation and text editing, financial investment planning, machine "vision" systems, factory controls, and computer hardware design.

The US government, through the Defense Advanced Projects Research Agency, continues to express confidence in the progress of AI research. AI will continue to attract attention—and jobs—for the foreseeable future.

**Computer Society of IEEE**
1730 Massachusetts Avenue, NW
Washington, DC   20036
(202) 371-0101

# ASSOCIATION EXECUTIVE

**Art History, Business Administration, Communications, English, History, Home Economics, Political Science**

There are thousands of professional societies and trade organizations through which interested individuals meet to discuss, learn, and do business. There have been numerous such organizations around for decades, but in recent years, their phenomenal growth has led to the development of a new type of professional—the association executive.

Association executives are the operational managers of business groups, most of which are non-profit, but many of which are multi-million dollar enterprises. The "business" of the group is providing services for members—holding annual meetings, publishing news about the profession, conducting conventions, holding educational seminars, or offering certification programs. A highly specialized function is lobbying state and federal government agencies.

In years past, it was common for a professional or trade organization to be headed by, and staffed with, practitioners of that trade or profession. A senior lawyer would head the local bar association, a master builder the state-wide builder's council. Now many organizations are so large and so complex that they can best be run by professional association executives.

Not surprisingly, such professionals now have *their* own organization, the American Society of Association Executives (ASAE).

According to ASAE statistics, there are 23,000 national organizations, a figure that has grown by four times since the early 1960s. The total revenue of associations and their members, from meetings, conventions, publications, and related activities, now approaches $25 billion. Associations are the third-largest business in Washington, DC (after the federal government and the travel/tourism industry), employing about 80,000 people.

Thus, it is now possible to attend graduate schools that offer specialized business-administration or public-administration programs leading to a degree in association management. It is also possible to develop a career without specific academic training, by choosing an employer where you can hone your skills.

A variety of specialized positions exist at the entry level for association executives. Since most associations regularly mail newsletters, magazines, and literature to their members, direct-mail marketers and editors are needed. Exhibitions or trader shows are big revenue generators and essential services; they require show managers. Meeting-planning is a skill necessary for the meetings and conventions. Finally, and perhaps most critically, the membership director must be able to keep current members satisfied (and willing to pay their annual dues) while seeking new members.

At smaller organizations, one individual may wear several hats; at larger ones, whole staffs may be devoted to each task. Those contemplating a career in association management should also be prepared to live in Washington, DC, New York, or Chicago, as those cities are the homes of the majority of associations. There are, of course, many more associations spread throughout the country, but they tend to be smaller and to have more local concerns.

Among the schools that offer training in association management are the MBA programs at George Washington University (Washington, DC) and DePaul University (Chicago). Salaries for entry-level positions are in the $20,000 to $30,000 range, depending on educational level and experience.

**American Society of Association Executives**
1575 Eye Street, NW
Washington, DC   20005
(202) 626-2723

# BANK ADMINISTRATOR

**Accounting, Business Administration, Economics, History,
Modern Languages, Political Science
(Some undergraduate programs, as well as MBA programs, offer
a degree in banking and finance.)**

The middle echelons of mid-sized to major banks are composed of ranks of financial managers, loan and credit officers (see **Mortgage Banker**), and marketing, administration, and information-management positions.

Bank officers follow one of two career tracks. The branch-management route involves managing a staff of workers at the local branches, and marketing savings or loan services to local customers. The other route, more national in scope, entails becoming involved with the commercial business of banks, working with the securities industry, real estate developers, and corporate clients. The latter path can be more lucrative, and a more direct route to the top levels, while the former offers more opportunities to work closely with people.

An MBA is the ticket for admission, especially on the commercial side. Banks invest heavily in their training efforts; new hires spend several months in rotating assignments, then are taught new skills periodically. Skills currently in high demand are marketing (which implies knowledge about sales and advertising), computers and information management, and foreign languages. The last is especially important in the growing business of international banking—for both US banks with overseas accounts and foreign banks setting up operations here.

The loan officer (Mortgage Banker) is the key operative in banking, representing the bank to the local business community and to home-mortgage customers. The bank seeks individuals who can represent the bank well: mature, cultivated, businesspeople who maintain a responsible demeanor. Loan officers still depend on the "Four C's" of banking—capacity, capital, conditions, and character—to decide who gets loans, but the business is now highly automated.

Overall employment in banking has not changed dramatically in recent years; Federal Reserve data show that commercial and savings banks combined went from about 1.97 million workers to 2.05 million between 1985 and 1989—a 4.2% increase. However, the number of professionals has actually grown at a faster rate; the figures reflect the loss of clerical and teller positions because of automated teller machines (ATMs) and other electronic-banking technology. The level of skills needed in banking will continue to rise, increasing the need for more training and education.

**American Banking Association**
1120 Connecticut Avenue, NW
Washington, DC   20036
(202) 663-5000

---

# BUSINESS ADMINISTRATOR

### Accounting, Business Administration, Economics, History, Home Economics, Political Science, Psychology

What does it mean to administer a business? There are so many facets of this kind of work, and so many different places and ways to do it, that the meaning is elusive. One element, however, distinguishes the true administrator from most other types of businesspeople:   leadership.

Leadership is important because the business administrator conducts an orchestra of specialists. Accountants keep the books, marketers and salespeople sell the product, engineers run the factories. A company needs an executive to pull all the pieces together. The executive needs the ability to convince people to make sacrifices for the common good, and to work with, rather than compete against, their peers within the company.

This is not to say that all Boy Scout troop leaders or all football captains make good business administrators (although employers do look for extracurricular activities like these among candidates). A career in administrative management usually starts with a position as a staff professional—often as an accountant or salesperson. Experience facilitates movement up the ladder to an administrative role.

Business administration is the most popular academic discipline —about 70,000 BA degrees are earned in "business administration and management" each year. Key elements of the education are accounting, economics, and management. Accounting is an especially critical skill since so many administrators' prime responsibility is keeping books.

Business administration has received its knocks in recent years, as many corporations have reduced the number of middle managers and staff employees not directly involved with making or selling a product. Nevertheless, the Bureau of Labor Statistics projects healthy growth for managerial and administrative occupations, with projected growth rates of 22–26% according to the specific job function. Depending on how you measure the category, there are as many as 9 million administrators.

Two career paths facing the administrator in the beginning: going to big companies, especially those that offer extensive training, or working for a small company (or for oneself). In the former case, the pay can be higher, at least initially, and the opportunities for personal growth strong. In the latter case, risks are higher (in the sense that the company or the business area may not be stable), but the opportunity to learn many different skills through hands-on experience is greater. When you join a small, growing company, you may have a real chance of striking it rich at some point.

**Administrative Management Society**
4622 Street Road
Trevose, PA 19047
(215) 953-1040

# BUSINESS-TO-BUSINESS SALESPERSON

**Allied Health Professions, Biological Sciences, Business Administration, Chemical Engineering, Chemistry, Civil Engineering, Communications, Electrical and Electronics Engineering, Industrial Engineering, Mechanical Engineering, Modern Languages, Psychology, Sociology**

In business-to-business selling, the salesperson doesn't have to deal with fashions in food, clothing, or entertainment. The customers are purchasing managers or similar executives at other corporations. The products may be tonnage quantities of raw materials, factory machines, office computers, or business services. The sales process is characterized by rigorous analysis of cost, reliability, technical characteristics, and deliverability.

This is not to say, however, that business-to-business selling is simply a matter of toting up the cost and quality numbers and making a selection. Personality, persistence, reputation, and other subjective elements enter the calculation as well. Thus a salesperson must be qualified to be successful.

Business-to-business sales often requires salespeople with a high level of training. Technological products—machine tools, construction equipment, computers and electronics, chemicals, design services—are often sold by engineers or scientists. Services such as telecommunications or property maintenance require representatives who can converse like equals with business managers. In addition, because the products are often multi-million-dollar machines that could require months to install and start up, the salesperson also has to be savvy about technical services. Often business-to-business salespeople start out with technical or business knowledge, then are given extensive sales training by the company.

As many American manufacturers push to increase export sales, more salespeople will need to understand foreign cultures, languages, and ways of doing business. While many companies get by with local representatives or business partners in other countries, more aggressive manufacturers are setting up their own staffs abroad.

Like their consumer-goods counterparts, business to business salespeople are in a hard-working, competitive environment. Companies invest heavily in staff training and motivation. Proof of strong competitive instincts, demonstrated by experiences such as participation in sports, is often sought.

Again, like consumer-goods marketing, most salespeople earn a base salary plus commission. The sales force may be organized by territory, key accounts, or product line.

The Bureau of Labor Statistics counted 629,000 "manufacturer's sales workers" in the mid-1980s and projects an increase of 22% during the 1990s.

Contact the professional or trade association of the industry that interests you.

A few examples are:

**Electronic Representatives Association**
20 East Huron Street
Chicago, IL 60611
(312) 649-1333

**Manufacturers Agents National Association**
23016 Mill Creek Road
Laguna Hills, CA 92654
(714) 859-4040

---

# CAMERA OPERATOR/ CINEMATOGRAPHER

### Performing Arts, Visual Arts

While many camera operators graduated from vocational schools or learned their craft on the job, cinematographers generally have a fine arts degree. They have technology in common—film or video making. Both cinematographers and camera operators are responsible for assuring the quality of a filmed event; generally, the former have a greater degree of artistic latitude in determining the proper look of a setting.

Technology is expanding the horizons of film-making. Cable networks offer dozens of channels; filling them with entertainment or information is challenging. Also, the video camera has made it possible to convey motion-picture equipment practically anywhere, so more things and events are being filmed than ever before.

The big time in film, of course, is Hollywood. Business there had been growing steadily until 1988, when the number of productions declined 12% from the year before, according to Department of Commerce data. Yet the dollar volume of theater receipts grew just over 5%, to $4.78 billion. The growth of the videocassette rental store has created a new source of revenue for movie producers. Movies are also an export powerhouse, generating about $2.5 billion for Hollywood.

Two out of three camera operators or cinematographers work in broadcasting, either for the national networks or at local stations. The remainder work in motion picture production and distribution, or for other communications media. Overall growth is pegged at over 25%.

Because it is such a collaborative and expensive media, breaking into film is not easy. Cinematographers study, then produce short films to show to producers or agents.

There is some career opportunity in "industrial" films, which often have nothing at all to do with "industry" (manufacturing). Industrials are films or videos that offer instruction or marketing information. Most of these pictures are produced by small, independent shops in New York or Los Angeles. Marketing and distribution channels for industrials vary widely, ranging from the instructional tapes for sale at your local hardware store to physical-fitness tapes sold on late-night television.

**Motion Picture Association of America, Inc.**
1133 Avenue of the Americas
New York, NY   10036
(212) 840-6161

# CHEMICAL ENGINEER

## Chemical Engineering, Chemistry

Nearly all manufacturing can be divided into two groups: discrete-parts assembly and processing. The former refers to putting together components, the way an automobile is produced on an assembly line. The latter refers to more or less continuous processes, as when fluid flows through a pipe; is heated, cooled, or treated with chemicals; and then is dispensed into tankcars or other containers.

By and large, the entire range of process industries is open to the chemical engineer. They include the obvious—chemicals, petrochemicals, pharmaceuticals—as well as the not-so obvious: pulp and paper, food processing, metals refining, energy generation and transmission, and semiconductors. Because many of the products of the process industries are hazardous, and because many of the treatment or disposal processes are very similar to the initial manufacturing steps, chemical engineers have an entree to the growing environmental-services professions. Chemical engineers are involved in the analysis of waste materials, the design of combustion or neutralization processes that eliminate the waste, and the cleanup of surrounding soil or water.

It all adds up to a solid career front for these engineers. Reflecting their high demand, the College Placement Council found in late 1989 that chemical engineers were receiving the highest average salary offers of the graduates of *any* undergraduate program —almost $33,000. Salaries are being boosted currently because enrollments in chemical engineering declined dramatically during the latter half of the 1980s, reversing a buildup that took chemical engineering to a peak graduating class of 7,685 in 1984. By 1989, the graduating class had dropped to below 4,000. Poor job prospects for graduates of chemical engineering programs in the early 1980s are the main reason for the dropoff in popularity now.

For the longer term, the Bureau of Labor Statistics projects that the number of working chemical engineers will grow at only an average rate—about 16%, to 57,000, over this decade. This growth will occur only if the decline in enrollments reverses itself.

The heart of chemical engineering work is process design. With a job title of either project or process engineer, these graduates develop new ways of combining equipment and chemistry to make products more efficiently, at lower cost, or with fewer environmental risks. Key to the design process is the construction of a "pilot" plant—a scaled-down version of a chemical process, which enables the engineer to run tests and gather data on reaction conditions, energy and material efficiency, and construction cost. The pilot plant represents a midpoint between the test tubes and beakers of the chemist and the acres-large commercial chemical plant.

Other chemical engineers work as plant managers, keeping the production lines running and seeking improvements in process efficiency. Still others act as quality control managers, monitoring the purity and chemical structure of the product.

**American Institute of Chemical Engineers**
345 East 47th Street
New York, NY   10017
(212) 705-7738

---

# CHEMIST

### Biological Sciences, Chemistry

It's a little silly to say that there are more chemicals than ever in our environment, simply because every material thing, including ourselves, is made of chemicals. On the other hand, it is true that the number of different chemicals is expanding all the time; the Chemical Abstracts Service, a central database of chemicals and their properties, has already counted over five million.

Knowing about chemicals and how they can be analyzed is at the heart of this growing profession. Thousands of chemists spend untold hours in laboratories analyzing the presence and effects of hazardous chemicals in our food, medicines, homes, and offices.

The Bureau of Labor Statistics projects a growth rate of 17% for chemists during this decade, their numbers reaching 93,000 by the year 2000. Thousands more chemists are needed as teachers, government regulators, environmental specialists, and sales and marketing professionals. Nevertheless, the number of chemistry students has been dropping for several years now, presaging a shortage.

Data from the National Science Foundation shows that about two out of three chemists work in industry. Chemists are heavily represented in the research and development laboratories of the chemical process industries, where new products are devised or the properties of existing products are further explored. Quality control, workplace safety, and manufacturing are also key employment areas. Typically, the chemist, having been trained in college to use a variety of analytical instruments, will use similar instruments to perform studies on the products of the employer. Although performing experiments—mixing chemicals together and analyzing the results—is the central element of chemistry teaching, only a small proportion of working chemists do this. Most are constantly looking at the existing products of their employers, trying to improve their quality or reduce their manufacturing cost.

Chemical manufacturing has been a powerhouse in the US economy lately, generating billions in export sales and high profits. Another growth field for chemists is environmental work in such areas as cleaning up contaminated soil or groundwater. This field is growing by 20% per year. Further opportunities will be created by the battery of environmental laws under which the chemical industry itself now works.

Starting salaries for chemists with a BS degree are around $25,000, while PhDs start at over $30,000. A PhD degree is often a requirement for the better research and development (R&D) jobs in industry.

**American Chemical Society**
1155 16th Street, NW
Washington, DC   20036
(202) 872-4600

# CIVIL ENGINEER

### Civil Engineering, Geology

Civil engineers build structures—skyscrapers, bridges, highways, airports. Many, but not all, such structures are on land, so they have to know how to deal with geological and groundwater issues. In turn, this familiarity with earth opens a major career avenue for civil engineers—environmental engineering.

On the whole, the 1980s were very good for civil engineers. A slow beginning early in the decade was followed by a boom in commercial and residential construction during the middle. In the latter half of the decade, environmental work relating to cleaner water, and to the removal of hazardous wastes from dump sites around the country, kept the job market bubbling.

Since then, the construction boom has moderated, as vacant space figures have risen in urban office districts, and the meteoric price rise of the housing market has slowed. Environmental work, however, appears to be taking up much of the slack. Federal money supports the Superfund program, an effort to clean up the dumps left by industrial activities from the past. These wastes, many of which were simply poured out onto open fields, are now percolating through the ground and contaminating wells and wetlands. Another program, for waste water treatment, has been going on for over 20 years; now, reduced federal money is being supplemented by state and city revenues.

A word almost as important as "environment" to civil engineers is "infrastructure." This term refers to all the highways, government buildings, transportation facilities, and related public works that help the private sector function. America's infrastructure is old and decaying. A spate of bridge collapses in the early 1980s called attention to the need for increased maintenance of existing structures, and the construction of new ones to meet high demand.

Typically, civil engineers work at large engineering firms, sometimes in conjunction with an architectural firm. Because the government requires that public works be built by licensed professional engineers, many civil engineers want to obtain this licensing shortly after graduation. Most cities or states, as well as the federal government, employ civil engineers to oversee construction projects. Most Fortune 500 companies, especially those in manufacturing, have civil engineering staffs to handle in-house construction projects. Finally, a small number of civil engineers work for manufacturers of building materials, helping maintain desired quality and seeking new ways to make or use construction materials.

In all these career opportunities, the common thread is the application of information learned in college about the properties of materials and how they are affected by physical stresses, and the techniques of building a structure.

There are about 186,000 civil engineers at work today, a figure that is expected to rise to about 219,000 by the end of the decade —just slightly above the average for all professions.

Because many civil engineers work in the lower-paying government offices, starting salaries are slightly lower than most engineering disciplines. In 1989, starting pay was around $27,000.

**American Society of Civil Engineers**
345 East 47th Street
New York, NY   10017
(212) 705-7496

---

# COLLEGE ADMINISTRATOR

**Classics, Education, History, Philosophy and Religion, Psychology, Sociology**
**(Education Administration is offered at the graduate level at many schools.)**

Many people say that the 4 years or so they spent in college were the best years of their lives—a tree-shaded campus, cultural events, the innocence and idealism of youth. College administrators, though, get to spend their entire careers in the idyllic setting.

That is undoubtedly one of the many reasons to consider a career as a college administrator. Another is pure ambition:

college and university education is a $151-billion-per-year indus-try, according to the latest data from the US Department of Education.

Just as a major corporation has dozens of divisions, the administration of many universities is divided into special functions. Administrators who aspire to running an entire university system usually spend the early years of their career as one of these specialists. These positions include directors of student affairs, alumni-relations, athletics, admissions, financial aid, community relations, and faculty affairs.

Salaries vary with the level of responsibility, the size of the school, and the educational background of the administrator. Some administrators rise through the administration ranks; others transfer from a teaching position. Generally a doctorate in education is required, especially at publicly funded universities. Average pay for experienced administrators ranges from around $30,000 to over $100,000. Over this decade, the number of all types of school administrators is expected to rise by 26%, to 236,000.

**American Association of University Administrators**
PO Box 870122
Tuscaloosa, AL   35487
(205) 348-4767

---

# COLLEGE PROFESSOR, LIBERAL ARTS

**Anthropology, Classics, Education, English, History, Modern Languages, Performing Arts, Philosophy and Religion**

A "slave market" is a regular part of the annual meetings of such organizations as the American Economics Association, the Modern Language Association, and the American Historical Association: graduate students seek to present papers and to make an impression on powerful departmental deans. The lucky few win appointments to teach for a few years at colleges and universities. A smaller, even luckier set of post-doctorates are picked for "tenure track" positions—those that offer a definite chance to win tenure, the lifetime job guarantee that means a professor has arrived. Competition is intense.

The slave market exists because there are many more graduate students than available teaching positions. This has been the case for decades in many of the liberal arts (except science), but the pressures have increased in recent years. Of academic postings, 40% are by contract or temporary (not tenure-tracked). Today's university administrators are looking at a declining number of college-age students, a trend which will continue through the late 1990s. (However, overall college enrollments remain high because older students are going back to college.)

These administrators are also under extreme pressure to keep a tight lid on educational costs, which have ballooned over the past decade. More professors—even non-tenured ones—obviously mean higher costs, which must be passed on to students in the form of higher tuition.

The result of these pressures is a less-than-average growth rate for college professors over this decade. The Bureau of Labor Statistics projects a 3% increase, to 869,000, by the year 2000.

However, don't pass up graduate school, or a career in teaching, for this reason only. Some fields are in high demand: some business school professors, for example, are hired with $100,000 salaries or more, simply because of their stature in the field.

Also, a 1990 study from the Andrew W. Mellon Foundation forecast especially critical shortages by the end of this decade in just those fields that have traditionally been thought of as the hardest to enter: humanities (literature, languages, art) and social sciences (history, political science, sociology, and so forth). That's because many of today's faculty will begin retiring during the 1990s, so there could be many job openings even though the overall field will grow only slightly. Moreover, it is becoming more common for schools to hire "adjunct" (part-time) professors of all types, leaving the academics freer to pursue outside interests.

In all but rare instances, a doctoral degree is a requirement for college-level teaching. The job titles run from assistant professor, to associate, to full professor. Salaries start at around $28,000, rising to the mid-40's with experience.

American Association of University Professors
Suite 500
1012 14th Street, NW
Washington, DC   20005
(202) 737-5900

---

# COLLEGE PROFESSOR, SCIENCE AND TECHNOLOGY

### Biological Sciences, Chemical Engineering, Chemistry, Computer Science and Engineering, Electrical and Electronics Engineering, Physics

Psst! Want a lead-pipe, dead-certain job, that pays fairly well and gives you a 3-month vacation every year? Be a professor of physics, mathematics, chemistry, biology or life sciences, or practically any of the engineering branches.

Well, nothing is absolutely certain, but nearly all signs point to a substantial shortage of professorial talent in the sciences and engineering (S/E) in coming years. If you were graduating from college this year, you could count on 4 to 10 years of graduate education, which would put you in the running for a university posting just when college-age students are expected to begin rising again, in the late 1990s. Add to this the fact that about half of all S/E advanced degrees are going to foreign nationals, many of whom return to their home countries after graduation. Then consider that the business community is calling for more scientists and engineers to do the research and development that America needs to compete in the world economy of the 21st century. Finally, factor in the graying of today's professorial ranks—many of the professors that began their university careers in the 1960s will be approaching retirement during the 1990s. The result of all these trends will be a shortfall of thousands of teachers with PhDs.

To be an S/E professor these days is to be a busy person. Professors teach, of course, the thousands of students intending to go on to medical school or to technical positions in industry, or to do research themselves. In addition, like most academics, they want to conduct their own research. With S/E professors, however, the big difference is that industry and the federal government are willing to spend tens of billions of dollars supporting that research.

Many professors involved in research highly valued by industry have found that their long hours in the laboratory can result in a sizeable wealth if their research is patented and commercialized. By comparison, humanities professors can only hope to publish books, only a few of which make money for their authors.

Not all is sweetness and light. The pressure to perform top-notch research is intense, and there will always be tough competition for the best academic positions. In addition, academics are generally paid 10–25% less than researchers in industry. However, salaries are still relatively generous, starting at around $30,000 for post-doctoral positions, $60,000–$75,000 for full professorships.

Contact the professional society for the appropriate type of science or engineering listed under other job titles in this section (for example, Life Scientist, Chemical Engineer). In addition contact:

**American Association for the Advancement of Science**
1333 H Street, NW
Washington, DC   20005
(202) 326-6400

**American Society for Engineering Education**
Suite 200
11 DuPont Circle
Washington, DC   20036
(202) 293-7080

---

# COMMERCIAL ARTIST

### Architecture and Urban Design, Visual Arts

Even in this era of video cameras and computer-aided drafting machines, there is a continuing need for drafters and other artists that put images on paper. The fine-art market (paintings, sculpture, etc.) runs on its own set of tracks. However, the business world needs artists to put an enormous amount of information into visual forms. This is the realm of the commercial artist.

About half of all commercial artists work in advertising or marketing. These careers can range from art directors at advertising agencies (see **Art Director**) to specialists in package design, mail package composition, or corporate logos. In publishing , artists are needed for book jackets, illustrations, and design of typography and layout. Many magazines spend as much money on the illustrations as they do for the words.

Another group of commercial artists designs instructional materials. These include, obviously, all the illustrations in textbooks for schools. They also include diagrams for assembling, operating, and maintaining machinery. In medical textbooks, the artistry of illustration is even more critical; medical students learn how to make their way through the human body through illustrations.

Commercial art in the broadest sense has a strong overlap with design (see **Designer**)—fashion design, interior design, product design, industrial design.

Regardless of the medium, the abilities to draw and to visualize abstract concepts are vital. Meanwhile, it is true that computerized drawing programs are increasingly important to commercial art.

The overall growth rate for art and commercial art is around 27%, according to the Bureau of Labor Statistics, which predicts that the number of professional positions will reach 274,000 by the year 2000. While there are many schools of commercial art offering specific training, many other art positions can be obtained by studying fine arts.

**Art Directors Club**
250 Park Avenue South
New York, NY 10003
(212) 674-0500

# COMPENSATION ANALYST

Accounting, Economics, Psychology, Sociology

American workers earn $4 trillion per year. Much comes from large companies and public institutions, some of whose bills run into the tens of billions of dollars. How do businesses keep a handle on this flow of money? Usually they call on the services of compensation analysts.

Compensation analysis is one of the linchpins of the human-resources function in businesses. The challenge is to structure wage scales so that the workers are motivated (which argues for maximum salaries) and the business as a whole remains profitable (which argues for minimum salaries).

Compensation analysts, under the direction of the senior management of a firm, establish pay scales, promotion policies, and benefits coverage for workers. The job is often a stepping stone to human-resources management. These analysts will probably share the same growth rate as personnel administration as a whole, which the Bureau of Labor Statistics rates at around 21%. Average earnings for experienced analysts, according to industry surveys, is around $40,000.

Over the years, a great number of guidelines, rules, and traditions for appropriate compensation have been established by individual corporations, and by the expectations of employees in general. Nevertheless, the field is constantly changing. One current trend—which will not go away soon—is the cutting back of health-care benefits due to their dramatically climbing cost. Compensation analysts counsel companies on restructuring health-care benefits without affecting their ability to attract and motivate employees.

Another new complexity in compensation is the legal issues relating to racial and sexual discrimination. A company that is not scrupulously fair in its compensation policies could find itself in court against its employees.

The smart company (and analyst) will study the business implications of many types of compensation structures before selecting one. For example, the process of salary negotiations with unionized workers is very different from the decision-making process concerning executive compensation. In some companies, commissions and sales incentives are vital; in others, the benefits package is the most important.

The American Compensation Association, with about 11,000 members, is the leading professional organization. It runs numerous seminars and provides certification of compensation-analysis skills.

**American Compensation Association**
6619 North Scottsdale Road
Scottsdale, AZ   85253
(602) 951-9191

---

# COMPUTER ENGINEER

**Computer Science and Engineering, Electrical and Electronics Engineering, Mathematics, Mechanical Engineering, Physics**

Since its inception, the computer has brought about a set of innovations in the forms of both hardware and software (programming). Computer hardware is easy to understand:  new types of micro-chips, different circuit arrangements, and new materials all lead to new computer designs. A new computer component can be patented. Computer software is a little less straightforward: instruction sets, data structures, do-loops and so forth, all written in a variety of languages that start from different assumptions of how logical thought patterns should be arranged. Some computer software is patented; most is copyrighted, much the way a book or a song is.

Electrical engineers are primarily hardware-oriented, while computer scientists are primarily software-oriented. The computer engineer, however, straddles both these fields. The computer engineering curriculum at colleges arose over the past 15 years or so as academic deans grappled with the conflicting demands of electrical engineering and computer science departments: in the former group, only a portion of the curriculum was applicable to computers specifically; in the latter, there was too little exposure to the special requirements of computer hardware.

Computer engineers, thus, focus on the design and operation of computers. What they gain by this narrower focus they lose in terms of having skills broadly applicable to all types of engineering or data processing. This can be a career problem during slow periods in the computer industry. At the beginning of the 1990s, the computer industry is undergoing a shakeout; most of the major manufacturers have announced layoffs, and growth rates have slowed.

However, such slowdowns have occurred before in the computer industry, and, eventually, it has always come roaring back as a new level of capability was built into the computers, thus increasing their potential market. With computers, what goes down always rises back up to an even higher level.

At the moment, much computer engineering expertise is being applied to a new type of computer chip, called reduced-instruction-set computing (RISC). RISC chips simplify the micro-circuitry of the computer, while putting more demands on the software that runs the machine. Users gain much faster data-processing speeds, and somewhat lower hardware costs. As RISC-based computers compete with more traditional designs, the entire computer business will grow in size and capability.

Many more computer innovations are on the horizon, ranging from optical computing (which uses light rather than electricity to switch circuits), supercomputing, so-called "neural networks," and others. It is easy to predict that computer design technology will continue to evolve for years to come, necessitating new generations of computer engineers to carry it forward.

**Computer Society of the Institute of Electrical and
  Electronics Engineers, Inc.**
1730 Massachusetts Avenue, NW
Washington, DC 20036
(202)371-0101

# COMPUTER PROGRAMMER

**Computer Science and Engineering, Philosophy and Religion, Physics, Psychology, Visual Arts**

Programming is the entry-level professional position in the computer world. It is not essential to have a BS or BA degree in computer science to be a programmer, but those who want to excel in the business will find that their career progresses faster with more education.

The basic task of programming, obviously enough, is to write computer programs. Today, more often than not, this entails customizing an off-the-shelf program, rather than writing a new one from scratch. Hundreds of key programs have now been developed. The programmer uses these programs to tailor a system to the needs of the client. Common business applications include databases, accounting spreadsheets or bookkeeping, telecommunications, and computer networks.

Although the industry is moving toward new types of computer software that are standard across a broad line of computer systems, plenty of customizing is still necessary. "The shortage of technical trained personnel has remained a serious constraint in the systematic computerization of many small and medium-sized corporations," said the Department of Commerce in its annual Industrial Outlook.

Moreover, businesses, research centers, and other heavy computer users have now invested billions of dollars in computer programs; they will not automatically discard this investment for the sake of a new computer language, no matter how beneficial the switch might be. This fact makes more work for programmers, who must spend time maintaining and servicing systems with older computer languages. Even Cobol, one of the oldest languages, is still common on business computers.

Notwithstanding all the computers spread throughout classrooms across the country, and all the computer programming jobs listed in newspapers, the number of computer-science majors is rising slowly, if at all. Only 1.6% of 1989's entering freshmen planned to major in computer science; 4.5% were in 1983, and the number has been declining ever since. While it is true that the computer field is not growing as fast as it was in the early 1980s, it has not slowed down by a factor of three. Starting salaries remain high—around $28,000.

Indeed, the Bureau of Labor Statistics projects a 48% increase in computer-programming jobs between 1988 and the turn of the century. That growth equals 1.2 million jobs in the year 2000. Computer programming is definitely a career with a strong future.

**Association for Computing Machinery**
11 West 42nd Street
New York, NY   10036
(212) 869-7440

---

# COMPUTER SERVICE ENGINEER

## Computer Science and Engineering, Electrical and Electronics Engineering

There are a variety of titles for those who service computers, from "technician" to "field service engineer." Because the types of educational backgrounds and work assignments vary so widely, there are many ways to describe this field.

Computer service engineers, to settle on one general title for this type of work, can be employed by the computer makers, by service organizations that offer contracts for repair and maintenance, by systems integrators (which assemble systems with components from a variety of manufacturers), or by the computer owners or users themselves. The work ranges from routine scheduled maintenance on the bevy of computers installed in the typical office, to highly specialized troubleshooting for computer systems.

Training and academic preparation show a similar range. Several national firms that sell computer equipment run training programs for their own hirees; this usually involves several months of classroom work followed by an assignment to a region. Technical schools and engineering technology programs at community colleges provide up to 2 years' academic training. A 4-year degree, in engineering, computer science, or information science can provide a broader foundation and higher pay.

The whole field is growing rapidly. The 40 million or so personal computers, and the billions of dollars invested in mini-computers, mainframes, computer networks, and heavily computerized factory equipment have created a strong demand for computer-literate workers. The Bureau of Labor Statistics projects that the number of positions for "electrical and electronics technologists" will grow by a hefty 38%, to around 471,000, by the turn of the century. Thousands more are working in software maintenance or on the peripheral equipment that keeps computers functioning.

At the beginning of the 1990s, the computer servicing industry is highly competitive. Many computer makers, wanting to expand their customer base, have offered to service the computers of other manufacturers, and sway customers to do so by offering lower prices. In addition, computers are simply more reliable and so need less servicing. Nevertheless, the rapid growth in the number of computers will keep the size of the maintenance pie growing.

Starting salaries are around $24,000 for technical-school graduates, and $26,000–$28,000 for 4-year college graduates. Bear in mind, too, that because "debugging" (the technical term for troubleshooting a piece of computer hardware or software) is an essential part of designing and building new computers, experience in maintenance, servicing, and troubleshooting could ultimately lead to the highly lucrative field of computer design.

**National Institute for Certification in Engineering Technologies**
1420 King Street
Alexandria, VA 22314
(703) 684-2835

# COMPUTER SYSTEMS ANALYST

**Chemical Engineering, Civil Engineering, Computer Science and Engineering, Mathematics, Philosophy and Religion**

Computer systems analysis is the next step up in the computer profession from entry-level programming jobs. Systems analysts deal with more complex challenges, have larger responsibilities, and earn more. Generally, systems analysts are concerned with multiple-computer networks or with situations where a computer (or computer program) must interact with a variety of peripheral systems, communications devices, or different types of users.

A good example of the systems analysis work is "LAN administration." Local area networks—LANs—are a combination of computer hardware and wires that enable a group of people to work on the same project, or with the same program, and to communicate with one another as if each computer station were simply an extension of one computer. Now that businesses and organizations have bought 30 million personal computers, they have to wire them together via LANs. Systems analysts can figure out how to arrange and maintain the network.

Systems analysis is important to the design and construction of computers, not just their use. A great variety of new computer designs are being developed currently, ranging from notebook-sized laptop PCs to behemoth supercomputers. The internal architecture of these computers is constantly being reevaluated by systems analysts.

Even stronger growth is projected for the systems analysis profession than computer programming; the Bureau of Labor Statistics foresees a 53% increase in positions by the year 2000. Currently, starting salaries are only a few hundred dollars above what computer programmers earn (about $28,000) but over a few years, the career path of the systems analyst will rise higher and faster than that of the programmer, with corresponding pay hikes. Average systems analyst salaries for experienced workers are in the $40,000–50,000 range, and can go above $100,000 for highly specialized positions.

**Association for Computing Machinery**
11 West 42nd Street
New York, NY   10036
(212)8699-7440

---

# CONSUMER-GOODS SALESPERSON

### Art History, Business Administration, Communications, English, History, Home Economics, Political Science, Psychology, Sociology

There are many terms for a salesperson in the business world: account manager, marketing manager, business-development manager, representative, product manager (see also **Business-to-business salesperson**). Regardless of the title, all salespeople need persistence and the ability to relate to and understand other people.

College degrees are not required for most types of sales work, and indeed, most salespeople lack them. Out of some 13.5 million salespeople at work in 1988, only 3.1 million, or 23%, had a college degree, according to the US Department of Labor. The best sales jobs, however, tend to be for well-trained professionals.

In particular, big consumer-goods companies require sophisticated business skills. The salesperson behind a department-store counter or knocking on a homeowner's door is only the last salesperson in a long chain of distribution and marketing personnel. At the intermediate steps—when a product is manufactured and delivered to wholesalers or warehouses—complex sales agreements are negotiated. In consumer-goods marketing, the producer's sales force targets purchasing managers of department-store chains, supermarkets, franchise networks, and the like. The ultimate buyer —the consumer—is reached through mass-market advertising, often on television.

At these major consumer-goods companies, the sales staff is a major arm of the marketing function. New hires are put through rigorous training, and the ones who establish a successful track record in selling are identified as the new marketing managers. With a college degree, the potential manager can keep moving up into areas of larger responsibility. The top sales and marketing positions are product (or brand) managers, and at this level, an MBA degree is required.

Sales is hard work; turnover can be high. Companies spend millions of dollars training and motivating sales staffs. Often they look for evidence of a strong competitive drive, such as participation in sports, among their job candidates.

Another hallmark of sales positions is that salaries are based on performance. Few professional jobs are as easily quantified as sales; the more you sell, the better a performer you are. For this reason, and because most people respond to pay incentives, the base salary is usually supplemented by a bonus or percentage of sales. In some organizations, the top salespeoples' salaries can exceed upper-management's. College-graduate surveys show that entry-level positions are worth around $24,000.

Sales positions for consumer goods have many specialized aspects, which usually makes sales training essential. The goal of many students interested in business careers is a position as a sales trainee by a company with a great training program. With that experience under their belts, opportunities for other types of sales work open up.

The Bureau of Labor Statistics projects that the total number of all sales positions will rise by 20%, to about 15.9 million, by the turn of the century. For retail sales specifically, the projection is 19%, to 4.5 million.

There are sales or marketing associations for salespeople in each type of business, for example:

**National Retail Hardware Association**
770 North High School Road
Indianapolis, IN   46214
(317) 248-1261

**Hotel Sales and Marketing Association International**
Suite 800
1300 L Street, NW
Washington, DC   20005
(202) 789-0089

For a general approach, try:

**American Marketing Association**
250 South Wacker Drive
Chicago, IL   60606
(312) 648-0536

---

# COPYWRITER

### Classics, Communications, English, History

Just as a movie is a collaboration between a screenwriter, a director, and a cinematographer, so an advertising campaign involves the copywriter, the account executive (see **Account Executive**), and the art director (see **Art Director**).

All good copywriters are good writers, in the broadest sense of the term, but not every good writer can be a good copywriter. The purpose of copywriting is to persuade someone to buy something. No amount of academic study can turn a writer into a good copywriter if a creative spark or inventiveness isn't there. So if you have written successful advertising copy, you will be hired, and if you haven't (or can't), your term of duty will be short. With a portfolio of actual work (or student assignments), the aspiring copywriter knocks on doors, networking and persisting until a job comes through.

Not all copywriting is done at advertising agencies. Many corporations have marketing communications departments (or full-blown "in-house" advertising agencies) where copywriting is performed. Many other companies, especially small ones, have copywriters who work as assistants to marketing and sales managers. In addition, some magazines and newspapers have staff members who help advertisers put their ads together.

There are many specialties within copywriting; they are usually defined by the type of product being advertised or the medium being used. Some specialties are:  medical, computer and electronics, financial, fashion, non-profit, and public information (i.e., for government).

Growth rates of the profession, and its pay scales, are hard to quantify because it is not formally organized. At advertising agencies, new copywriters can earn $15,000–20,000, while senior writers can earn well over $50,000.

**American Association of Advertising Agencies**
666 3rd Avenue
New York, NY 10017
(212) 682-2500

# CORPORATE SECURITY SPECIALIST
## Computer Science and Engineering, Civil Engineering

Like nations, major corporations have security forces. Providing security for businesses and private organizations has been a growing industry during the past couple of decades, and the indications are that it will continue to expand.

Part of the reason for this growth is that crimes against people and property are generally increasing. Also, corporations' liabilities are greater than ever before—it is the corporation's duty to protect its employees in the workplace. Security has come to be combined with occupational safety, fire protection, and other safeguards. At many companies, the same people who oversee insurance and health-care policies also manage the security forces.

Corporate security is also a growth area for private firms or consultants that provide security guards and management advice for a fee. Security is an especially hot area for computer consultants, who offer protection from the many ways interlopers can break into computer databanks. Usually these break-ins are little more than pranks, but sometimes they turn into vandalism or thievery as data are trashed or financial records rewritten.

The professional contemplating a career in security usually starts by working for the government, as a police officer or court official, or in the military. As the field grows, it is attracting the attention of colleges, who are expanding their programs in criminal justice or in business administration to include corporate security.

Forget about James Bond-like secret weapons or sensational escapades; the work of a corporate security manager is more like an insurance industry executive's. Managers institute and review policies, attend to government regulations, and fill out a seemingly endless series of forms for security problems and workplace hazards. Because providing security is an expensive overhead item, corporations usually seek to minimize costs, while keeping a close eye on trends in the insurance industry, security technology and criminal activities.

**American Society for Industrial Security**
Suite 1200
1655 North Fort Myer Drive
Arlington, VA   22209
(703) 522-5800

---

# CORPORATE TRAINER

### Allied Health Professions, Communications, Education, Home Economics, Psychology, Sociology

Guess what—your education doesn't stop when you receive your sheepskin. In many ways, a college graduate really begins to learn *after* college, under the guidance of corporate managers. Many of the people that carry out this type of education are corporate trainers.

Corporate training is getting a boost these days from the sorry state of public education. Many companies are finding that new entry-level workers don't have basic verbal or math skills.

Corporate trainers work primarily at major corporations and at consulting firms whose clients are major corporations. They teach everything from basic education to highly specialized programs in technology, computing, market research, sales, or management.

Many corporations pride themselves on the amount of money they invest in the training of their employees; indeed, the American Society for Training and Development (ASTD) estimates that $40–60 billion is spent annually by private corporations.

In noting that the pool of young people in America is shrinking, ASTD says that "employers, who used to skim the most qualified from an oversized labor pool, increasingly will have to make rather than buy skilled workers." They "make" a skilled employee through training and experience.

For a teacher, corporate training represents a dramatic alternative to regular classroom education. Motivational problems are small; the students are there to learn. There are no grades, although at some firms, especially those in banking and financial services, the level of performance in the training program figures into promotions.

Individuals with a background in teaching and education—whether or not they actually have teaching experience—are prime candidates for corporate training positions. An alternative route is to gain experience in a particular phase of business or industry, such as manufacturing or quality control. A third route is to take advanced academic training in such fields as psychology or sociology, and offer consulting services to corporations. Many college professors find extra income, and sometimes insight into their academic work, by conducting corporate training seminars.

The range of programs being taught by corporate trainers is vast. An imaginary "Fortune 500 University" would have departments relating to motivational training for sales and marketing people; interpersonal skills for managers; technical skills for machine operators and factory-floor workers; computer training; and programs unique to a corporation and its business philosophies and practices. The largest department, though, would concentrate on basic and remedial skills.

Corporate trainers can earn about $25,000 to start; salaries are dependent on the level of education and experience. The long-term growth is above average: the US Bureau of Labor Statistics forecasts a 21% growth, to 286,000, for the "personnel, training, and labor relations specialist" job category.

Depending on how corporate America confronts its future workforce needs, corporate training could become a much faster-paced field. In dealing with the problems of local schools, some corporations are devoting resources to helping the school systems, or are bringing promising candidates into the corporate headquarters for on-the-job training. Both these activities involve the training specialists. Expansion of these efforts in the future will require a larger training staff.

**American Society for Training and Development**
Box 1443
1630 Duke Street
Alexandria, VA   22313
(703) 683-8100

---

# COST ESTIMATOR

### Accounting, Civil Engineering, Economics

What will it cost to build something, do something, or take some business action? This may seem to be a straightforward question, but it often requires the special knowledge and skills of the professional cost estimator. Two-thirds of cost estimators work in the construction industry. The rest oversee government contracts, help businesses plan for growth and change, and evaluate new products as part of a manufacturer's design-development team.

In the construction industry, most training occurs on the job, although there are engineering-technology programs for construction that provide a strong background. In construction, experienced workers earn $30,000 to $40,000. In manufacturing, the more education one has, the better the career prospects. These cost estimators commonly have degrees in civil or industrial engineering, and possibly an MBA.

Salaries vary, based on the type of industry that the estimator is employed in.

Cost estimating requires familiarity with existing materials, labor practices, union and workplace rules, and sources of supplies. Estimators do extensive research, and they need sharp math and accounting skills to keep track of the myriad details of a design or structure. Typically, the cost estimator works with construction engineers to evaluate the costs of a project before the first earth is turned. Accuracy is vital because the estimation of the firm's construction costs determines its bid on the project. In manufacturing and government contracting, cost estimators help project the cost of a new type of product or a new manufacturing method.

Over the next decade, the career prospects of the majority of cost estimators will be tied to the swings in the real estate market, which was booming through the mid-1980s but which has slowed down considerably since. An upturn may be years away. The Bureau of Labor Statistics projects an average 15% growth over this decade, to 194,000 jobs.

**American Society of Professional Estimators**
Suite 230
6911 Richmond Highway
Alexandria, VA   22306
(703) 765-2700

# DANCER/DANCE THERAPIST

### Education, Performing Arts—dance

To be a dancer is to have two careers:   one as a performing artist, and one as a wage-earner to pay the bills. Only the exceptionally talented and lucky are able to make a living solely by performing.

The career picture is not as bleak as it sounds, however. As part of a general upswing in improved health-care, physical education, and therapy, dance is coming into its own as a profession. More opportunities are appearing in schools and health-care facilities. Anyway, even the best dancers have usually begun supplementing their performing work with teaching by the middle of their careers (which, for dancers, is usually in their 30s).

Dance therapists help the handicapped or those with emotional or psychiatric problems. Patients develop self-esteem through practice and training. Dance therapists, while not usually licensed by state authorities, can be certified through the American Dance Therapy Association. Certification requires study in both dance and psychology or dance therapy itself, plus experience. Dance therapy is taught at about a dozen schools at the undergraduate and graduate levels.

Kinesiologists use dance and other forms of physical exercise to help the elderly and to provide physical education for the young. The line between physical education and kinesiology is blurry; the distinguishing factor is that kinesiologists apply the principles of dance and dance training.

According to the Bureau of Labor Statistics, about 10,000 dancers are working *at any one time;* thousands more are "in between" performances.

Professional dancers usually earn the salaries set by the American Dance Guild; single-performance minimums are about $200, while weekly salaries start at about $450. There are always more dancers who want to work than jobs available, so assignments are usually filled competitively.

**American Dance Guild**
31 West 21st Street
New York, NY   10010
(212) 627-3790

**National Dance Association, American Alliance for Health,**
   **Physical Education, Recreation and Dance**
1900 Association Drive
Reston, VA   22091
(703) 476-3436

**American Dance Therapy Association**
Suite 320
2000 Century Plaza
Columbia, MD   21044
(301) 997-4040

# DEMOGRAPHER

### Economics, Mathematics

There are over 5 billion people on Earth. The population has doubled since 1950 and will reach 6 billion by the end of the century. Demographers are occupied with how populations grow; what patterns of education, health-care, job development, and governance develop; and what the future human-services needs will be.

Demography requires a knowledge of culture, social patterns, and economics along with a solid grounding in statistics. According to literature from the Population Association of America, Inc., demography is a "data-hungry enterprise, [and] its basic tool is the computer."

About half of all demographers or *population specialists* work at universities and colleges. Usually they are part of departments of statistics, economics, sociology, or public health, since there are only a few departments devoted exclusively to population research. In an academic setting, demographers teach undergraduates, conduct research, and act as advisors or consultants to population studies sponsored by private organizations.

Most levels of government also need demographers. The federal government's Bureau of the Census is an obvious example; others not so obvious are research centers for education, health statistics, and immigration. States are also developing demographic expertise to guide policy-making and economic development. Meanwhile, a host of international aid or research organizations employ demographers to cope with the statistical needs of the Third World, and as part of internationally sponsored health-care and development efforts.

Finally, private industry supports a growing number of demographers through its ever-expanding need for market-research data. Forward-thinking consumer-goods companies, for example, use demographic information to make decisions about new markets to explore or products to reposition. Some private-industry demographers are on the staffs of the largest manufacturing corporations.

Alternatively, demographers can work at marketing-services firms that act as consultants to industry.

Demography is a specialized field, with only a few thousand participants. Salaries in academia begin at $30,000 and rise to $50,000 or so with experience. In private industry, salaries are generally higher (although the practice of academics consulting for industry tends to blur this difference.) In government, the usual salary range is around $35,000 to $50,000.

**The Population Association of America, Inc.**
PO Box 14182
Washington, DC   20044
(703) 684-1221

**Population Reference Bureau, Inc.**
Suite 800
777 14th Street, NW
Washington, DC   20005
(202) 639-8040

---

# DENTIST
### Biological Sciences, Chemistry

Dentistry isn't what it used to be. It has had to adjust to the shrinking number of children (the primary receivers of dental care), and the better care young and old are able to provide their teeth. The Bureau of Labor Statistics projects that dental careers will grow by only 13%, to around 189,000, by the year 2000; this is a couple of points below the average for all professions. (This number is greater than the actual number of dentists who will be working then, because many dentists hold two jobs:   a private practice and a staff position at a hospital or clinic.)

Like physicians, dentists take 4 years of graduate school. If their budgets can stand it, and if their ambition is high enough, the new dentists establish their own practices after completing training.

Often, however, new dentists work with those having existing practices or buy out the practice of a retiring dentist.

Roughly 85% of dentists have general practices; the remainder specialize in one of eight categories certified by the American Dental Association. These include orthodontics (for straightening teeth), periodontics (care of gums), oral surgery, and others. The specialty practices have seen the most change in recent years: for example, cosmetic dentistry, including teeth brightening and straightening of adult teeth, is growing in popularity. Unquestionably, the growth area of coming years will be prosthodontics—the making of artificial teeth and dentures—due to the aging of the American population.

Experienced dentists earn about $75,000, and $100,000 or more if they specialize.

**Council on Dental Education**
American Dental Association
211 East Chicago Avenue
Chicago, IL 60611
(312) 440-2788

---

# DESIGNER, INDUSTRIAL
# AND FASHION

**Architecture and Urban Design, Art History, Home Economics,
Industrial Engineering, Mechanical Engineering,
Performing Arts—theater, Visual Arts**

Reflecting the importance of good design to American consumers, *Business Week* magazine now has an annual issue that lauds the best-designed products of the previous year.

The challenge facing industrial designers is that they must be concerned with both aesthetics and business. Manufacturers must be able to reproduce their products in large quantities. The designer has to take into consideration the cost of materials, their assembly, and whether or not they are "manufacturable." Even for custom goods such as jewelry or haute couture clothing, it must be possible to reproduce the designer's vision.

The designer, therefore, has to know how manufacturing works, how materials function during use, and how the products will be used by the consumer. The designers check with manufacturing specialists to see what variations are possible, and especially what new possibilities are opened up by novel materials or methods.

Newness is an important element in design; people don't like to buy things that look like holdovers from a few years before. Very old things, however, have their own appeal, so designers spend a lot of time researching the look of products in the past. Design has a history, and many designers succeed by becoming familiar with earlier traditions.

According to the Bureau of Labor Statistics, the design professions will enjoy a strong 28% growth during the 1990s. This growth will be spread across a number of specialties, including furniture design (where 11% work); retailing, including floral or antique shops (22.5%); engineering and architectural services (7.5%); and advertising, business, and personal services (the remaining 59%).

Industrial Designers Society of America
1142–E Walker Road
Great Falls, VA   22066
(703) 759-0100

---

# DESIGNER, INTERIOR

**Architecture and Urban Design, Art History, Home Economics,
Performing Arts—theater, Visual Arts
(A few schools offer degrees in interior design specifically.)**

Over a third of all designers work in interior design, at furniture manufacturers and dealers, antique shops, architectural firms, or individual consulting firms. Interior design is enjoying a renaissance, partly because of the growth in residential and commercial construction, and partly because American lifestyles call for it. The baby-boom generation is now ensconced in homes that are considerably more expensive than 10 or 15 years ago, and many homeowners have decided that they want richly finished interiors that correspond to the elevated value of their homes. There is a turf battle brewing between interior designers and architects over who gets to dictate the look of the insides of buildings and offices. It appears that interior designers will become an integral component of the team that designs and constructs new buildings.

It's hard to say exactly how many interior designers there are because many work independently of consulting companies or retail stores.

Successful interior designers have both knowledge of materials and art and the ability to persuade customers; only a satisfied customer will pay bills and come back for more business.

Training in interior design is offered at many schools, and additional experience can be acquired by working at retail stores, antique dealers, or building-supply firms. The goal of many designers is to work independently, but they usually develop a base of clients before striking out on their own.

**American Society of Interior Designers**
1430 Broadway
New York, NY 10018
(212) 944-9220

# DIETICIAN/NUTRITIONIST

**Home Economics (Some schools offer a program in this field independent of the home economics department.)**

How's your cholesterol level? Are you getting enough fiber or vitamins? As never before, people today worry about their diet, their weight, and the wholesomeness of the foods they buy. The professionals with the answers are the nutritionists. Working with physicians, the nutritionist or dietician attempts to find products that are nutritious, tasteful, and healthful. A growing part of dietary science is developing foods for special situations: setting weight-losing diets, meeting the special needs of the elderly, getting food to the poor or home-bound.

Dietary science is almost exclusively a profession of women (97%). The Bureau of Labor Statistics projects 28% growth, to 51,000 workers, by the year 2000. In a survey of its membership, the American Dietetic Association (ADA) found that 37% of its members work as clinical dieticians at hospitals or other health-care facilities. A quarter are in "management practice," the ADA term for planning meals at schools, cafeterias, and the like. About 18% are in private practice, and the remaining 20% provide community services or teach.

In practice, the dietician assesses the particular dietary needs of a restaurant, hospital, or cafeteria, then assembles a menu of foods that, it is hoped, are satisfying while healthful. The need to meet budget allocations challenges the inventiveness of the dietician. In hospitals, "therapeutic dieticians" work closely with doctors and nurses to devise diets that help the injured or diseased. Therapeutic dieticians may need special training, depending on the job and state.

To establish yourself in this profession, ADA recommends the Registered Dietician (RD) status, which is attained by earning a bachelor's or master's degree in dietetics or nutrition, gaining clinical experience, and taking an examination.

A growing trend in the dietary profession—indeed, in the lives of all of us—is prepared foods in packages that can be microwaved at home or in a restaurant. Food-processing companies and fast-food chains have been hiring more dieticians to help devise new recipes and delivery systems. Pay scales for nutritionists are rather low—starting salaries are around $20,000, and average salaries for the experienced are around $30,000. This situation may change, however, because of the greater need for dietary consulting by health-care facilities and private industry.

**American Dietetic Association**
216 West Jackson Boulevard
Chicago, IL 60606
(312) 899-0040

# DIRECT MARKETER

**Business Administration, Communications, Psychology**

Pick up nearly any magazine or newspaper and go to the classified pages, or to the section where small fractional-page advertisements are printed. There you will see the current crop of direct marketers in action. The products involved are usually unusual— say, gimmicky gift items or time-shared apartments in some exotic place. Month after month, year after year, someone is using these "direct" channels to market and sell a product or service to consumers.

Classified advertisements are not the only medium; the other primary method is "direct mail"—i.e., junk mail (a term direct marketers hate, preferring the phrase "direct-response advertising"). Americans are inundated with junk mail, almost from the moment an address is established. The third major direct-marketing medium is telemarketing—selling over the telephone.

The people and companies that use these marketing channels are direct marketers, and the operating conditions of the business are different enough from the types of selling (such as retail stores or personal contact) that they have their own professional organization, the Direct Marketing Association, Inc. (DMA). DMA represents 3,200 companies and has over 6,000 members.

As new communications media grow in acceptance, new marketing channels open up as well. Good examples of recent innovations include home shopping programs and home-computer-based networks.

In each case, the direct marketer has to be able to target an audience, find the right products, and minimize the cost of connecting the two to each other. General marketing training is valuable, as is a major in business administration. Several business schools offer a concentration in direct marketing, including Northwestern University, the University of Missouri, and New York University.

Direct marketing covers a broad range of businesses. At one

extreme is the entrepreneur with an idea, who grows a business from a garage or kitchen tabletop. At another is the corporate marketer, who works for large firms, including the largest banks in the country (who are becoming sophisticated telemarketers). There are also independent marketing-services agencies (akin to advertising agencies) that perform the function for clients. A 1984 survey by DMA showed that salaries of executive direct marketers were as high as $80,000.

**Direct Marketing Association, Inc.**
6 East 43rd Street
New York, NY  10017
(212) 689-4977

---

# EARTH (PLANETARY) SCIENTIST
### Biological Sciences, Geology, Physics

Is the greenhouse effect real? Are lakes and streams becoming more acidic because of air pollution, or some natural cause? With the introduction of new technology, can the oceans provide more food and minerals? These are some of the questions that occupy the time of today's earth scientists.

The earth sciences—geophysics, oceanography, geochemistry, atmospheric science, and seismology (see **Geologist**)—have traditionally been the realm of academic researchs. Scientists pursued pure knowledge in hopes of getting a better fix on how the earth was formed, and how oceans, rock strata, and the atmosphere function. Today, with the upswing in concern about the environment, there are more research dollars available, more private foundations being formed, and more consulting to industry. The career options have widened.

Nevertheless, the bulk of job opportunities remain with universities and with government-sponsored research institutes. Dr. Richard Paull, a geoscientist at the University of Wisconsin, says that "For the next 5 to 10 years, academic employment opportunities in the geological sciences will be modest but stable." In a report for the Geological Society of America, he said that "many retirements occur about the time a current freshman completes a PhD."

Over the years, earth science has also become planetary science (i.e., the study of Earth and other planets), for the simple reason that much of its data comes from satellites, space flybys, and astronomical observation. Most planetary science depends on the programs of the National Aeronautics and Space Administration (NASA), which, at the moment, is concentrating most of its work on the space shuttle and on the construction of a space platform. There is a growing debate on the value of a manned mission to Mars; if this were to occur in the next decade or two, hundreds of job opportunities would be created for planetary scientists.

Earth scientists have created opportunities for themselves in private industry by adapting satellite observational equipment to commercial needs. Originally developed for military spy satellites, photogrammetry (the mapping of earth features using aerial photography), and remote sensing are now being used to survey land masses for mineral deposits, agricultural resources, or environmental problems. Sometimes they are even used for highway construction projects.

The total effect of all these trends is a gradual increase in opportunity. The membership of the American Geophysical Union, for example, has risen from around 12,000 in 1980 to almost 23,000 in 1990. The Bureau of Labor Statistics, which estimated the number of geologists and geoscientists at about 42,000 in 1988, projects a 16% growth to 50,000 in the year 2000.

**American Geophysical Union**
2000 Florida Avenue, NW
Washington, DC   20009
(202) 462-6900

# ECOLOGIST

### Biological Sciences, Chemistry

Ecology is the branch of biology that deals with systems of living things. While a microbiologist, for example, would be concerned with specific types of plankton in the world's oceans, the ecologist would try to establish what makes plankton colonies flourish and which plants and animals depend on them for their own existence.

Growing environmental concerns will keep ecologists busy in coming years. For example, one of the clearest indicators of environmental problems is a sudden decrease in the population of plants and animals, but no one will know that a decline is occurring unless someone goes into the field to count the populations. Studies then have to be performed to try to pinpoint the causes of the decline.

Some of these studies are featured in today's newspaper headlines: is acid rain indeed affecting the fish population of lakes and the tree population of forests? How would global warming change the mix of agricultural plants that we depend upon? How is over-harvesting affecting the resources of fish and other protein from the sea?

Ecology can be studied at undergraduate as well as graduate levels, usually as part of a biology program. For positions in academia, where most of the jobs are, an advanced degree is required. At universities, biological researchers can earn $45,000 to $60,000, depending on their level of experience. Over the long term, there will be many additional opportunities in private foundations, government, and industry.

**The Ecological Society of America**
9650 Rockville Pike
Bethesda, MD   20814
(301) 530-7005

# ECONOMIST

### Business Administration, Economics

Economics, "the dismal science," is looking a little brighter these days. The projected job growth during the 1990s, according to the Bureau of Labor Statistics, is 27%, well above the average for all professions.

Prospects haven't been too bright recently. During the late 1970s and early 1980s, many large corporations shut down the economics departments that used to provide specialized forecasts and analyses. It was more cost effective to purchase these services from consultants and economic-forecasting agencies. Then, during the mid-1980s, a wave of corporate restructurings, mergers, and staff reductions eliminated hundreds more positions.

However, there is a seed of good news in those changes. The fact that businesses were willing to buy consulting services, obviously enough, led to a growth in such consulting firms. Meanwhile, the great surge of interest in business-related careers on college campuses and graduate business schools has meant more positions for academic economists. Roughly one out of three economists is a college teacher.

The employers of economists at the beginning of the 1990s are a mix of Wall Street, Washington, Madison Avenue, and the academic ivory tower. The financial services industries have traditionally depended on economic forecasting services to get a better fix on what is about to happen to stocks, commodities, and currencies. With the overall growth of financial services remaining fairly steady (tempered by downturns in stock prices), economists will find that the audience for their projections is larger. In the nation's capital, meanwhile, increasing complexity of the federal budget, tax laws, and industry/government relationships has created a high demand for economic expertise. About one out of five economists works for the federal government; another 10% work for state governments.

Finally, the importance of economics to advertising and marketing is being realized. As market researchers and demographers look more closely at consumers' needs, the economist can use this information to draw general conclusions about the marketing of consumer goods. These conclusions can, for example, help determine the level of inventory necessary to satisfy demand.

Most economists spend a lot of time these days in front of a computer screen. Vast amounts of data that economists compile can be quickly analyzed by a computer.

**American Economic Association**
1313 21st Avenue, South
Nashville, TN 37212
(615) 322-2595

**National Association of Business Economists**
28349 Chagrin Boulevard
Cleveland, OH 44122
(216) 464-7986

---

# EDITOR, BOOK

**Art History, Classics, English, History, Modern Languages, Performing Arts, Philosophy and Religion, and most other liberal arts programs**

In the broadest sense, editing involves reviewing a manuscript before publication, making sure that it is grammatical, truthful, and legally sound. At the major book publishers, junior editors and special copy editors now do the line-by-line editing. Senior editors spend their time acquiring new books for the publisher and helping to make marketing decisions.

Book editors start as editorial assistants/secretaries. They slowly move up as they gain experience by working closely with an editor —a process rather like an apprenticeship. Salaries tend to be lower in book publishing than in other industries, but editors find much satisfaction in working with ideas, books, and writers. Editors tend to move from house to house frequently in search of more money and greater opportunity.

The publishing business in general is doing very well, although there are areas where business conditions and job growth are terrible. Book publishing is a good example. Most of the major publishers are going through a period of contraction and staff turnover. There are many other publishers of books, however: the hundreds of small presses scattered throughout the country; university presses; technical and professional organizations; textbook developers; medical and legal publishers; and publishers of genre fiction, including children's books, romances, science fiction, and mysteries.

Even though everyone laments the falling literacy and book-buying habits of Americans, around 60,000 new titles are published each year, and that number continually rises. According to the Department of Commerce, there are roughly 20,000 publishers, although 90% of all books are published by 2,300 firms that produce four or more titles per year. Employment in the entire industry has risen to 75,500. For the general category of writers and editors, the Bureau of Labor Statistics projects a 23% increase in employment by the year 2000.

**Association of American Publishers, Inc.**
220 East 23rd Street
New York, NY   10010
(212) 689-8920

---

# EDITOR, MAGAZINE

**Art History, Business Administration, Communications, English, History, Home Economics, Modern Languages, Political Science, Philosophy and Religion, Sociology
and most other liberal arts programs**

In the newspaper world, a distinction is often made between news (or "beat") reporters and feature writers. The former report news as it happens; the latter take time to reflect on what trends are developing, and write longer, more analytical, more stylish pieces.

The same distinction holds true in the magazine world, except that the great preponderance of journalists are feature writers. The usual format of a magazine—a weekly, monthly or even annual publication, with long lead times and many pages to fill—demands more feature writing than news reporting. Also, as compared to book editing (see Book Editor), many more magazine editors are working writers. Book editors at publishing houses—especially the larger ones—spend much more of their time planning publication schedules, reviewing proposals, or researching bookworthy topics than putting words on paper.

The upshot of these comparisons is that, if you above all enjoy writing and striving to write stylishly (as opposed to simply reporting facts), the world of magazines beckons.

There are roughly 12,000 magazines being published in the US today, and about 500 new ones start every year (most of which are destined to fail within 5 years). Most of these are the well-known "consumer" magazines sold at newsstands across the country. About a third of the total are "business" publications, which are rarely sold on the newsstand and therefore are all but invisible to most people. This field "constitutes a dynamic growth industry with a major need for trained professionals," according to the Association of Business Publishers.

The training for both consumer and business publications varies. Many editors seek writers with specialized training or experience in the topic of interest—travel, entertainment, banking, engineering, science, and so on. Others argue for good writers with a general background, the better to translate specialized information into something of interest to the general reader. Thus, attending journalism school can be a help for a magazine career, but is by no means essential.

Salaries tend to be low—in the $20,000–25,000 range to start, rising only to the $25,000–45,000 range for experienced editors. Top magazines pay considerably more. According to the Bureau of Labor Statistics, there are 219,000 "writers and editors;" the category is projected to grow by an above-average 25% over this decade.

**Society of Magazine Editors**
575 Lexington Avenue
New York, NY 10017
(212) 752-0055

**Association of Business Publishers**
Suite 1912
205 East 42nd Street
New York, NY   10017
(212) 661-6360
(This organization also manages a group called the Business Press
  Educational Foundation, Inc., which provides information,
  internships, and educational materials.)

---

# ELECTRICAL ENGINEER

### Computer Science and Engineering, Electrical Engineering, Physics

Electrical engineering is the largest branch of engineering. Nearly
one out of three engineers at work or in school today is an electrical or electronics engineer. Moreover, the field of electrical engineering is expected to grow the most—by 40%, to reach 615,000
professionals by the turn of the century.

There is one reason for this dominance:   the impact of microelectronics on how we live, work, transport ourselves, communicate, and entertain. Microelectronics began in the 1950s with the
development of the transistor. Microelectronics continually advances in capability, decreases in price, and shows up in more
aspects of our lives.

The most obvious result of the microelectronics revolution is the
computer. When the computing microchip was developed in the
early 1970s, the hand-held calculator appeared, soon to be followed by the personal computer. Now there are microchips and
associated electronics in cars, planes, nearly all of our communications equipment, household appliances—indeed, houses themselves.

Most electrical engineers are involved in the design of circuits.
These circuits may be the microscopically small patterns on a silicon chip, or the wiring in an airplane or car. Each advance in
computer technology requires a new round of circuit design and

development of electronic components that can handle the ever-faster operating speeds of the microchip. The original purpose of electrical engineering—the generation and use of electrical power—is now a small specialty.

The only cloud on the electrical engineering horizon is that at least a third of them are employed by defense contractors, who will be hurt by the reduction in the federal defense budget due to lessening of tensions between the superpowers. Electrical engineers work not only on the electrical equipment and controls of tanks and jet fighters, but on radio, remote sensing, and communications gear.

Besides design work in electronics and electrical equipment, electrical engineers are involved in materials science—the development of new ceramics, alloys, and polymers. Besides making computers, electrical engineers also write programs. A specialty within the profession that is now beginning to develop its own academic and professional identity is computer engineering; at many schools, this is still part of the electrical engineering department.

The great concentration of electrical and electronic equipment in factories makes electrical engineers valuable there, too, even when the products of those factories may be such non-electrical things as paper or chemicals. Automatic control equipment and, to a lesser degree, robots are going into factories across the country. The electrical engineer helps design, install, and maintain these systems.

Institute of Electrical and Electronics Engineers, Inc.
345 East 47th Street
New York, NY   10017
(212) 705-7900

# ELEMENTARY/HIGH SCHOOL ADMINISTRATOR

**Education, English, Political Science, Psychology, Sociology**

The number of elementary school students will continue to grow until the late 1990s. The trend for high-school-age students, whose number declined through the 1980s, will reverse itself in the next couple of years and grow through the turn of the century. More schoolrooms, more teachers, and more administrators will be needed at both levels.

Furthermore, education is turning into a national priority. Funding for elementary/high school education is growing at a 6.9% per year clip, up from 6.4% in 1987.

The individuals who decide how these funds are best spent are school administrators, including principals. Most of us probably feel that school administrators are the cops of the schoolrooms, keeping both students and teachers hewing to the straight and narrow. Unquestionably, they are responsible for the smooth functioning of the overall system. However, the administrators can do just as much, if not more, than the most popular and innovative teachers by their hiring, funding, and scheduling decisions.

Besides organizing and overseeing teaching duties, school principals set up guidance, counseling, and athletic programs, perform community relations, set overall budgeting goals, and monitor school costs and quality. The job calls for a multi-talented generalist who can act as a business manager, accountant, public relations specialist, booster, and, in the final analysis, teacher.

A great number of administrators began working as teachers, then accumulated the necessary experience and education to qualify as administrators. Others simply continued their education in college-level education departments, then joined school systems as assistant principals, counselors, or other administrators. Generally, a master's degree in education is the minimum; some go on to obtain a PhD.

The Bureau of Labor Statistics projects a 26% growth for all types of school administrators, and the projected decline in college-level positions probably means that the growth rate is even higher for elementary/high school administrators. Salaries for experienced administrators averaged between $40,000 and $70,000 in 1988; for principals, the average range was $40,000–50,000, according to the Educational Research Service (Arlington, VA).

**National Association of Elementary School Principals**
1615 Duke Street
Alexandria, VA   22314
(703) 684-3345

National Association of Secondary School Principals
1904 Association Drive
Reston, VA  22091
(703) 860-0200

---

# ENERGY ENGINEER

### Chemical Engineering, Civil Engineering, Electrical and Electronics Engineering, Mechanical Engineering, Physics

Energy engineers are concerned with both sides of the energy equation—producing it and using it. The field enjoyed widespread popularity during the 1970s, as continuously climbing energy costs made its production and conservation valuable tasks. During the low-energy-cost 1980s, the career's growth was stunted. A sharp observer will note however that in January 1990, petroleum imports topped 50% of US consumption for the first time ever—and greater imports are all but inevitable. When imports hit the 40% level in 1973, the OPEC embargo followed, causing the first of the US's energy crises. The warning signs indicate that energy will again become a crucial economic issue during the 1990s.

Energy—power generated by gasoline, fuel oil, water, steam, wind, or the sun—keeps the wheels of commerce turning, and keeps us warm, illuminated, and entertained in our homes. Energy engineers work at utility companies where electricity is generated and natural gas coveyed, as well as at refineries where oil is transformed into gasoline and other liquid fuels.

Many other energy engineers "produce" energy by conserving it. They are especially common in factories and in the commercial building industry. So-called HVAC (heating, ventilating, and air-conditioning) engineers try to minimize energy consumption in a commercial building through insulation, energy management systems, and the application of advanced technologies such as solar energy. Most types of factories, however, use much more energy than office buildings. Energy engineers make the factory's production more efficient, often with the use of computers.

Energy engineers are becoming more concerned with the environmental aspects of energy production and consumption—for example, they may do research on the exhaust gases from power plants and automobile tailpipes to find opportunities to conserve energy and to reduce pollution.

Industrial, mechanical, electrical, and civil engineering are all common routes to energy engineering. Academic study mates the theoretical understanding of energy with a knowledge of the conventional equipment and machinery that use energy. Starting salaries are in the $28,000 to $30,000 range, depending on the type of employer.

**American Society of Energy Engineers**
Suite 420
4025 Pleasantdale Road
Atlanta, GA   30340
(404) 447-5083

**American Society of Heating, Refrigerating and Air-**
  **Conditioning Engineers, Inc.**
1791 Tulie Circle, NE
Atlanta, GA   30329
(404) 636-8400

---

# EXECUTIVE SEARCH CONSULTANT

### Art History, Business Administration, Communications, Modern Languages, Performing Arts, Political Science, Psychology, Sociology

Over the years, executive search consultants have tried—with some success—to establish themselves as a cross between a business consultant and a job counselor. The profession continues to fight its reputation as "headhunters"—people who try to move an executive from one job to another merely to win a fee from the new employer. The more reputable search consultants seek to establish a long-term relationship with employers, and sometimes even to provide advice on how to structure the compensation and responsibilities of a job.

If you are a gadabout, a socializer, a person who has lots of friends and continually meets new ones, you have the potential to be an executive search consultant. The business works almost exclusively by personal referrals. The challenge is to become well-known in a certain city or line of business in that city so that both top employers and top job candidates will come to you for advice and guidance about job-hunting.

The job involves selling skills because the consultant must try to paint the best possible picture of the employer to the job-seeker, and vice versa; some people term the process "executive matchmaking." For the consultant, the result of all this bringing-together can be a very lucrative salary. Commissions are 10–15% of the first-year earnings of the new employee (the fee is paid by the employer, never by the employee). Annual commissions over $100,000 are not unheard of.

Most executive recruiters begin as professionals in a particular line of business, such as data processing, engineering, publishing, sales, banking, finance, or management consulting. With that experience, and with the constant networking that goes on, the aspiring search consultant has a base for moving into the business. Other search consultants start out in human-resources management and parlay that experience into the search business. Most search firms are based in major cities.

It's hard to say precisely how many search consultants there are, as the field is one in which people are constantly on the move. *Business Week* magazine estimated 1989 revenues for the profession at $2.5 billion. The Association of Executive Search Consultants, Inc. had a membership of 83 companies at the end of 1988.

**Association of Executive Search Consultants, Inc.**
17 Sherwood Place
Greenwich, CT    06830
(203) 661-6606

# EXPERIENTIAL EDUCATOR

Allied Health Professions, Communications, Education, Home
Economics, Performing Arts, Philosophy and Religion, Visual Arts

"I graduated from the school of life," used to be the refrain of successful businesspeople who had avoided formal education. Notwithstanding the efforts you are making, or are about to make, in college or professional school, experience is indeed a valuable form of learning. Now there is a profession, the experiential educator, to help you get the most from it.

Experiential educators set up, administer, or evaluate a wide variety of alternative educational methods: internships, summer programs, cooperative education, public-interest educational foundations, athletic or sports programs, and short-term efforts like Outward Bound (a program that combines camping with team-building).

Hard numbers on experiential educators are difficult to obtain, as the field is relatively new and remains somewhat disunited. There are about 1,200 members of the National Society for Internships and Experiential Education (NSIEE), but thousands more are involved in experiential education part-time. Most are affiliated with schools (for example, through a co-op program at a high school or college), private foundations for rehabilitation, child-care programs, or the vast number of programs for personal growth and self-improvement.

A 1988 survey of the NSIEE's membership revealed that about 60% were female, and that 80% were affiliated with post-secondary education. The members are often administrators of two or more different programs, and the majority of those programs enroll between 31 and 300 students. These educators themselves have a high level of training; 57% have master's degrees, and of those, half have a doctorate as well. On the other hand, slightly more than a third of the survey participants had no formal college-level educational training at all before they began working in the field.

No salary data are available, but it is an open question as to how useful averages would be, since the programs vary so much in size and quality. Full-time experiential educators who are employed by educational institutions seem to be paid about as much as starting teachers—in the neighborhood of $18,000–24,000.

Education in America is being critically reviewed as never before. A glaring example of failure is the dropout rate in high schools, and it seems certain that experiential education is one alternative form of teaching that can help mend these kinds of failings. Big things are in store for the field.

**National Society for Internships and Experiential Education**
Suite 207
3509 Haworth Drive
Raleigh, NC   27609
(919) 787-3263

---

# FILM/VIDEO ENGINEER

### Communications, Electrical and Electronics Engineering, Performing Arts, Visual Arts

Film is, well, film that is exposed at a steady rate to a moving image. Video is the use of electronic devices to record moving images. Because of technical differences between the two media, whole careers in this field can be spent in one or the other. Film and video engineers, who also go by the titles of motion-picture and television engineers, apply engineering-design principles to the machinery that records, transmits, and receives moving images. They set up film studios, develop novel recording or filming techniques, and oversee the quality of film reproduction and transmission.

While it is true that the majority of television sets, camcorders, videocassette recorders, and projectors sold in the US today come from the Far East, it is not true that film/video engineering is dead in this country. One acronym serves to highlight the dynamism of this field: HDTV (high-definition television). HDTV is the much-debated technological leap from today's grainy, blurry television and video images to brighter, clearer images. Billions of dollars are riding on the decisions of electronics companies, broadcasting enterprises, and national governments over how HDTV will be applied. HDTV is being offered as a replacement for the decades-old National Television Standards Committee (NTSC), whose technical details define how we see television today.

A subject like HDTV will affect the employment of film/video engineers as new methods of recording, transmitting, and displaying visual images are developed. The most promising forecasts tell of a revival of US-based research and manufacturing in television and film technology.

Television is the biggest market for film/video engineering talent, but it is by no means the only one. Hollywood, with its troops of special-effects personnel, beckons. There are also numerous applications of imaging technology in fields ranging from space research to high-speed photography of industrial experiments to television advertisements. Meanwhile, the broadcasting companies, ranging from the national networks to the local UHF stations, and including the growing number of cable-television companies, also need technical professionals in film/video engineering.

Only some film/video engineers have an engineering degree. Many do, however; of these, there are an especially large number of degrees in electrical or electronics engineering, but degrees in physics, mathematics, or image technology are also appropriate. Regardless of how one approaches the field, dealing with electronics will be essential, as so much of film and video recording and broadcasting involves electronic equipment.

The film/video field is enjoying the same growth as television (including cable), video, and the motion-picture industry. The rapid advance of new technology raises the value of professionals who are able to understand the latest innovations.

These professionals work cheek by jowl with film technicians and cinematographers. The former are the primary users of the products of film/video engineers, and serve as camera operators and broadcast technicians. The latter are the "artistes" that get credit for the recording quality of a motion picture. With the appropriate desire and training, it is possible for the film/video engineer to work as a technician (although possibly at lower pay than as an engineer) or as a cinematographer.

**Society of Motion Picture and Television Engineers**
595 West Hartsdale Avenue
White Plains, NY   10607
(914) 761-1100

---

# FINANCIAL ANALYST

### Accounting, Business Administration, Economics, Mathematics

Is investing in Wall Street like gambling in Las Vegas or Atlantic City? Not if you talk with any financial analyst. These analysts stake their reputations on their ability to ferret out value in stocks, now and for the future. To a certain extent, analysts help *define* the value of stocks; if a corporation decides, for example, to get out of one line of business and get into another, Wall Street may consider the move ill-advised and recommend that current stock owners sell the security. The stock's price can nose dive as a result.

Financial research is the key activity of the analyst. By continually poring over government documents, annual reports, and newspapers and magazines, and by regularly talking with corporate executives, the analyst draws conclusions on the current and future performance of a company or type of investment. These conclusions form the basis of recommendations to buy or sell a stock.

As analysts' careers progress, many begin to specialize in a specific industry, such as steelmakers, food processors, or transportation. Then their time is spent following the leading firms of that industry and paying attention to larger social or business trends that will affect it.

The opinions of financial analysts are so important that many companies employ staff people simply to maintain contact with the analysts, a type of public relations work known as "investor relations" (see **Investor Relations Manager**).

Advanced study in business and finance is usually obligatory for the financial analyst—getting a master's degree is usually the first step. It is common for financial analysts to begin their careers with the major securities dealers, where their recommendations are used by brokers to trade stocks. Many analysts go on to work for mutual funds, private banks, or pension-fund-management firms, where their recommendations are used to guide the purchase of investments.

There are about 25,000 financial analysts currently, and this number will grow only slowly during the early 1990s, as so many securities dealers are going through a difficult financial period. According to the Institute of Chartered Financial Analysts, 38% of these analysts work at investment firms, 21% at brokerage houses, and 16% at banks (the remaining 25% are spread throughout the workforce). The increasing complexity of the financial services industry, combined with its growing international structure, should create many opportunities in the near future, however.

Starting salaries vary widely on the basis of the background the analysts bring to their positions. With several years' experience, salaries can reach $60,000 and more. Additional status is obtainable by earning certification through the Institute of Chartered Financial Analysts; less than half of those working currently have been chartered.

**Financial Analysts Federation**
PO Box 3726
Charlottesville, VA   22903
(804) 977-8977

**Institute of Chartered Financial Analysts**
PO Box 3668
Charlottesville, VA   22903
(804) 977-6600

---

# FINANCIAL PLANNER

### Accounting, Business Administration, Home Economics, Political Science

In simpler times, the head of a household considered a standard set of options when planning a family budget. A fixed-rate mortgage, whole life insurance, a savings plan (often with US savings bonds), and perhaps a few shares of stock covered most situations. These days, mortgages are fixed, adjustable, ballooning, or convertible; insurance is whole, single-life, universal; savings are tax-free, high-dividend, or tax-deferred; and the stock market is a crazy carnival of stocks, options, funds, bonds, you name it. Enter the financial planner.

Financial planning guides customers—usually individuals—in setting up their insurance, minimizing their taxes, and saving and investing for the future or for retirement. Only rarely do the financial planners sell the actual financial products; instead, the planner serves as a sales agent for a variety of banks, insurance companies, and investment houses. The planner will "run the numbers" on the client's budget and aspirations, then make suggestions. Many financial planners are sole practitioners who may offer accounting or investment services as well as overall planning.

The International Association for Financial Planning estimates that there are 30,000 planners today, many of whom it has certified. (When it comes to personal financial arrangements, there are many opportunities for unwise if not illegal actions, so the association spends a lot of time policing the activities of its members.) However, the total number of planners could be as high as 50,000, because many leading insurance companies, investment houses, and banks now provide planning services as an adjunct to their main product lines.

The profession is subject to business trends; when the stock market was rising rapidly and the economy was growing during the mid-1980s, many more people gravitated toward the field than at the beginning of the 1990s. The rising complexity of taxation, savings, and investment, however, will make a permanent place for many financial planners.

Many financial consultants start their careers with insurance firms, banks, or investment brokers. Training in accounting, tax policies, and securities provide a big career boost. It is also possible to study planning and gain some degree of certification through the two academic centers for this work: the College of Financial Planning (Denver, CO) and the American College (Bryn Mawr, PA).

Depending on the type of planner and the wishes of the client, planners earn a flat fee, or one based on the value of the investments they help the individual set up. Earnings start around $20,000.

**Institute of Certified Financial Planners**
2 Denver Highlands
Suite 320
10065 East Harvard Avenue
Denver, CO 80231
(303) 751-7600

**International Association for Financial Planning**
Suite 800
2 Concourse Parkway
Atlanta, GA 30328
(404) 395-1605

---

# FOOD SCIENTIST/TECHNOLOGIST

**Biological Sciences, Chemical Engineering, Chemistry (A number of schools offer specialized programs in food science.)**

Watching the birth, growth, and retirement of food and diet trends is getting to be an entertaining spectator sport. Since the 60s, many foods have been touted as the keys to a longer and happier life—from granola to mineral water to fiber, to oat bran, to psyllium, to who-knows-what. The evolution of dietary habits seems to be quickening, which should benefit the food science/technology profession dramatically.

Food science and technology involves the production, packaging, and serving of prepared foods. It devises everything from ways to put new flavors on snack foods to new techniques for feeding hundreds of people at a time in institutional settings.

Although many consumers are pushing harder and harder for "all natural" foods, the difficulties and expense of delivering totally unprocessed foods are rising. This push for natural foods is only another boon to the food scientist/technologist, who may be devising new flash-freezing techniques to deliver fresher food more quickly, or developing processed foods that taste every bit as good as that coming off the vine or stem.

In college, food scientists/technologists study those topics specifically, or nutrition or agricultural sciences. Home economics and restaurant administration are also entry points to the field. A similarly diverse range of job opportunities awaits graduates. The giant food-processing firms that produce bread, cereals, meats, and prepared foods employ food scientists/technologists to devise new ways of harvesting, cleaning, sterilizing, and packaging all types of foods. These professionals are also at work devising special diets or food-delivery systems for those who need to lose weight, or are hospitalized, or have unusual dietary requirements.

By the end of the century, the food science/technology field will have grown by 21%—comfortably above the average for all professions—according to the Bureau of Labor Statistics. Although the food business grows only at about the same rate as the US population, greater needs for engineering and processing expertise in food preparation will create job openings.

Currently, starting salaries are about $22,000, with the highest salaries in private industry and substantially lower pay for the college teacher and those working in institutional food services.

Institute of Food Technologists
221 LaSalle Street
Chicago, IL 60601
(312) 782-8248

# FOREIGN LANGUAGE TEACHER

## Anthropology, Classics, Modern Languages, Philosophy and Religion

For years, Americans have been notorious for their ignorance of foreign languages and customs. The problem starts with a lack of interest in languages in high school and goes all the way to the top —the United States is said to be the only country in the world whose ambassadors are not required to be able to speak any foreign language, let alone the appropriate language for an overseas posting.

This state of affairs has not only distanced us from the rest of the world, but has helped to cause annual trade deficits of billions of dollars a month. Now American corporations are striving to expand their overseas operations and to become better exporters. Thus the need for foreign-language knowledge is very great.

After a long decline, interest in foreign-language courses and programs is rising among high school and college students. Most educators agree that learning a language should be a goal of all students, especially those in college.

As part of a push to improve education at all levels, school districts, cities and states and, to a small extent, the federal government have expanded teaching budgets; this is creating new opportunities for language teachers.

Meanwhile, business is strong for private teachers of foreign languages, who work with business executives about to begin overseas postings. Opportunities in this line of work, as well as in translating, are being generated by the increasing volume of international trade.

It is hard to predict which languages are going to be hot. Whenever there is a change in America's relationship with other countries, the call usually goes out for the appropriate language experts. In the early 1970s, following detente with the Soviet Union, Russian was a popular choice. In the past decade, Japanese and Chinese have been in intense demand. Presumably, the changing relations with Eastern Europe will open up opportunities in Polish, Hungarian, Czechoslovakian and other Eastern European languages. However, the low state of nearly all foreign language learning in the United States will create a need for all types of language teaching.

For public schools and universities, language teachers must meet the same requirements as other teachers: graduation from an accredited college, internship as a teacher in training, and licensing by the state in which one wants to work. Salaries appear to be considerably higher than the average teacher's, however, the College Placement Council reported in late 1989 that foreign language graduates were receiving average offers over $21,000.

**The American Council on the Teaching of
   Foreign Languages, Inc.**
6 Executive Boulevard, Upper Level
Yonkers, NY   10701
(914) 963-8830

---

# FRANCHISE MANAGER
### Business Administration, Home Economics

Franchising, an American invention, combines the benefits of an independent enterpreneur with the support of a large corporation. A phenomenal amount of retailing today is done through franchises—around $700 billion, which is more about four times the volume of department-store sales. The main advantages for young job-seekers are that they can start a business with a relatively small investment and then can maintain some advantage over conventional retailers or service companies.

First, some definitions. The franchisor is the company that offers franchises, which are usually established for certain territorys or regions. A "product and trade name" franchise involves the purchase of a brand name and some supplies; a "business format" franchise includes cooperative marketing arrangements between the franchisor and franchisee, and a stricter set of guidelines for conducting the business. Gas stations, auto dealers, and soft-drink bottlers are examples of the former; fast-food restaurants and computer-retailing chains are examples of the latter. Business-format franchises are growing more strongly.

Typically, an entrepreneur pays a fee to the franchisor and agrees to return a certain portion of sales. In return, the franchisee obtains supplies, advice on how to run the business, and the support of national advertising campaigns. Franchisors increasingly seek to define the style of the building where the service will be offered, the pricing policies, the sources of supply, and the methods of providing service. In this way, the franchisor controls the quality of the product or service.

The initial investment can be substantial; a franchise with an established chain, such as McDonald's, can cost several hundred thousand dollars. Franchise chains just starting up will have much lower startup fees. Franchise promoters like to say that only 5% of new franchises fail in the first year, which is much lower than conventional businesses. However, this number has never been reliably proven. Although professional franchise organizations police their members, the franchising business attracts more than its share of fast-buck artists.

The actual work of the franchisee is business administration and marketing. The best-run franchisors will offer training and advice to franchises, thus creating a learning opportunity for the franchisee.

Aspiring franchisees can study franchising as an MBA specialty at a few business schools, including the University of Nebraska. Lacking a pot of money to invest, the job-seeker might consider working for another franchisee as a store or business manager to learn the ropes of the business and accumulate enough cash to strike out independently. Pay scales are highly variable, as in any new business undertaking, but substantial earnings are possible.

International Franchise Association
Suite 900
1350 New York Avenue, NW
Washington, DC   20005
(202) 628-8000

---

# GEOLOGIST

### Geology, Physics

Geology took it on the chin in the 1980s, but appears poised for a comeback in the 1990s. True, the Bureau of Labor Statistics projects growth of 16% (to about 49,000 practitioners), just a hair above the average for all professions, but job opportunities should be great because enrollments in geology nose-dived by 46% during the middle years of the 80s, to around 3,300 BS graduates per year.

The main reasons for the plunge were the combined collapse of domestic oil exploration and minerals mining. Both these industries depend on geologists to find and develop energy and mineral sources. As the decade wore on, both industries began to improve. Now, at the outset of the 1990s, there is an increase in hiring.

The career prospects of geologists are also being improved by environmental activities (see **Earth Scientist**). Whether the issue is the siting of garbage landfills for cities or the remediation of toxic-chemical dumps from the past, or the development of new groundwater sources, geologists are needed to perform tests, analyze results, and guide construction activity. The specialty of *hydrogeology* is especially important; this field involves the study of how water interacts with soil and rock. Hydrogeologists can determine the pollution level of an underground water source and how to arrest and correct the contamination.

Other sources of jobs for geologists are state surveys and the US Geological Survey. These government organizations oversee the sitting of highways, bridges, and other public-works structures, and help private industry evaluate new mineral sources.

According to a 1988 publication of the American Geological Society, new bachelor's graduates at that time were receiving offers of $24,000 to over $30,000 from the mining and petroleum industries. State and federal survey organizations offered $17,000 to over $25,000.

The oil industry is becoming more lively, especially in offshore exploration, which will create job opportunities in coming years. The same is true, to a lesser extent, for mining companies. Much of the work in both areas is moving to remote locations around the world, so student geologists can help themselves by studying foreign languages and cultures.

**Geological Society of America**
PO Box 9140
3300 Penrose Place
Boulder, CO    80301
(303) 447-2020

# HEALTH-SERVICE ADMINISTRATOR

### Allied Health Professions, Psychology, Sociology

Doctors are the key professionals at hospitals—no one else takes primary responsibility for the care of sick or injured patients—but doctors don't actually run the hospitals. Health-service (hospital) administrators do.

Like business managers, health-service administrators must make sure customers are satisfied, must market the services of the organization, and must keep the books in order. Like a public administrator, the hospital manager knows that, one way or another, society covers the bill for the hospital, so there are responsibilities to the community that are not driven solely by ability to pay. Unlike any other administrator, the hospital administrator knows that the ultimate goal of the business is to save lives. It is impossible to compromise the quality of health-care. That puts an extra responsibility onto the administrator's shoulders, but is also one of the major satisfactions of the job.

Hospital administration is taught at both the undergraduate and graduate levels by a large number of schools. The number of managerial roles in the US health-care system has risen dramatically in recent years, even faster than the rise in the cost of health-care. (The country's bill for health-care in 1990 is estimated at a truly astounding $661 billion.)

Pressures are rising throughout the health-care system because of the rise in its cost. Corporations who fund employee health plans, the federal government's Medicare and Medicaid programs, and the insurance industry are all grappling with health-care costs. As a result, the job outlook is very good in hospital administration. The best-run, most efficient hospitals will ride out the current crisis.

About 55% of health-service managers work in hospitals. Another 17% are at nursing homes, and the remainder work at doctor's offices, laboratories, and outpatient-care facilities. Industry data show that salaries are tied to the size of the organization, with top managers at the largest hospitals earning nearly $150,000. Starting salaries for master's-level graduates are around $32,000.

**American College of Health-Care Administrators**
325 South Patrick Street
Alexandria, VA 22314
(703) 549-5822

---

# HISTORIAN

### Classics, History

History stands out as one of the academic majors that is perennially popular with college students, and yet has few direct job possibilities. About 17,000 students earn a history degree annually; the number of openings for teachers of history at high school and college levels is only a few thousand, and the number of non-teaching history occupations only a few hundred. The number of positions for historians outside academia is too small for the Bureau of Labor Statistics to record.

This has been true for a long time, and thus the history student knows to look elsewhere. However, there are some openings for those trained in history and who wish to continue historical work outside the academic context.

First, some details on teaching: there are an estimated 25,000 faculty in the nation's collegiate history departments; openings develop at the rate of about 2,500 (10% of positions) per year. A somewhat larger number of instructorships become available, but they are generally short-term. According to data from the College and University Personnel Association, new assistant professors earned average salaries of $25,500, while instructors earned $23,000.

Teaching positions are tied to demographics: the situation coming up in this decade is a slight shrinkage at the university level, a slump in high schools that begins to rise toward the end of the decade, and higher demand at the outset of the 1990s for elementary school teachers (see **College Professor, Liberal Arts** and **Teacher, K–12**).

Outside the classroom, there are positions for the historian at public-policy institutes, community or state-funded history projects, and specialized business professions. A somewhat informal profession of "contract historian" has developed in recent years; this individual, who often works for corporations, will research and write a historical perspective of individuals, companies, or social or political trends.

A special field that generally falls under the umbrella of historian is the *archivist* or *curator*. These individuals combine history-research skills with the cataloguing or organizing skills of the librarian to assemble documentation for some event or entity. The average earnings of archivists working for the federal government in the mid-1980s was about $36,000, according ot the Bureau of Labor Statistics. Most have advanced degrees.

The history student who wants to develop a career in this field must be inventive and entrepreneurial. Jobs exist to be filled, but it is also true that, like artists and other creative people, historians create their own opportunities.

**American Historical Association**
400 A Street, SE
Washington, DC   20003
(202) 544-2422

---

# HOME ECONOMIST
### Home Economics

Our society tends to belittle homemaking for many reasons—not the least of which is that few people are paid directly for it—but running a household, or tending to the well-being of a family, is complex and economically important work.

Sales of hundreds of billions of dollars are controlled by homemakers—in consumer goods, appliances, real estate, home furnishings, and energy. Home economists study and develop this market.

The scope of home economics has widened in recent years. Traditionally, home economists worked for consumer-goods suppliers in consumer marketing, food styling, and public relations. In recent years, they have become involved in consumer activism, home safety, and social work.

According to Home Economists in Business (HEIB), a professional group, home economics is taught under 58 different titles in college, ranging from human ecology to family science.

There are at least 25,000 professional home economists—the current membership of the American Home Economics Association. About a third of these teach, especially in high schools. A large portion of the rest work in community affairs and social work.

Thousands more work in industry. The industrial jobs for home economists include marketing and marketing research, advertising, consumer information, and writing or editing. Many workers in these field have other types of academic backgrounds. A number of positions that are unique to home economics graduates includes:

- running a test kitchen for food or appliance manufacturers, to research and test the value of new products
- offering customers service for supermarkets, utilities, and manufacturers
- consulting in kitchen or home-furnishing design
- food styling for photography

The prospects for home economics are good, reflecting the general upswing in consumer-goods marketing and consumer protection. Salaries range from $15,000 (for teachers and civil servants) to over $50,000 for consumer-goods marketers. many home economics graduates pursue graduate training in health-care, nutrition, or journalism.

**Home Economics in Business**
5008 Pine Creek Drive
Blendonview Office Park
Westerville, OH   43081-4899
(614) 890-4342

**American Home Economics Association**
1555 King Street
Alexandria, VA 22314
(703) 706-4600

---

# HORTICULTURIST

### Architecture and Urban Design, Biological Sciences

"If you like plants, you can make decent living as a horticultural scientist," says the American Society for Horticultural Science (ASHS). This underwhelming statement is certainly true, but it fails to illustrate the dramatic effect of biotechnology on the field. A quiet revolution has been going on in the plant sciences.

Horticulturists are using the very latest techniques in tissue culturing, gene splicing, and other genetic manipulations to create new strains of agricultural plants; to extract useful compounds from plants; and to understand better how plants live, grow, and regenerate.

Horticultural scientists and agricultural scientists have similar concerns, but with an intriguing difference. Where the agricultural scientist is most concerned with the volume and quality of production from plants, the horticultural scientist is concerned with seeds —the potential of the plant. Both types of scientists plant, grow, harvest, and study plant life, but the horticulturist will look at genetic changes from generation to generation, while the agricultural scientist will focus on the combination of growing conditions that lead to a successful harvest.

Horticulture is dominated by agriculture, but the field has considerably more to offer. Subspecialties include floriculture (flowers) and pomology (fruit trees). Related to floriculture is the vast field of landscaping and decorating; many who study horticulture are employed as landscapers or gardeners.

Just over half the ASHA's members are in education (including so-called extension programs, which assist people or organizations with their plant problems). About 20% work in industry, either at seed companies or biotechnology firms, or as providers of plants and landscaping services, or as consultants to these groups, and about 15% work for government, including the Agriculture Department and the array of services offered to farmers.

Horticulture is usually taught as its own department at many colleges, especially the land-grant universities of the Midwest. At other schools it is combined with biology or landscape architecture. Those who remain in academia perform research, just as most life scientists do, by growing generations of plants, analyzing their chemistry and biology, and performing tests.

In private industry, the range of activities widens. At landscaping firms, horticulturists oversee the production of marketable plants such as shade trees, shrubs, and flowers. They will also serve as consultants to architects who seek to landscape a plot of land, or to dress up the interior of a building (some landscape architects get their degrees from schools of horticulture). At seed companies, they maintain the quality of seed products—especially vegetables —and experiment to improve the generative properties of seeds. Many agricultural-chemical companies (which provide fertilizers and pesticides) hire horticulturists to help develop new products.

Salaries vary according to the type of employer. In academia, professors usually start at around $28,000, and can reach median incomes of $50,000 to $60,000. In private industry, salaries are lowest at the plant harvesters and highest at the agricultural-chemical companies.

Plant science will grow more important in the near future because of concern over the environment, especially that of tropical forests, grasslands, and other stressed areas.

**American Society for Horticultural Science**
701 North Saint Asaph Street
Alexandria, VA   22314
(703) 836-4606

# HOTEL MANAGER

**Business Administration, Civil Engineering, Home Economics, Modern Languages, Sociology**
**(Hotel administration specifically is offered at a few schools.)**

Inkeeping has been around for a long time, but it is getting a new look today. Modern hotels are major real estate projects, and more are being tied to shopping districts and convention centers, or being used for both recreation and business meetings. Managing a hotel means a lot more than answering the telephone and passing out room keys.

The field's growth is actually being constrained by a shortage of workers. A "serious problem facing the lodging industry is the shortage of labor. . . . Most firms are developing aggressive recruitment and retention programs to attract and keep their share of new applicants," says the US Department of Commerce.

The basics of hotel management are easy to understand: arranging reservations, booking people in and out, making sure supplies are on hand, and overseeing the staff. The hotel manager acts as a property manager, making sure that the facilities are in proper working order and handling vendors.

Hotels are seeking to expand their business in many directions. More travelers are depending on hotels to arrange for tours or recreation. Businesspeople increasingly use hotels as an extension of their offices, taking blocks of rooms on a permanent basis for use by a steady stream of visitors to the company, and all sorts of people—including those who aren't even renting rooms—look to hotels for dining and entertainment.

These expansion objectives require the hotel manager to be an expert marketer. Complex lodging/meeting room arrangements require the manager to negotiate favorable rates.

For this decade, the Bureau of Labor Statistics projects that the number of job slots will rise by 29% (including food-service managers). Starting salaries are around $20,500.

**American Hotel and Motel Association**
1201 New York Avenue, NW
Washington, DC   20005
(202) 289-3100

---

# HUMAN-RESOURCES MANAGER

**Anthropology, Communications, English, History, Home Economics, Industrial Engineering, Performing Arts, Philosophy and Religion, Political Science, Psychology, Sociology**

Despite its factories, buildings, inventories, patents, consumer lists, and money in the bank, a company is nothing more than its managers and employees. Especially in industries like banks, airlines, advertising agencies, and securities firms, a substantial investment is made in the selection, training, and rewarding of workers. The human-resources manager oversees these tasks.

Human-resources, which used to go by the simple term "personnel," means a lot more today than the hiring, firing, and retiring of workers. Increasingly complex legal and regulatory issues are at stake. Equal opportunity laws and the sincere desire by employers to be more representative of society at large means that extra efforts must be made to attract and keep female, minority, and handicapped workers.

A number of specialty positions in human-resources management are professions in their own right, and serve as stepping stones to managerial slots. These include compensation analysis (the development of pay scales, promotional qualifications, and fringe benefits; see **Compensation Analyst**), recruiting and counseling (see **Job Counselor**), labor relations (important in heavily unionized businesses), and training (see **Corporate Trainer**). Some individuals pick up experience in several of these areas, then move up into management.

It is also possible to study fields related to human-resources in college. A number of schools offer bachelor degrees in organizational behavior, labor relations, counseling, or personnel administration. A background in psychology, sociology, or business can also help career prospects.

Typically, human-resources managers oversee the various activities of the department; advise upper-management on areas needing change or improvement; and keep abreast of industry and national trends in hiring, promoting, and providing compensation. Many conduct classes ranging from teaching secretarial skills to grooming upper-management trainees.

Some make career moves from a corporate position in human-resources to independent consultant. Some become executive recruiters (see **Executive Recruiter**). A number of management-consulting firms also specialize in human-resources.

Many manufacturers today are pushing to raise productivity so they can compete in the international arena. Automakers, electronics firms, defense contractors, and most other manufacturers have instituted quality circles, worker-management teams, automation, and other techniques to help workers improve productivity and raise the quality of goods. This drive represents an across-the-board challenge to human-resource managers, who must find ways to train and motivate workers accustomed to less rigorous standards. Much improvement has already been achieved, but no one is saying that the upgrading is finished. The long-term prospects for human-resource managers in nearly all types of business enterprises are good.

There are over 750,000 professionals in the human-resource occupations according to the Bureau of Labor Statistics. Projected growth is between 22% and 25%. Starting salaries are about $23,000.

**American Society for Personnel Administration**
606 North Washington Street
Alexandria, VA   22314
(703) 548-3440

**Employment Management Association**
Suite 1100
5 West Hargett Street
Raleigh, NC   27601
(919) 828-6614

# INDUSTRIAL/MANUFACTURING ENGINEER

### Chemical Engineering, Chemistry, Computer Science and Engineering, Electrical and Electronics Engineering, Industrial Engineering, Mechanical Engineering

An athlete—say a sprinter—pays close attention to his performance. He knows his peak speed to the hundredth of a second, and he constantly analyzes his take-off, his stride and his breathing to improve that speed.

The same sort of analysis can be performed on the operation of a factory or business. How much raw material winds up in the final product, and how much as waste? How many hours of labor produce a finished article? Which machines perform efficiently, and which function poorly or break down often?

Industrial/manufacturing engineers answer these and a host of other questions. This field has undergone revolutionary changes in the past decade, with further change to come during the 1990s. The reason: intense competition with foreign manufacturers who have been able to offer better products at lower prices. Traditionally, business assumed this was possible merely because foreign workers are paid substantially less than American workers, but today's manufacturers no longer believe this, and they are re-evaluating the production methods from top to bottom. The industrial/manufacturing engineer carries out this investigation.

Reflecting this focus on manufacturing technology, the society of Manufacturing Engineers more than doubled between 1977 and the late 1980s. For the future, the Bureau of Labor Statistics projects an 18% growth rate, to about 155,000, by the end of the decade.

This projection, however, doesn't reflect the many ways industrial engineering expertise can be applied. Industrial engineers are showing transportation companies, food-service firms and financial-services organizations how to organize their employees and technology. College-graduate surveys show that industrial engineers are getting jobs in accounting firms, retail stores, government, and consulting firms. Salaries range from the low 20s to around $30,000.

Industrial engineers study an intriguing combination of human and mechanical capabilities. One of the earliest types of industrial engineering, developed from 1900 to 1920, was "scientific management." This usually involved defining and timing the motions of a worker on an assembly line. By reducing these motions to their essentials, the industrial engineer was able to show how best to perform a job. Such "time-and-motion" studies have become but a small part of the analysis of today's industrial engineer. More often, the engineer will be measuring energy and raw material costs, or evaluating the potential effect of automating a job function.

As an academic program, industrial engineering is a full-fledged engineering discipline, with the same heavy dose of math and science as all engineering programs. Manufacturing engineering, on the other hand, is often considered part of the engineering-technology program. Math and science requirements are reduced, and in their place are courses tailored more specifically to certain industries or types of work. Generally, the industrial engineering degree is more prestigious, but in many cases, the insight that engineers are able to bring to their work washes out many distinctions after a few years.

**Institute of Industrial Engineers**
25 Technology Park/Atlanta
Norcross, GA   30092
(404) 449-0460

**Society of Manufacturing Engineers**
Box 930
1 SME Drive
Dearborn, MI   48121
(313) 271-1500

# INFORMATION BROKER

### Computer Science and Engineering

No, information brokers don't work on Wall Street selling facts instead of stocks. They are a new type of researcher—part librarian, part detective, and part computer jockey—adept at ferreting information out of computer databases.

A database is nothing more than a collection of data, which may include anything from the transcripts of court cases to the texts of past issues of magazines or newspapers. There are many, many specialized data bases of important business information, such as stock or real estate transactions, government contract bids, or scientific bibliographies.

Using some of these databases can be challenging. Many have a user's guide, which allows the researcher to select items from a menu or choose key words, and then instruct the computer that houses the data to search for the appropriate items. There are many ways to conduct a search, and often a skillful researcher can assemble a new database out of an existing one simply by refining and organizing the information to fulfill a different function. Enter the information broker, who sets up these databases and searches through them for clients.

The field of electronic information services is large and growing rapidly. The Department of Commerce estimates revenues in this business at $7.5 billion in 1989. There are about 3,500 individual databases, accessed through telephone lines and so-called "gateway services," whereby one telecommunications company offers to transmit messages to another. The revenues come from fees that users pay per minute to access the database, as well as fees for the telephone.

The field is so new that there is little academic training for it. Library science is probably the closest academic program; many schools are developing data base training as part of a curriculum in information science or management of information systems (MIS; see **Information Specialist**). Experience is the key right now.

**Association of Information Systems Professionals**
Suite 201
104 Wilmot Road
Deerfield, IL   60015
(312) 940-8800

**Association of Independent Information Professionals**
PO Box 71053
Shorewood, WI   53211
(415) 524-3212

---

# INFORMATION SPECIALIST

**Art History, Business Administration, Classics, Computer Science and Engineering, English, History**

MIS, management of information services, is one of the hot buzz-words of the business world. It assumes that there is a mother lode of information—piles and piles of data that, if presented in the right way to business management, will make the managers see how much more profitably the business could be run, or reveal to them new, profitable ventures.

Indeed, more than a few companies have been able to develop new markets through the savvy use of their computer resources. The airline industry, for example, has devised a system called "load management" that enables them to juggle the number of full-fare passengers with discount-fare bargain seekers, thereby filling the plane while obtaining the maximum revenues. Load management is now being tried in the hotel industry, and who knows—you may someday be buying your groceries at prices that vary according to daily demand and availability.

MIS workers are concerned with the business applications of computers rather than computer technology itself. Appropriate training may be in computer science, business administration, or information science. MIS workers need to know how businesses gather information, and how important they hold the timeliness or precision of a set of data. Minute-by-minute fluctuations in the stock markets, for example, could be exploited, through the use of the right computer programs, to extract profits from rapid buying and selling of shares.

The MIS function also has a more day-to-day aspect. Businesses have invested billions of dollars in hardware and software; the cost of computerization is a major element in the overall health of some kinds of enterprises. Business organizations need executive-level judgment to determine which computer investments are worthwhile, and how the computer systems should be maintained.

For manufacturers, computerization takes on a different aspect. The people on the factory floor have elaborate control systems that help run the manufacturing processes. The business managers have computers that record sales and expenses, crank out quarterly profit reports, and write out employees' paychecks. By marrying the two systems, the manufacturer gains to-the-minute awareness of the cost and profitability of production processes. This is called "computer integrated manufacturing" or CIM. Manufacturers are racing to develop more powerful CIM systems that will help them gain better control over the quality and scale of production processes. Inventories could be reduced, and inappropriately designed products could be minimized if the two computer systems were more closely coupled. CIM involves industrial and electrical engineering as well as computer or information science. This aspect of MIS is growing dramatically at present, and is likely to continue to do so for some time to come.

Entry-level MIS specialists earn somewhat less than computer programmers or systems analysts—around $24,000 to $26,000. Like those other computer professionals, however, their careers will see dramatic growth in coming years.

**American Society for Information Science**
Suite 404
1424 16th Street, NW
Washington, DC-20036
(202) 462-1000

# INSURANCE AGENT

**Accounting, Business Administration, Civil Engineering, Political Science, Psychology**

Selling insurance to individuals and businesses has been one of the vast training grounds for future sales and marketing managers. The work is hard, but success comes to those who persist, and who are on top of the trends in new insurance products and new insurance needs.

Selling insurance is also a severe test of one's determination to succeed. The dropout rate, according to some industry estimates, is 90% within 2 years. For whose who make it through the first few years, however, the rewards can be substantial, with salaries rising well over $50,000 for the most successful.

There are two major ways to approach the profession of selling insurance, especially life or personal insurance. The usual course is to join one of the major national firms, which handle life, auto, and property insurance. New hires receive their training, pass state examinations, then begin working lists of names. Each actual or potential client is asked for references, and more sales calls are made. At various times, the corporate management run marketing campaigns to attract more potential clients.

A second route is to work as a so-called "multi-line" agent, offering a variety of insurance products to individuals or businesses.

Salaries are set at a basic rate for trainees or beginning agents, and very quickly are replaced by a commission based on the volume of sales. Business built up over a period of years adds to the earnings.

Many insurance agents, after obtaining valuable experience, strike out on their own as insurance brokers. These professionals, who usually market their products locally in a town or neighborhood, offer the insurance products of several different insurance companies. The brokers can receive commissions on each sale, according to their sales agreements with the various product companies.

Self-confidence, ambition, and skills in interpersonal relations are the key ingredients to success. Academic training need not be specific to insurance, but courses in accounting, business, and economics help.

The bureau of Labor Statistics counted 423,000 insurance agents and brokers in 1988, and expects that total to rise by 14%, to about 481,000, by the year 2000. That growth is about average for all professions. In 1988, 45% were involved in life insurance, 36% worked as brokers, and the remainder provided fire, marine, and casualty insurance, or insurance services.

Because insurance is such a critical part of most families' financial planning, insurance sales also offers an entree to other types of investments, savings, and tax planning. Many financial planners (see **Financial Planner**) started out in insurance sales, and the major insurance companies themselves have branched out into such areas as tax, retirement, or investment planning.

American Council of Life Insurance
Suite 500
1001 Pennsylvania Avenue, NW
Washington, DC  20004
(202) 624-2000

---

# INVESTOR RELATIONS MANAGER

### Business Administration, Communications, Economics, Political Science

Investor relations is a specialty within public relations that requires special knowledge of how finance and business investment works. Like other public relations managers, most investor relations managers work at corporations; some work for consulting firms located in New York near the major stock exchanges.

Investor relations managers target the financial analysts (see **Financial Analyst**) who follow the stock prices of an industry or line of business. They promote the pluses of corporate performance, at the same time minimizing the damage that is caused by financial losses or poor performance.

The secondary audience for investor relations managers is investors themselves, some of whom are the managers of billion-dollar pension or mutual funds. When a company is "in play," as during an attempted takeover, the investor relations manager works overtime to win the majority of stockholders' views over to that of the corporate management. Conversely, the company attempting the takeover hires investor-relations artillery to convince the stock owners of its point of view.

As in all types of public relations, skills in writing and communicating are of paramount importance. In 1985 a third of the members of the National Investor Relations Institute (NIRI) had a background in communications/public relations. The largest number had a financial or accounting background. Because of the intricate ways investments are analyzed, and the way companies are described to investors, experience as a stock broker or financial analyst is valuable. Some companies feel that investor relations is so important that the function is reserved for senior managers of the firm.

Salaries vary widely, depending on the size of the company and the experience of the practitioner. An NIRI survey showed that average salaries ranged from $56,000 to over $67,000.

National Investor Relations Institute
1730 M Street, NW
Washington, DC   20026
(202) 861-0630

---

# JOB COUNSELOR

**Anthropology, Education, Philosophy and Religion, Sociology**

One of the reasons you are probably reading this book is that it's a job to get a job. Many people find the services of a job counselor essential. Some ultimately wind up giving job advice to others—as job counselors.

Job counselors are part of the triangle of corporate human-resources managers (see **Human-resource Managers**), government job offices, and schools. Each part of this triangle matches job candidates and jobs. Most job counselors (67%) work at schools; the remainder work at state employment offices or private employment agencies. A small portion of the last group is executive search consultants (see **Executive Search Consultant**). At the college level, job counselors usually go by the title of "placement officer."

The long-term prospects for job counseling are quite good. The Bureau of Labor Statistics projects that the number of positions will rise by 27% through the year 2000, reaching 157,000. In public secondary schools, the pay is around $33,000, according to 1988 data from the Educational Research Service (Arlington, VA). Earnings at the college level are slightly higher, depending on the size of the school and whether it is private or public.

The 55,000-member American Association for Counseling and Development (AACD) is an umbrella organization for 16 counseling specialties. The two largest are the American School Counselor Association and the American Mental Health Counselors Association, each representing about 22% of AACD members.

It is the responsibility of the job counselor to keep informed of hiring trends locally or for certain specialties throughout a region. Training in the assessment of individual skills and interests is also necessary. Many counselors perform their best work by acting as an adviser, getting to know the student or job-seeker personally and making recommendations about lifestyle, level of training, and capabilities. The goal is a good match between the individual's desires and capabilities, and the job's responsibilities and opportunities.

**American Association for Counseling and Development**
5999 Stevenson Avenue
Alexandria, VA   22304
(703) 823-9800

**College Placement Council**
62 Highland Avenue
Bethlehem, PA   18017
(215) 868-1421

**Career Planning and Adult Development Network**
4965 Sierra Road
San Jose, CA   95132
(408) 559-4946

---

# JOURNALIST

### Anthropology, Art History, Biological Sciences, Business Administration, Chemistry, Classics, Communications, Economics, English, History, Modern Languages, Philosophy and Religion, Political Science, Psychology, Sociology

Does news happen if no one is there to report it? Preventing that riddle from being posed is the goal of journalists, who hunt down the news for newspapers, magazines, networks, and newswires. At times, it seems that there is nothing left to report, since there are so many news organizations covering every aspect of American life and commerce; but just then a sharp, ambitious journalist will uncover a story that shakes up the status quo.

The archetypal journalist was captured in *The Front Page*, a play that has been made into numerous movies: a hardbitten, all-knowing reporter will do anything to get a story. That romantic image, fueled by untold numbers of spy thrillers, murder mysteries, and melodramas, has attracted generations of aspiring writers to the journalism business. While that vision comes true for some reporters, the great majority of journalists work at more mundane tasks: analyzing business and government trends, traipsing to City Hall, sitting through chicken-and-mashed-potato dinners to report speeches.

Business has been pretty good for the news organizations that employ journalists. Newspaper sales have risen (although the number of papers has fallen), more magazines are started every year, and the number of broadcasting organizations has grown. Because of high interest among college students for careers in journalism, however, job competition is always fierce.

The usual advice for journalists starting their careers is to get a job on a local newspaper, then work up to bigger papers, finally reaching one of the national papers. This tradition has been altered by the growth of newspaper chains, some of which move their top staffers around within the organization, with greater responsibilities at each move. Journalists work crazy hours, so the field tends to have more appeal to younger workers; the older ones tend to move into editing.

The long-term prospects for journalism are average: the Bureau of Labor Statistics projects a 16% increase by the turn of the century, to 82,000 positions. Starting salaries are around $18,000; experienced workers average around $35,000. The larger or national news organizations pay better than local ones.

American Society of Journalists and Authors
Suite 1907
151 Broadway
New York, NY   10036
(212) 997-0947

---

# LANDSCAPE ARCHITECT

### Architecture and Urban Design

The "natural" beauty of many of our parks and public spaces is actually the result of intensive work by landscape architects. These professionals work with building architects, urban planners, real estate developers, and conservationists to plan and execute landscaping projects such as the lawns or public areas around skyscrapers, highway borders, municipal parks, golf courses, and the grounds of planned communities. There is a growing business lately in providing landscaping services for the owners of luxury homes.

The first landscape architects in the United States were the developers of the large municipal parks (and cemeteries!) during the late 1800s. Such names as Frederick Law Olmstead, the designer of Central Park in New York City, are still revered in the landscaping profession. During this century, landscape architecture developed from a branch of architecture into a separate profession with its own educational and licensing requirements. Nevertheless, there is still close cooperation between the two professions, and many architects trained in building construction also perform landscaping work.

The work requires skill in design and drafting (like any architectural work) plus a knowledge of plants, water, and land. For example, the landscape architect must know what types of trees flourish in direct sunlight on city streets, and which are proper and appealing for shaded enclaves. At the same time, the landscape architect must be concerned with proper water drainage and the effects of erosion. The designs have to fulfill the needs of the landowner, or of the users of public areas for meeting, walking, or recreation.

According to the American Society of Landscape Architects (ASLA), 75% of its members are in private practice, 20% work for the government and the remaining 5% teach. The private practitioners work in sole practices, with large landscaping firms or with architectural firms. A small number are employed by manufacturers of landscaping equipment or horticultural firms that supply trees and other plants.

Starting salaries for landscape architects are around $18,000; in a 1987 survey, ASLA found the median income of its members was about $45,000.

The study of landscape architecture involves many courses in design and drafting, so good art skills are a plus. In addition, students take courses in biology and botany to learn about plants. A 4-year degree is customary, although many obtain a master's. After beginning work, the next big hurdle is to obtain state licensing, which requires 3 years of experience and the passing of an examination.

The long-term projected growth for landscape architecture is good, according to the Bureau of Labor Statistics, which predicts that the number of professionals will rise 29%, from 18,000 to about 25,000. There are many reasons to believe that growth may be even stronger:  it is more and more common that the success or failure of a major land-use project, such as a housing project or resort complex, rides on how well that project is integrated with its environment. The project may never get underway unless strict land-use commissions approve it. When the project is completed, purchasers or users (e.g., homeowners in a planned community, or vacationers at a resort) vote with their pocketbooks on the quality of land use.

Even in inner cities, efforts are being redoubled to improve the parks, passageways and other public-use areas. The rising consciousness of our environment, too, requires wiser conservation of land, forested areas, and shorelines.

**American Society of Landscape Architects**
1733 Connecticut Avenue, NW
Washington, DC   20009
(202) 466-7730

---

# LAWYER

**Business Administration, Chemical Engineering, Classics, Electrical and Electronics Engineering, History, Philosophy and Religion, Political Science, Psychology, Sociology**

"I'll see you in court!" After this gauntlet is thrown, one of the 600,000 lawyers in this country swings into action. The practice of law has grown to be much more than handling court cases. The legal profession can be a stepping stone to careers in government, business management, real estate, and public policy.

This potential is undoubtedly one of the reasons for the continued popularity of the law among college students. Following a slight decline in the early 1980s, graduating classes have grown to more than 36,000, according to the Department of Education.

Another reason, simply put, is money—law is one of the highest-paying post-graduate career choices. The average salary of a beginning lawyer is $32,000, and every year, there are newspaper stories about leading law firms tempting the top graduates with offers over $75,000.

A final reason for the continued growth is the generally bright prospects for the profession. The Bureau of Labor Statistics projects a 31% increase in the number of working lawyers by the turn of the century.

What are the common tracks for starting lawyers? Nearly three-quarters go into private practice; most of the remainder go to work as employees in state or federal government. The private-practice field is dominated by law firms, where starting lawyers spend long hours at work, competing for a chance to become a partner. Law firms were getting bigger and bigger (both through internal growth and through mergers) but that appears to have crested for the moment. There are a few dozen firms with over 500 lawyers, and the 100 to 500 category is now showing a stronger growth.

Courtroom appearances are only a small part of the work at law firms; much more time is spent in negotiations over contracts, providing documents to government or to other agencies, and handling such matters as tax policies, filing patents, and simply providing advice to business managers.

Partnerships are offered only to the lucky few at most law firms; after about 5 to 8 years of work, most law firms indicate to their junior members whether or not they have a real chance at a partnership. Those that do not often move on to other types of work, especially corporate law. Corporations are the main clients of most law firms, and the lawyers that work on the client side can lead a somewhat more normal life, with fewer 80-plus-hour work weeks.

**American Bar Association**
750 North Lake Shore Drive
Chicago, IL   60611
(312) 988-5000

---

# LIBRARIAN

**Art History, Classics, Education, English, Philosophy and Religion
(Library science specifically is taught at both the undergraduate
and graduate levels.)**

If you haven't visited a good library in a while, you are in for a surprise. There are still librarians who concentrate on the Dewey decimal system, sending "past due" notices, and removing chewing gum from the bottom of seats. But a growing number are concerned with online databases, fax machines, or computer-scanned texts. Library science is being profoundly affected by the computer revolution.

The changes in library science are creating different specialties. The librarians most familiar to us work in conventional public libraries in most towns. Specialized skills are usually not required, salaries are low, and technology is being applied slowly. In special libraries, however, salaries are higher—around $35,000—and the intellectual challenges more demanding. One common type of special library is that found at the headquarters of major corporations, or at their research and development centers: the business library. Business libraries offer special services such as obtaining the texts of periodicals or financial documents by using computers linked by telephone. Other special libraries may be operated for a law department, a research laboratory, or a government institute.

At a research laboratory, the librarians doing literature searches may need to be conversant with the technical language of engineers and scientists. They also have to be familiar with special periodicals. Other special libraries may be used to research patents, legal references, or trademarks.

To obtain these types of information, librarians now use a broad array of directories and computerized services. The information may come from videotape, microfilm, computer links, or digitally stored files accessed through a compact-disc player. Words on paper are only one way to store information today.

The Bureau of Labor Statistics projects a growth rate of around 10% for professional librarians, whose numbers will reach 157,000 by the year 2000. Pay scales are low for the average librarian—around $18,000–$20,000. This is especially low considering that most professional librarians have to have a master's degree before being hired. Experienced workers have earnings from $28,000 to $40,000.

**American Library Association**
50 East Huron Street
Chicago, IL 60611
(312) 944-6780

**Special Libraries Association**
1700 18th Street, NW
Washington, DC 20009
(202) 234-4700

# LIFE SCIENTIST
### Biological Sciences, Chemistry

According to the Bureau of Labor Statistics, 57,000 biologists are working today. As 36,000 belong to the American Society for Microbiology (see **Microbiologist**), that leaves about 19,000 other kinds of biologists. These specialists, most of whom have advanced degrees, concentrate on specific types of higher life forms.

There is a formal name for practically every type of specialist: botanist (plants); ornithologist (birds); herpetologist (reptiles); entomologist (insects); zoologist (the general class of animals), and more. The study of the interaction of life with its environment is the province of the ecologist. Those who study ancient, extinct life forms are paleobiologists or paleontologists.

For many years, some of these fields had an eccentric air about them; they often appeared to be hobbies unrelated to the main stream of academic science. With the powerful techniques of genetic manipulation and with evolutionary theory firmly in place, the action was in microbiology. This is changing, however, mostly due to the rising concern over environmental problems.

There is little mistaking the fact that pollution and other environmental assaults shows up rapidly in the health of certain species: fish, insects, birds, trees. Now government research institutes, private companies, conservation groups, and others are calling on all the specialized scientists to help figure out what is going on, and to provide solutions.

Rising environmental concerns are also showing up in other ways. Companies that provide agricultural chemicals, such as pesticides and fertilizers, now realize that they have to produce less environmentally harmful products. Food producers and pharmaceutical companies (which base many of their drugs on extractions from rare plants) are intensifying the search for new knowledge of plants and animals.

Thus opportunities are increasing for life scientists. The work ranges from field research in jungles or coastal waterways to complex laboratory experiments. In the latter case, these scientists are joining forces with the microbiologists that are leading the biotechnology revolution.

In most cases, an advanced degree, usually a doctorate, is required for the life sciences. Currently, enrollments in these programs are declining, but the importance of environmental protection, and the increase in commercial opportunities from life forms, are expected to fuel a boom in life science careers. Overall growth is projected at 22% by the Bureau of Labor Statistics.

**American Institute of Biological Sciences**
1401 Wilson Blvd.
Arlington, VA 22209
(703) 527-6776

---

# MANAGEMENT CONSULTANT

**Accounting, Anthropology, Business Administration, Communications, Computer Science and Engineering, Economics, Industrial Engineering, Manufacturing Engineering, Operations Research, Political Science, Psychology**

One sector of the US economy that has grown steadily over the past decade, and is forecast to continue growing, is "business services"—assisting other firms, including manufacturers. One of the strongest parts of the business services field is management consulting—advising and doing evaluations for corporate managers.

Management consulting is not without its critics, who wonder what the managers of a firm are being paid for, if so many of their decisions are arrived at only after a management consultant has been brought in, for a hefty fee, to give an opinion. Nevertheless, most of the better-run companies actively hire consultants to look at hiring and promotion practices, productivity, new ventures, and corporate strategy.

The practice has become more common in recent years, as the

largest corporations have shed many of their middle-managers. With fewer staff people available, upper-managers are compelled to hire consultants to research business situations and provide advice. In more than a few cases, the consultant is the very individual who was let go by the firm.

So one career track for the aspiring consultant is to become a seasoned executive who is familiar with a business area. The other track is to attend a well-known business school, then join one of the large management-consulting firms. Such firms as McKinsey, the Boston Consulting Group, Arthur D. Little, Inc., and Booz, Allen & Hamilton, Inc., tend to hire the cream of the business-school crop, pay them extraordinary salaries ($70,000 and up), and groom them in their particular style of doing business.

The consultant will usually visit a client to discuss a particular objective, then set to work researching it. The research could involve studying the overall market size, the practices of competitors, or the policies that are carried out on the assembly lines or in the offices of the client firm. A report is issued, and the consultant goes on to the next objective, or next client. It is not uncommon for consultants to become so intrigued with, and knowledgeable about, a particular business that they join a firm, or start their own, to practice what they've been preaching.

The hours are long, and travel is extensive. At senior levels, consultants can become partners, sharing in the profits of the firm. At prestigious firms, the competition for partnership is intense.

There are about 100,000 management consultants today, says the Institute of Management Consultants, Inc.; their firms earn about $10 billion.

**Institute of Management Consultants, Inc.**
Suite 810
19 West 44th Street
New York, NY 10036
(212) 921-2885

# MARKETING MANAGER

**Anthropology, Art History, Business Administration, Communications, English, History, Modern Languages, Performing Arts, Political Science, Psychology**
**(Many business-related colleges offer programs in marketing management specifically.)**

Marketing management is one of the central functions of any manufacturing corporation; marketing expertise is also coming to the fore in many other areas of commerce, such as banking and financial services, non-profit organizations, health-care and even government.

For this reason, it is not surprising that tens of thousands of college students study marketing in school; in the late 1980s, almost 35,000 were obtaining a degree in it each year—one of the largest academic programs around. It is open to question, however, whether a marketing degree is better preparation for a career as a marketing manager than a liberal arts degree with a minor in marketing. The paramount ingredient for success in marketing is the ability to understand why consumers or customers make the choices they do.

Sales knowledge and experience are always essential parts of marketing. So it is customary, but not universal, that marketing executives rise through sales or market-research positions before being handed management responsibilities. At many companies (especially small ones), however, the marketing manager and the sales manager are the same person.

For a new product introduction, the marketing manager of a large consumer-goods company first assembles sales or audience data from market research; gets cost data from manufacturing and accounting; and chases down the details of advertising themes, media, and product-distribution methods. With all the data at hand, decisions are made on how the product will be priced, where it will be sold, and how it will be advertised. These decisions make all the difference between a successful product introduction and a failed one.

For existing products, marketing managers constantly survey their customers and competitors to keep ahead of rapidly evolving markets. When a new fashion trend or technology appears, it often affects the market for existing products. If sales begin to falter, the product must be made or sold a different way.

Excellent communication skills are needed for success in marketing because of all the coordinating that goes on. In addition, a strong competitive drive is desirable, if not essential. Marketing managers love to keep score and to win.

Salaries start at around $24,000 for sales or marketing-trainee positions, and can go as high as corporate America is willing to pay for successful product marketers. At present, the Bureau of Labor Statistics projects a 26% growth for marketing and public-relations management positions. However, keep in mind that marketers get (and get to keep) their jobs through the success that they demonstrate.

**American Marketing Association**
250 South Wacker Drive
Chicago, IL 60606
(312) 648-0536

---

# MARKETING RESEARCHER

### Anthropology, Classics, Communications, Economics, Home Economics, Mathematics, Philosophy and Religion, Psychology, Sociology

In 1989, there were a record 12,055 new food and drugstore products, according to an industry newsletter called Gorman's New Product News. There were also thousands more new products in other areas. Behind each of those products was a team of market researchers who polled potential customers; helped fine-tune the product's taste, packaging, and pricing; and determined the "selling points" that formed the theme for the advertising.

Most of those products will fail nonetheless, but for the few that hit big, a $100-million market can be created almost overnight. Therein lies the need, and opportunity, for market research. By uncovering markets for a new or improved product, the market researcher performs an essential function in the business world.

Market research lives on data, but most of the analysis doesn't require more than simple arithmetic. (If you *have* acquired a deep understanding of statistics, you can go far in market research.) Market researchers poll consumers in shopping malls, send product samples through the mail, and pore over mailing lists of buyers to find the right match. The basic tool of the market researcher is the fill-in-the-blanks survey form.

Market researchers are most common in consumer-goods companies, but many of the same methods can be applied to book and magazine publishing, financial services, banking, industrial products and non-profit organizations. The latest trend is the development of products for overseas as well as domestic markets.

Preparation for the field varies. It is possible to specialize in market research as part of a marketing degree. Others take extra courses in math and statistics while majoring in one of the liberal arts. Much of the specialized training is carried out on the job. Training in psychology or sociology is often useful at agencies that conduct personal polling (or when several people are interviewed simultaneously in a "focus group").

While entry-level researchers earn $19,000 to $24,000, senior researchers reach $60,000 or more.

Employers range from all the major corporations (who are continually polling their customers) to advertising agencies and marketing-services firms that do research on behalf of clients.

**American Marketing Association**
250 South Wacker Drive
Chicago, IL   60606
(312) 648-0536

# MATHEMATICIAN

### Mathematics, Physics

Math—yeech! That's the usual reaction of people contemplating the courses they are required to take in college. For the lucky few with a genuine knack for manipulating numbers, however, a math career can be an attractive goal.

There are about 46,000 mathematicians and statisticians at work these days, a total that the Bureau of Labor Statistics projects will rise by 32%, to 61,000, by the year 2000. Most of the 46,000 are doctorate scientists. The National Science Foundation defines the profession differently, as "mathematical scientist," and puts the number at a much larger 131,000. That total breaks evenly among workers with bachelor's, master's and doctorate degrees.

Mathematicians and statisticians (see **Statisticians**) work with numbers, and where there is a concentration of numbers, you will find these professionals. A large number of mathematicians work in scientific research, either in math itself ("pure" math) or with biologists, materials scientists, physicists, and others ("applied" math). Mathematical applications in medicine are a hot research area today.

Many mathematicians work for the federal government, especially in all its organizations that compile data:   the Departments of Defense, Health and Human Services, and Energy, as well as the Office of Management and Budget, the National Aeronautics and Space Administration, the Bureau of the Census, and the Bureau of Labor Statistics. In the private sector, very similar work goes on in actuarial science, statistical forecasting, and the like. In the go-go 1980s, Wall Street had a dalliance with mathematicians, but things have quieted there since.

Among the products of technology, mathematicians are perhaps most at home with electronics and computers. The design of electronic devices and circuits is usually an exercise in math, even for electronics engineers. In computers, the similarities between math and computer programming are also strong. In telecommunications and other forms of signal transmission, math is an important contributor to new understanding. For example, some of the most exciting mathematical developments of recent years have come out of the math teams at Bell Labs.

Whether in research, government, or private industry, the mathematician's work has changed dramatically due to the computer. Analyses that used to take hours on a mainframe computer (where the user would have to wait while his program was completed in batches) now takes a few minutes at a desktop PC. At the same time, the enormous power of supercomputers has given mathematical researchers a new window on number manipulations; several important math theories have already been confirmed by the programming strength of such machines.

In a 1989 survey of new graduates, the American Mathematical Society found that salaries for doctorate-level mathematicians ranged from a low of $29,500 in academic research to $44,000 in business and industry.

**American Mathematical Society**
PO Box 6248
Providence, RI   02940
(401) 272-9500

---

# MECHANICAL ENGINEER
### Industrial Engineering, Mechanical Engineering

At the heart of most technology is a machine—one as common as an automobile or as rare as an orbiting telescope. Where machines exist, usually there are mechanical engineers at work, designing, operating, or maintaining them. Mechanical engineering is one of the oldest and largest fields of engineering, and mechanical engineers find employment opportunities in most sectors of the economy, including manufacturing, transportation, utilities and in the many businesses where there are a concentration of computers.

A great number of mechanical engineers are employed as designers. Most vehicles, appliances, tools, and mechanical systems need constant updating as manufacturing costs, materials, and styles change. For example, a new car design may use more plastic than previous models, and will have modifications in, say, its engine, suspension, or pollution-control systems. Mechanical engineers conceive and design these components, and other mechanical engineers integrate all the new technology into a smoothly running (and selling!) car.

The American Society of Mechanical Engineers, the central organization for these engineers, is organized into subgroups that suggest where mechanical engineers work: manufacturing; energy conversion (i.e. power generation); materials and structures; environment and transportation; and systems.

There are about 225,000 mechanical engineers at work today, according to the Bureau of Labor Statistics, and the total is projected to rise to 269,000 (a 19.8% increase) by the year 2000. Demand is strong wherever manufacturing sectors are experiencing solid growth. Currently, these include the computer industry, aircraft (especially civil aircraft), chemicals, paper and food processing. Many of the engineers at work in these industries are less concerned with design and more concerned with getting the most efficient production from the machinery that cranks out the rolls of paper, barrels of chemicals, or jars of food.

Starting salaries for bachelor-level graduates are around $31,000, according to placement-office surveys. The average experienced mechanical engineer earns about $48,000, according to the Engineering Manpower Commission.

**American Society of Mechanical Engineers**
345 East 47th Street
New York, NY   10017
(212) 705-7722

---

# MEDIA PLANNER

### Anthropology, Communications, Performing Arts, Sociology

John Wanamaker, one of the inventors of the department store, is said to have once complained, "I know that half of my advertising dollars are wasted. Now, if only I knew which half. . . ." It is the role of the media planner to minimize that waste.

All advertising must be delivered through some medium, whether it is a small-town newspaper or a million-dollar, 60-second television spot during the Super Bowl. The media planner helps advise other executives at an advertising agency, and the client who is footing the bill, on which media to use. The media planner knows which programs or publications will best convey the advertising message and best reach its intended audience.

A few years ago, the *New York Times* reported that media planners, many of them young college graduates, were making and breaking magazines. If they declared that a new magazine was "in" with the right crowd of readers, it would be showered with millions of dollars of advertising. Another magazine, suddenly on the outside, could quickly go into a tailspin.

The debate continues over whether new magazines or shows succeed because they should, or because the all-important media planners decide that they should. In any case, the media planner has to support the recommendations with facts and research; the decisions are not arbitrary. Media planning can be considered a part of market research (see **Market Research**); the planner usually spends many hours studying the demographics of readership or audience for some event or publication. Then the cost of appearing in that outlet is assessed. The all-important ratio is the "CPM" (cost per thousand viewers) of showing an advertisement.

The job also requires good marketing judgment, since the type of reader or viewer must also be analyzed. Market researchers are drawing a finer and finer bead on potential customers for products; the media planner must then attempt to match that customer profile to the profile of the audience reached by the medium.

Media planning is carried out not only at advertising agencies, but also at major consumer-goods manufacturers. Also, savvy publishers and broadcasters have their own staffs of planners who show how the demographics of specific audiences can be assessed.

In general, the future prospects in media planning should match the growth in marketing, which is around 26%. Training in advertising and business administration is a plus when job-hunting.

**American Association of Advertising Agencies**
666 3rd Avenue
New York, NY 10017
(212) 682-2500

# MEDICAL TECHNOLOGIST

## Allied Health Professions, Biological Sciences

These days, the inside of a hospital can look like a NASA control room. There are flashing screens, beeping lights, humming electronic boxes and more tubes, pipes and wires than you could shake a catheter at. Modern medical care is largely dependent on electronics and instrumentation. Machines monitor the condition of a patient, control medications or therapies, and assist nurses and doctors in completing their work.

This mass of instruments needs constant maintenance. As electronics technology advances, specialists are needed to develop new or improved instruments to continue to raise the quality of care. Thus the medical technologist has become important.

Medical technology is a crossroads in technology and training. Some medical technologists are trained as doctors and surgeons, some as engineers (especially biomedical) or electronics engineers), and some as engineering technologists and technicians. Whatever their background, medical technologists are much in demand. The Bureau of Labor Statistics projects a 38% growth, to 471,000, for the general class of electronics technicians and technologists, and a 19% growth for the subspecialty of clinical technologists and technicians, to 288,000. (Technologists involved in the direct care of patients, such as therapists, are treated separately here.)

It's easy to see why medical technologists need a higher level of competence than other types of technologists. If a factory instrument breaks down, the company loses only the product that passed down the line until the instrument's fault was noticed. In a hospital, however, lives are at stake, practically every moment. Instruments have to work perfectly.

It is for this reason, among others, that the medical technology field is seeking to upgrade its professionalism. The leaders in the profession want to be identified as "clinical engineers" and to have licensing and certification procedures similar to those of other health-care professionals.

Currently, salaries are in the range of $22,000 to $30,000, depending on the level of training and the employer. Just under half of the medical technologists who belong to the Association for the Advancement of Medical Instrumentation work at hospitals; the remainder are at manufacturers, colleges and laboratories, government, and doctors's offices.

**Association for the Advancement of Medical Instrumentation**
Suite 400
3330 Washington Boulevard
Arlington, VA   22201
(703) 525-4890

---

# METALLURGICAL AND MATERIALS ENGINEER

**Chemical Engineering, Civil Engineering, Mechanical Engineering, Physics**
**(A few schools offer degrees in metallurgical engineering or materials science specifically.)**

Until a generation ago, the formal study of materials was primarily concerned with metals, especially steel. Since then, the steel industry has shrunk dramatically in the United States, and less research and development of steel technology is conducted here. Most metallurgical and materials engineering programs shrank along with the steel industry, and for a while, job opportunities were thin.

Those conditions are changing now. Materials engineering programs have broadened to include polymers (plastics), ceramics, and semiconductors. Even more significantly, the technology for new types of materials is zooming ahead. For example, engineers have produced:

• "warm" superconducting ceramics, which can conduct electricity with essentially no power loss

- diamond films, easily and cheaply manufactured, to be applied to knife edges, microelectronic components, or other specialty materials
- polymeric membranes, sheets of plastic that contain holes so small the membrane can separate one molecule from another

Most exciting of all, engineers are working on a method by which a block or sheet of material can be formed atom by atom to achieve highly specific (and often seemingly magical) properties.

Not all these technologies are being propelled forward by those with a metallurgical/materials engineering degree. Electrical engineers, heavily involved with microelectronics, are participants, as are physicists and chemists. Some civil engineers become experts at ceramics through working on new types of brick or concrete.

Generally, metallurgical/materials engineering is oriented toward research, and advanced degrees are common. Knowledge of the basic properties of matter must be combined with an understanding of state-of-the-art production equipment. The challenge is usually to take some intriguing new material out of the laboratory, where it might be produced in gram quantities, to the factory, where pounds or tons of it are to be made.

Traditional employers such as steel and metals refiners, building materials manufacturers, and plastics and fibers producers continue to hire these engineers. Growth areas for the future include microelectronics companies, aerospace firms, and high-technology research and development organizations. The Bureau of Labor Statistics projects a 13% growth rate, to about 22,000 positions, by the turn of the century, but this forecast uses traditional definitions of materials engineering involving steel or plastics. Growth outside the traditional employers should be far more dramatic.

Starting salaries, according to industry surveys, are around $30,000.

**Society for the Advancement of Materials and Process Engineering**
Box 2459
1055 West San Bernardino Road
Covina, CA   91722
(818) 331-0616

# MICROBIOLOGIST

## Biological Sciences

Biology is a big field and is very popular among college undergraduates, many of whom use the training as preparation for medical school. There are, however, a growing number of career opportunities in biology itself.

Biologists train and specialize at the graduate level, where a diverse array of fields exists, organized according to life forms. Microbiologists, simply put, study what is usually seen only under a microscope—single-celled life forms such as bacteria, or algae, fungi, and other plant forms. (See **Life Scientist** for other types of biologists.)

The American Society for Microbiology, 36,000 members strong, is the largest professional society of biologists; microbiology is the broadest field of biological study. The specialty is so popular for a good reason: a single microbe reveals much of what goes on among all life forms. For example, bacteria have been likened to "microchemical factories" that crank out myriad compounds as they adjust to their surroundings. By studying microbes, biologists gain insights to the functioning of nearly all other life forms.

The big news in microbiology is the array of techniques that have come to be called "biotechnology." Biotechnology, now a multi-billion-dollar business, became prominent in the 1970s with the first manipulation of genetic material. By splicing, transferring, or snipping genetic strings in microbes, it has become possible to create organisms that produce a desired biochemical composition, or that are resistant to certain chemicals, or that can digest synthetic materials (such as petrochemicals). Over the 1980s, an impressive group of new companies were formed to exploit these abilities; in the 1990s, many of them are bringing new pharmaceuticals or diagnostic techniques to market.

Microbiologists aid this effort by spending long hours in laboratories, running chemical analyses on genetically altered microbes, testing improved production techniques, or devising new methods of analyzing or categorizing biological functions. Much of the work is very similar to the way biology is learned in college; experiments are run, and junior scientists meet with senior scientists (i.e., their bosses) to analyze the results.

It has also become common for the microbiologist to spend time in the field: in the middle of a swamp, at the seashore, atop a city dump, in the jungle. The reason is that biotechnology is also providing insights into environmental problems, and even offering ways to clean them up. Many chemical spills are now being treated by specially developed microbes that literally eat the offending compound. With billions of dollars being committed to environmental cleanup, microbiologists have an opportunity to aid these efforts while gaining further knowledge of how life functions. The same is true for improving the flow of oil from underground reservoirs, for reducing the volume and toxicity of garbage dumps, and for improving the fertility of agricultural lands.

Starting salaries for bachelor-level biologists are around $21,500, according to recent surveys. However, well over half of biology majors go on to graduate schools (indeed, to become a microbiologist specifically, it is almost essential). For the overall field of biology, the Bureau of Labor Statistics projects that employment will rise by 26%, to around 68,000, by the year 2000.

**American Society for Microbiology**
1325 Massachusetts Avenue, NW
Washington, DC  20005
(202) 737-3600

---

# MORTGAGE BANKER

**Architecture and Urban Design, Business Administration**

Banks do many things, from serving businesses to setting up checking accounts for individuals. One of the central activities, however, is the management of home mortgages or real estate loans. This business is so large that it has developed its own profession, the mortgage banker. Note , too, that many mortgage bankers do not work at banks, but at financial organizations that amount to credit agencies: they provide mortgage money, but none of the other services we traditionally think of as banking.

Mortgage bankers are specialists in evaluating real estate and the credit worthiness of potential homeowners, and in managing the process of obtaining money to lend. The Bureau of Labor Statistics estimates that there are 172,000 loan officers and counselors, and that their numbers will grow to about 209,000 by the turn of the century, a 22% growth.

Having a home of one's own is still a central part of the American Dream, and for roughly two out of three families, it is a reality. By the late 1980s, some $3 trillion was wrapped up in home and business-property mortgages. Also by then, the annual rate of new mortgages reached about $450 billion. (Not all of these dollars are under the control of mortgage bankers; the majority is managed by commercial banks and other lending institutions.)

At the beginning of the 1990s, the mortgage banking industry is in turmoil, due primarily to the sickness of one of the key components of the American banking system: savings and loan associations. These banks have run up a debt (in terms of unserviceable loans) on the order of $300 billion. Yet because of the contorted logic by which banking is administered, many of these banks are still active mortgage providers. Their low loan rates create competition for healthier lending institutions.

At some point soon, the "savings and loan crisis" will come to a head, causing a new round of changes in how banks are administered. Until then, uncertainty will be the rule of the day. Even so, it is certain that the mortgage banking business will continue to exist in some shape or form. The simple reality is that a large portion of America's wealth is tied up in its homes.

To be successful at mortgage banking, training in finance and banking is strongly preferred; an MBA degree can help. Mortgage banking is divided into two activities: loan production (obtaining customers) and servicing. The former involves extensive managerial and marketing skills, while the latter involves financial analysis, data processing, and customer contact. The Mortgage Banking Association (Washington, DC) provides training and certification in both areas.

**Mortgage Bankers Association of America**
1125 15th Street, NW
Washington, DC 20005
(202) 861-6562

---

# MUSICIAN

### Performing Arts

To millions of people, music is like air or water—they couldn't live without it. That creates opportunities for the more than 200,000 professional musicians in America; it also creates one of the main problems. There always seems to be more musicians on hand than openings available. Getting steady work is a constant challenge.

The near-term prospects may be even dimmer due to a revolutionary change in music technology. The advent of powerful synthesizers capable of reproducing a dizzying array of sounds, is believed to be reducing opportunities for some types of performers. With the right equipment (whose cost is continually declining) a single musician or composer can simulate the sound of an entire symphony.

Obstacles like these have always challenged aspiring musicians. It still remains true that with the right mix of determination, talent and luck, a performer can go from a penniless nobody to a rich celebrity practically overnight.

As a result of the difficulties of earning a living, musicians have traditionally sought alternative or complementary careers. Teaching—in school systems or privately—is an obvious choice. There are over 60,000 music teachers, according to the Music Educators National Conference, a professional group. Working in musical media—radio, television, advertising, recordings, musical equipment, theater—represents another possibility.

The most prestigious professional music occupations are with symphonies, of which there are about 1,600 in the country. Reduced federal support of the arts, and generally lower charitable contributions, make life precarious for many symphonies. The most potentially lucrative option, of course, is to go for the gold with a pop music recording. There are dozens of other opportunities, which take a lot of digging to uncover. One of the largest of these is religious or choral music. Live music is performed at everything from nightclubs to weddings; these performances are essentially arranged on a freelance basis, with short-term contracts that pay a few hundred dollars per performance.

A college-level music education is not essential for most musical positions, except for teaching. Studying music at college provides valuable training time and the opportunity to network with teachers, professional musicians, and agents.

**Music Educators National Conference**
1902 Association Drive
Reston, VA   22091
(703) 860-4000

---

# NUCLEAR ENGINEER
### Chemical Engineering, Mechanical Engineering, Physics
### (A few schools offer degrees in nuclear engineering specifically.)

Hope seems to spring eternal that nuclear energy will come back into fashion. Ever since the accident at Three Mile Island in 1978, there has been no new order for a commercial nuclear power plant in the United States. Nuclear engineering departments have dwindled; epic battles have been fought over the startup of some new plants that were ordered in the mid-1970s, but completed only in the 1980s.

A very big "however" is that the career possibilities of nuclear engineers are not tied solely to commercial power production. True, that represents the largest existing or potential opportunity, but there are a variety of others. The US military, for one, uses a considerable number of nuclear power plants for ships, submarines, and satellites, and, not to be forgotten, nuclear weapons. In the commercial sector, nuclear medicine is a large and thriving field, involving chemotherapy for cancer patients and a variety of analytical technologies.

The biggest potential in the near future, however, is, ironically, in environmental work. The US Department of Energy faces a cleanup job whose cost has been estimated at $100 billion to be spread over the next decade or so, to correct the problems that have developed at a network of nuclear-material production facilities in operation since World War II. Moreover, we must dispose of the spent nuclear fuel from commercial plants—and the plants themselves, once they are worn out. Both these activities will employ large numbers of nuclear engineers in the future.

Finally, the few remaining commercial contractors of nuclear power plants have regrouped and are attempting to garner interest in so-called "inherently safe" power systems. The ongoing debate over acid rain and the greenhouse effect—two forms of air pollution tied to conventional non-nuclear power production—may make nuclear power more attractive in coming years.

For the present, only a few hundred nuclear engineering graduates come off college campuses every year, joining the approximately 14,000 working nuclear engineers. Projected growth is 1% or less, according to the Bureau of Labor Statistics. Starting salaries, though, are high—in the neighborhood of $30,000.

Nuclear engineers study a series of courses similar to chemical or mechanical engineers, learning about all types of power generation and conversion, and specifically how radioactivity is started, sustained and shut down, and what materials are suitable for containing it. Much of this training is applicable to non-nuclear power production, so nuclear engineers have job possibilities even at non-nuclear utilities. The federal government, through the Department of Energy and the Nuclear Regulatory Commission, employs large numbers of nuclear engineers and continues to hire new ones.

**American Nuclear Society**
555 North Kensington Avenue
La Grange Park, IL   60525
(312) 352-6611

# OCCUPATIONAL THERAPIST

### Allied Health Professions

Occupational therapists help people disabled by mental illness, disease, handicap, or aging to establish or regain control over their lives by teaching them basic living skills (dressing, cooking, driving a car, etc.). Over the longer term, therapists also help people regain cognitive skills.

Occupational therapy, like other types of therapy, will be growing rapidly in coming years because of the rising number of aged people. The Bureau of Labor Statistics projects a 49% growth, to 48,000 practitioners. Starting salaries are around $21,000, and can raise to about $40,000.

In school and in practice, occupational therapists usually specialize in a type of patient: the injured, the mentally disabled, the aged, or children. About half of all occupational therapists work at hospitals.

**American Occupational Therapy Association**
PO Box 1725
Rockville, MD    20850
(301) 948-9626

# OPERATIONS/SYSTEMS RESEARCHER

### Computer Science and Engineering, Industrial Engineering, Mathematics

Consider a modern, large-city airport. The problems of getting airplanes in and out are obvious, especially when weather turns bad or when a rush-hour backup begins. Also consider everything else that makes an airport function: fuel, supplies, food, workers, package shipments, automobiles, mass-transit systems. How can they all work together smoothly?

Such questions occupy operations/systems researchers. Typically, they deal with the logistics of delivering or receiving large quantities of things—money, goods, equipment, or people. They see to it that the things and people are processed rapidly and efficiently, and sent on their way.

Operations/systems research originated in military planning, especially during World War II, when we had to work out the logistics of sending hundreds of thousands of soldiers around the world and supplying them with essential resources.

Today operations researchers are involved in a wide range of logistical issues. They work at securities firms or banks, managing the flow of customer orders and financial deposits. Many also work at organizations that concentrate on transportation—airlines, trucking companies, mass transit systems. Some still work in the military. A growing number are employed by firms that offer computer data processing; in this case, the issue is how to manage the flow of information into and out of the firm's computer banks.

The computer in turn is also an essential tool for modern operations/systems research. Many questions on the distribution of objects and activities are being resolved by analyzing computer models.

The operations research curriculum includes heavy doses of math and statistics; more than a few mathematicians find employment in the field. Although baccalaureate degrees can be earned in operations research, employers prefer those with master's degrees or even a doctorate. Pay starts rather low—around $20,000 —although it can rise dramatically during a career, since the issues the field addresses concern upper-management.

Dramatic growth is projected for this field—a whopping 55%, according to the Bureau of Labor Statistics. There will be around 85,000 operations researchers by the turn of the century, the bureau predicts. Student interest has also been rising, with class sizes around 2,500 at the baccalaureate level.

**Operations Research Society of America**
Mt. Royal and Guilford Avenues
Baltimore, MD   21202
(301) 528-4146

# OPTOMETRIST

## Biological Sciences

Almost three out of five Americans wear glasses or contacts. That fact may depress the rest of us, but it makes optometrists happy. These are the medical specialists who examine eyes and prescribe lenses or treatment. (Optometrists are not to be confused with "dispensing opticians," as they are called, who are the technicians at the optical store who fill the prescription and help select frames or types of contacts.) The other optical specialist is the ophthalmologist, who is trained to perform eye surgery or diagnosis of disease as well as prescribe lenses.

As America's population ages, optometry will grow. That is one of the reasons that the projected growth rate is 16%—slightly above the average for all professionals—to 43,000 job slots. The actual number of working optometrists is somewhat less, because many of them hold two jobs; a position at a hospital or clinic and a private practice. Some 54% are sole practitioners exclusively.

Optometrists receive six to eight patients per day, according to data from the American Optometric Association. They perform a diagnosis using equipment that measures visual acuity, which can then be used to select the proper eyewear prescription. Some states now permit optometrists to prescribe certain medications for eye conditions.

Like dentists, at the outset of their careers optometrists can try to start a practice, or can buy into the existing practice of a working optometrist. Initial earnings are around $30,000, rising to an average of $60,000–70,000 for those who have built up a practice.

There are a relatively small number (18, including two in Canada) of schools that provide education in optometry, which usually consumes 4 years. Most students already have their baccalaureate, although it is possible to go into a "pre-optometry" program that reduces the number of undergraduate years. An admissions examination is required to enter any one of the schools.

**American Optometric Association**
243 North Lindbergh Boulevard
St. Louis, MO   63141
(314) 991-4100

---

# PARALEGAL

## Classics, English, History, Political Science

The relatively new paralegal profession (a.k.a. *"legal assistant"*) was one of the fastest-growing professions of the 1980s. Its growth has been fueled by the corresponding growth of lawyers and law firms; both are the beneficiaries of the much broader role of legal and regulatory activities in our society.

Critics have noted that suing and counter-suing usually does not add much to society at large, and that other countries, notably Japan, have a much much lower level of lawsuits, court cases, and regulations. These things may be true; nevertheless, future growth of the paralegal/legal assistant field is expected to continue at a rapid clip.

The Bureau of Labor Statistics' projection for 1990s growth is 75%, up to 145,000 practitioners—one of the highest growth rates of any professional occupation. Community colleges, universities, and trade schools are all expanding their programs; with such dramatic growth forecasts, and with such a high level of student interest, it probably won't be long before the field is flooded with applicants.

One of the nagging concerns of the paralegal profession is the extent to which lawyers will allow them significant, responsible work, as opposed to clerical and secretarial tasks. Many paralegals complain that they are treated (and paid) hardly any differently from a secretary. Yet others have positions of high responsibility, even including contact with the clients of the law firm. Their responsibilities include performing research in case law (to find precedents for various legal actions), conducting interviews, compiling reports, and managing the flow of information that piles up with most cases.

All these things require some special knowledge, which is now being taught in college programs. The candidate paralegal can also make himself or herself more valuable by specializing in some area of law, such as malpractice, patent law, public policy, or estate planning. Specialization does present some risk, though, as one's area of expertise could become outmoded.

For the time being, the message seems to be: look closely at a law firm before deciding to join it. Find out whether paralegals have room and incentive for professional growth. There are also other employers to consider, such as hospitals, insurance companies, government, and the courts. All these organizations need to manage the flow of information that keeps the legal eagles flying.

A 1988 survey by the National Association of Legal Assistants (of both members and non-members) revealed that 91% of paralegals had more than a high school education; 34% had a bachelor's degree or better. Average total compensation was $26,023; in large cities, the average was over $30,000.

**National Association of Legal Assistants, Inc.**
Suite 300
1601 South Main
Tulsa, OK   74119
(918) 587-6828

**National Federation of Paralegal Associations**
Suite 201
104 Wilmot Road
Deerfield, IL   60015
(408) 940-8800

# PETROLEUM ENGINEER

**Chemical Engineering, Chemistry, Geology, Mechanical Engineering**
**(Several schools offer programs in petroleum engineering specifically.)**

The early 1980s were something like an extended New Year's party for the petroleum business. Skyrocketing prices led to a lot of new drilling activity; each well that came in with a sufficient flow made overnight millionaires. The party came to an end around 1982 when, instead of continuing a march toward a projected price of $45 per barrel, oil slumped to $12. It has since recovered, but the US oil industry is still a little hung over from the good times.

This recent history affected the fortunes of the petroleum engineering profession. When the times were good, students flocked to the engineering programs; graduating class sizes reached 1,550 in 1985 (the students had started their engineering program in 1981). By 1987, it had dropped to 1,064, and there is yet to be an upswing in numbers of students or, indeed, jobs.

That's the bad news. The good news is that the United States remains one of the world's largest oil producers. The majority of the largest oil firms are American, and while most of the action in oil is occurring overseas, there is a distinctly American flavor to much of the oil business. There will be new jobs for graduating petroleum engineers indefinitely into the future. Indeed, while the number of job offers extended to BS petroleum engineering graduates remains well below its historic highs, the salaries are around $33,000—near the top of all college graduates.

Typically, a working petroleum engineer is either analyzing the results of preliminary drillings, or actively managing a drilling project. In school, would-be engineers study geology and petrology—the actions of oil in the ground—and become familiar with the equipment used to explore for and recover crude oil and gas. When a field is discovered, "reservoir engineering" determines how it should be exploited for maximum yield. A growth area for the future is enhanced oil recovery, the injection of steam or carbon dioxide to raise the productivity of the process.

One of the problems that petroleum engineers encountered when the job market fell apart was the dearth of alternative careers outside the oil-producing business. Some engineers were able to transfer their skills successfully from oil to environmental work, especially in the removing of a hazardous chemical from groundwater or from deep in the soil. There is still a possibility of studying petroleum engineering and then going to work in the environmental remediation business, but the more direct route is to study geology or civil engineering.

Another common tactic is to prepare oneself to work overseas. This can be done by studying a foreign language while in school, and by emphasizing an understanding of the geology and oil-extraction practices of other parts of the world. In the US, according to federal data, the number of working petroleum engineers will remain stagnant at around 23,000.

**Society of Petroleum Engineers**
c/o American Institute of Mining, Metallurgical and Petroleum
  Engineers (AIME)
345 East 47th Street
New York, NY   10017
(212) 705-7695

---

# PHARMACIST

### Biological Sciences, Chemistry

Roughly $50 billion worth of drugs and pharmaceutical preparations are dispensed each year in the US, according to the Department of Commerce. A key figure in this distribution is the pharmacist, who prepares the dosage and provides instruction to the user.

We usually know pharmacists as the people behind the tall counter at the drugstore; about three out of four pharmacists work there. The remainder are employed at hospitals and clinics, in education, and in industry. The drugstore pharmacist often shares drug-dispensing duties with the responsibilities of owning a small-business (the drugstore). Those responsibilities include meeting a payroll and keeping inventories.

Drugstore retailing is about a $70-billion-per-year business, with more than half of that volume from "Group II" stores, defined by the Department of Commerce as those with 11 or more establishments. In the latter case, the pharmacist is usually a salaried employee of the chain, which means that the pharmacist has fewer business-management worries. On the downside, these pharmacists lose some of their independence.

Universities offer a 5-year program for the bachelor degree; it is also possible to attend a program for 6 years and graduate with a Doctor of Pharmacy (D. Pharm) degree, which is desirable for clinical work. College students majoring in something other than pharmacy can attend these graduate schools for about 3 years to get the D. Pharm.

Pharmacy had been losing popularity among college students, but this trend reversed itself in the late 1980s. It's a good thing, because Bureau of Labor Statistics projections show that 27% more pharmacists will be needed by the end of the century, a growth rate well above the average for all professions. Starting salaries are around $27,000.

**American Association of Colleges of Pharmacy**
1426 Prince Street
Alexandria, VA 22314
(703) 739-2330

---

# PHOTOGRAPHER

**Architecture and Urban Design, Art History, Communications, Performing Arts, Visual Arts**

Notwithstanding the growing popularity of film and video (see **Cinematographer**), the photography profession is much larger and is projected to grow at about the same rate. The Bureau of

Labor Statistics estimates the number of photographers working in 1988 at 94,000, and projects an 18% growth to 111,000.

Just over a third of all photographers work at portrait studios; some of these are employees of studio chains, and the rest are independent businesspeople. We can count on our own vanity to keep photo studios in operation—who doesn't want at least one professionally produced photo?

There is, of course, much more to photography, including photography that winds up in museums and galleries. For "fine" photography, the usual career path begins by becoming an assistant to an established photographer. While lugging lighting equipment and cameras around, assistant photographers learn the ropes and gradually develop their own styles and clientele.

Communications media, including newspaper and magazine publishers, news organizations, advertising agencies, and public relations firms employ large numbers of photographers. These photographers generally earn more than the independents (at many newspapers, their pay scales are set by unions), and of course, the work is steadier.

Going to college or attending special schools is not required to become a photographer—about 45% of the photographers who are members of the American Society of Magazine Photographers have no advanced training. More school certainly can't hurt, however, especially when it comes to keeping abreast of the rapid changes in photographic technology. Students also gain greater access to photo labs and teachers, and can get started on building a network of contacts.

**American Society of Magazine Photographers**
419 Park Avenue South
New York, NY   10016
(212) 889-9144

**National Press Photographers Association**
Suite 306
3200 Croasdale Drive
Durham, NC   27705
(800) 289-6772

# PHYSICAL THERAPIST

## Allied Health Professions

Physical therapy, which can accelerate the mending of injuries or lessen the effects of aging or sickness, is growing faster than practically all other professions. According to the Bureau of Labor Statistics, the number of physical therapists will increase by 57%, to 107,000, by the year 2000.

Physical therapy involves the manipulation of injured joints, massage, and guidance for exercise by the patient. The therapist must usually have a high level of physical strength, stamina, and a knowledge of how exercise affects the body and spirit. Most physical therapists work at hospitals, and about 20% have a private practice. Only a few states, though, permit the therapist to work independently of a medical doctor.

A 4-year degree is the usual training for this job; some schools offer second-baccalaureate programs (in which one obtains a bachelor degree in some general field, then has specific training for physical therapy) or master's programs. Salaries start at around $22,000 to $24,000. The highest earnings are possible with a private practice.

**American Physical Therapy Association**
1111 North Fairfax Street
Alexandria, VA   22314
(703) 684-2782

# PHYSICIAN (MEDICAL DOCTOR)

## Biological Sciences, Chemical Engineering, Chemistry

Well, of course. What bright student hasn't thought, briefly or for a long time, about becoming a doctor? The field is high-profile and high-earning. It's no wonder that medical school applications are so high.

Doctors are the central figures in America's $661-billion health-care industry. In fact, doctor's services themselves cost an estimated $137.5 billion, according to the US Department of Commerce. While starting salaries for interns at hospitals (where they complete their residency prior to licensing) are around $24,000, the average salary of all doctors is in the neighborhood of $150,000.

We know what doctors do from our experiences in their examining rooms or in hospital beds. What we don't see are the high liability-insurance policies today's doctors must carry, the paperwork, and the hunt for more patients. Salary growth today isn't what it was 5 or 10 years ago.

Doctors can specialize in many kinds of patients, from pediatrics to geriatrics. Others specialize in various parts of the body—cardiology (the heart); surgery; dermatology (the skin); neurology (the brain); endocrinology (the hormone system); and so on—almost as many specialties as there are parts to the body. These days, only about 13% of working physicians have general or family practices; specialization usually provides a higher income.

Most larger colleges and universities have special pre-med programs, or have academic advisors that help guide students on to medical school. Many different undergraduate majors can be studied while the strong requirements for a medical school application are fulfilled (mostly chemistry and biology courses).

Most students spend 4 years in medical school, then undertake 3 or more years of residency. Specialties combine residency with more study. The number of graduations from medical school has held fairly steady for the late 1980s; while roughly the same number of students are being admitted, there have been fewer applications to medical school, so the chances of being admitted are marginally better today.

The turn-of-the-century projection for physicians' occupational growth is 28%, well above the average for all professions. So even though there is talk of a glut of doctors, and fears that earnings growth will be constrained by strict budgeting by insurance companies and the federal government, medicine will be a solid career opportunity for years to come.

**American Medical Association**
535 North Dearborn Street
Chicago, IL 60610
(312) 645-5000

---

# PHYSICIST

### Mathematics, Physics

Physics has been the king of sciences since the turn of the century. The prestigious training provided by a physics program is broadly applicable in a range of industries, including electronics, materials sciences, geotechnology, and instrumentation.

Roughly 5,200 BS degrees are awarded each year in physics. According to the American Institute of Physics, roughly half of these graduates go on to jobs, about a third attend graduate school in physics, and the remainder enter other types of graduate programs.

Most industrial physicists work in research, either as principal researchers on materials or electronics technology, or as the specialists that operate complex analytical devices and computers for a wide variety of industrial research projects. In 1988, average salaries were $26,500 for those in industry, and $23,200 for all types of BS degree holders. At the master's level, the overall average was $31,200, and at the PhD level, the average ranged as high as $40,800, depending on the permanence of the position.

A strong background in math is essential to a physics degree; in fact, physicists divide themselves between the "theoretical" camp, where nearly all the study and work is mathematical in nature, and the "experimental" camp, where analysis of the properties of matter and energy is stressed. The latter group has a better chance of landing jobs, by a two-out-of-three margin.

In practice, the physicist may be running the experiments necessary to build a new type of electronic component, an energy-conversion system, or a new analytical instrument that exploits some property of matter and energy to provide a desired result.

Physicists in production may run the complex photographic and chemical-processing equipment used in manufacturing electronic components, or operate a specialized instrument to study materials.

Physics has enjoyed a renaissance in the past two years, with some potentially revolutionary discoveries. One of these is the discovery of "warm" superconductors, which can conduct electricity with virtually no power loss. Another is the use of light in optical fibers, which is well on its way to replacing copper wires for telephones, and thereby creating a new multi-billion-dollar industry. This has proven to be a boon to telecommunications, automation equipment, and sensors and instruments.

Many physicists also teach; at the master's level, about 10% of the degree-winners in 1988 wound up in education, while at the PhD level, the number rose to 25%.

Over this decade, the number of physics positions is expected to rise by 13% (roughly the average for all types of professions), reaching 20,600 in the year 2000. This figure from the Bureau of Labor Statistics, however, doesn't include all the physicists working as researchers or production personnel.

**American Institute of Physics**
345 East 45th Street
New York, NY   10017
(212) 661-9404

# PHYSIOLOGIST

### Biological Sciences

Were you nauseated or thrilled at the prospect of dissecting a frog in your high school biology class? If you eagerly grabbed the scalpel, you may have the makings of a physiologist.

Physiologists study how life functions in plants and animals. While much of the research is directed at the cellular level, like microbiologists' work, the core of physiology is organs and systems. The results of physiological research can be seen in new surgery techniques, improved medications and treatments for disease, and more complete rehabilitation of handicaps.

There are about 7,000 physiologists at work today, based on the membership of the American Physiological Society (APS). More than half work in research, mostly at medical schools and clinics. While it is possible to study physiology as an undergraduate, the great majority of working physiologists have advanced degrees: PhD, MD, or combination.

The day-to-day work of the physiologist is very much like that of most scientists: long hours in the laboratory conducting experiments and analyzing samples through a microscope or other scientific instrument. A considerable amount of work is done with animals (alive or dead), and for this reason, APS and others have been under siege from animal-rights activists.

Physiologists have many specialties: cardiovascular (the largest), cell/tissue, endocrine, environmental, gastrointestinal, muscle/exercise, neural, renal, and respiratory. There are also general or comparative physiology researchers.

According to a 1988 survey of its academic members, APS found that the starting salary for an instructor is about $24,000, assistant professors earn an average of $33,000, while experienced professors and departmental chairs earn between $50,000 and $100,000.

With the general increase in funds supporting medical care and research, there should be no problem finding a job in the future. APS, in fact, is growing concerned about a looming shortage of trained physiologists in the early years of the 21st century.

**American Physiological Society**
9650 Rockville Pike
Bethesda, MD   20814
(301) 530-7164

# POLITICAL SCIENTIST

### History, Political Science

Since ancient times, people have debated over the appropriate ways of governing citizens, yet political science became a specialty apart from philosophy only in this century, and primarily at American universities.

Political science is a popular college major, with about 28,000 BA graduates each year. It is clearly ideal preparation for those contemplating a career that will interact with state or federal government or the elective and governing processes. Those who want to work specifically as *political scientists* will need a PhD.

Most political scientists work at universities and colleges. There are about 6,000 faculty across the country, and the number is not expected to rise during this decade.

College-level teaching is not the *only* thing political scientists do, however. Some are involved in community services, business, or government. Political scientists can be effective lobbyists for trade or professional associations, administrative specialists for the legislative or executive branches, or leaders and strategists for community-action groups. All these positions use their interest in, and familiarity with, the governing process.

Courses in political science stress the importance of gathering data through surveys or research. The numbers are often prepared and analyzed by computer. This training helps political scientists weigh the benefits of one course of government action over another. These analytical skills can also be used in non-political fields such as market research, advertising, fundraising, or social work.

Many political science faculties are part of a larger department, often called public affairs. Public-affairs training leads to administrative roles in city, state, or federal government.

The possible career directions can be summed up by the largest groups within the American Political Science Association (APSA): intergovernmental relations; urban politics; political organizations and parties; and laws, courts, and judicial processes.

A 1989 survey of political science faculty performed by the APSA showed that the average salary of a full professor was around $49,000; assistant or associate professors earned between $27,000 and $36,000. Overall growth is likely to mirror that of all the social sciences, which the Bureau of Labor Statistics pegs at 239,000 jobs by the turn of the century, up 23% from the 1988 figure.

**American Political Science Association**
1527 New Hampshire Avenue, NW
Washington, DC   20036
(202) 483-2512

# PROPERTY MANAGER

### Architecture and Urban Design, Civil Engineering

Without taking inflation into consideration, real property values doubled from the mid-1970s to the mid-1980s. Many people made fortunes while values were going up. The new owners have a larger stake in their properties now, however—more personal or business assets are tied up in owning land and buildings. They need to take care of this property, and to run it efficiently. Enter the property manager. This profession, which applies the skills of the modern business manager to real estate, is expected to grow by 19% during this decade, reaching 267,000.

Property management is a good way to become familiar with the forces that drive the real estate business—how buildings fit the needs of their tenants, what choices tenants make, and what makes a tenant loyal to or dissatisfied with a property owner.

The day-to-day work of a property manager depends on the type of project being managed, and the nature of the management company. A *resident manager* controls the services and facilities of a building. In an apartment building, for example, the manager makes sure basic services are provided, budgets for additional services, and keeps an eye on the sale or rental of unoccupied apartments. In commercial property, the manager makes sure that the tenants are abiding by the building's rules and reviews the needs of tenants. (A common need today, for example, is for updated wiring to support all the computers and communications equipment.)

An *asset manager*, on the other hand, is a higher-level executive more concerned with the overall profitability and financial health of a project than its day-to-day operations. An asset manager may be the representative of a deep-pocketed investor, who wants a certain rate of return for an investment but is too far removed from the real estate business to know how to maintain the property's value.

According to the Institute of Real Estate Management (IREM), almost three-quarters of its members have a bachelor's degree or better. IREM sponsors a certification process (requiring 5 years of management experience and a series of examinations); managers who are in training for this trademarked CPM designation earn between $25,000 and $42,600. Experienced managers can earn $50,000 or more.

**Institute of Real Estate Management**
430 North Michigan Avenue
Chicago, IL   60611
(312) 661-1930
(This organization is affiliated with the National Association of
   Realtors)

---

# PSYCHOLOGIST

### Philosophy and Religion, Psychology

A growing number of counselors and therapists help us deal with the complexities of modern life. While many of the 40,000 psychology graduates each year were attracted in part by the opportunity to learn about themselves, as professionals they focus on helping others understand themselves.

A bachelor-level degree is good preparation for a wide variety of professions where it helps to understand the way other people think, including marketing research, advertising, sales, human-resources management, and counseling. Professional psychologists, though, need a master's or doctorate degree and a state license.

The psychological specialty within the business world is industrial psychology which studies people in a working environment. Industrial psychologists help factory or office managers allocate work appropriately among staff, and devise new ways to motivate people to cooperate for maximum effectiveness.

Personal counselors are usually called clinical psychologists. They may specialize in family psychology, child, or adolescent psychology, or therapy for criminals, substance abusers, or the handicapped. The psychologist usually holds a consultation with the individual or family, sometimes in a group setting. The psychologist analyzes the situation, then recommends various types of therapy, medical care, or changes in lifestyle. Whereas psychiatry and psychotherapy emphasize internal, intrapersonal problems and issues (and usually require a greater degree of medical training), psychology emphasizes external, interpersonal concerns. There is, however, a certain degree of overlap, especially in clinical psychology. Bear in mind, though, that the training of a psychiatrist usually takes a much different track when compared with psychologists; the former are medical doctors who take years of additional training.

Salaries for graduate-level psychologists in private practice are between $30,000 and $50,000, depending on the type of therapy and amount of experience. A generally bright future is projected for psychologists, according to the Bureau of Labor Statistics:   the number of jobs will rise by 27%, to about 132,000, by the year 2000.

**American Psychological Association**
Educational Affairs Office
1200 17th Street, NW
Washington, DC   20036
(202) 955-7600

# PUBLIC ADMINISTRATOR

**Accounting, Architecture and Urban Design, Communications, Economics, Education, History, Political Science, Sociology (Schools of public administration, primarily at the graduate level, are also available.)**

"Bureaucrat" is a job title that is often spoken in frustration. Yet these professionals are essential to our society, and worthwhile and significant careers can be found in the public sector.

Some people in politics are elected to their jobs, others appointed. We will consider the latter—the public administrators who manage 1.2 trillion in federal revenues and $600 billion in state and local funds.

Local government is the largest kind, with 10 million civil servants. There are about 4 million state employees and 3 million federal ones (not including the military), according to the Department of the Census. Despite years of "cost-cutting" and "belt-tightening," all levels of government have grown larger in recent years. The largest part of this labor force is education, with over 7 million (including 4 million teachers). Health and hospitals is second (1.65 million); the Postal Service is third (754 million); and police services are fourth (760 million).

Among professional administrators of all that government, the most common background is financial administration and accounting. The government needs to keep the books and to manage service agencies, construction budgets, and the like. Jobs in agencies administering the police, health-care or natural resources require special training, usually at the master's level. Lawyers are sprinkled throughout all levels of government.

To prepare for a career in one of the specialized government functions, it is best to obtain an advanced degree, such as public administration, followed by a specialization in health-care, natural resources, or whatever.

Pay is almost categorically lower in government than for comparable positions in the private sector. Job security, however, is much higher. While many people feel that civil service is a dead end as a career, the smart ones realize that it is very wise to obtain valuable experience in government service while young, and to turn that experience into a lucrative private-sector career later. Such institutions as the district attorney's office for courtroom lawyers, or taxation and zoning bodies for income and real estate, are well-trodden pathways to high-profile, high-paying private sector jobs.

One growth area during the past several years has been private-public partnerships, which are quasi-governmental organizations that combine resources and personnel from the private sector with government officials. These organizations are improving schools and low-income housing, and are pioneering in "privatization" (the contracting-out of what are traditionally considered to be public works).

The range of salaries in the public sector is broader than one might imagine. According to the College Placement Council, the lowest starting salaries were in social services counseling (about $17,700) and the highest were in finance and taxation ($24,200).

Only minimal growth is expected for civil service over the next decade, but rapid turnover is one of the marks of the field, so opportunities for job-market entrants will continually appear.

Most civil service jobs are posted at city or state personnel offices, and regional Federal Job Centers. Federal job information may also be available at local offices of Congresspeople. Several of the key executive-branch agencies, such as Treasury, Environmental Protection Agency, Federal Bureau of Investigation, and National Security Agency, visit college campuses.

**American Society for Public Administration**
1120 G. Street NW
Washington, DC   20005
(202) 393-7878

# PUBLICIST

**Art History, Classics, Communications, English, Performing Arts, Political Science, Visual Arts**

Today, good public relations (PR) is essential to companies, non-profit organizations, and government agencies. Companies need PR professionals because their products face stiff competition; charities need them to help fight for contributions; and the government needs them to help establish new policies.

In the corporate world, public relations creates a favorable impression that becomes the foundation of advertising campaigns and direct selling.

Most public relations professionals do work for businesses. Many work at PR agencies that handle the needs of a company or organization for a fee. Other public relations professionals work in government, where they're called public information officers. Public relations for the financial community is called investor relations (see **Investor Relations Manager**).

The Bureau of Labor Statistics estimates that 91,000 publicists were working in 1988 and projects growth to 105,000 by the turn of the century—on the button for average growth for all professions.

Writing is the central skill of the publicist. Most entry-level positions involve drafting press releases or scripting filmed or live presentations. Speech writing is also sometimes called for. For these reasons, journalism school is often the desired educational background. Actual experience on a newspaper or other public medium is even better. Any liberal arts program with strong writing requirements can also serve as background. For highly technical fields such as medical products or electronics, training in science or engineering is often sought, but good communication skills must be proven.

Salaries vary with educational background, employer, and region of the country. The average for entry-level positions is around $18,000 to $20,000.

With experience, the publicist learns to handle different media, and to package a message so that it appeals to a certain publication or television program. With additional training in business management—in school or on the job—the publicist working at an agency can become an account executive, the manager who maintains primary contact with clients and leads a team of publicists.

**Public Relations Society of America**
33 Irving Place
New York, NY   10003
(212) 995-2230

---

# PURCHASING AGENT

### Accounting, Business Administration, Civil Engineering, Industrial Engineering, Mechanical Engineering

Before a manufacturer finally sells a product to a customer, a lot of intermediate goods are bought and sold. Businesses buy raw materials, production equipment, building materials, typewriters, and paper clips. The purchasing agent is responsible for making the best purchases for the best prices.

One might think that a purchasing agent simply reads part numbers out of a catalogue, writes up an order, then goes to lunch, but consider this:  if a factory's raw materials aren't delivered on time, it might have to shut down until they arrive. You can buy a rug or chair this week or next month—but corporations need their deliveries in a timely manner. Thus the purchasing agent must be familiar with the character and capability of suppliers, not just the price and type of goods being purchased. Also, the supply contracts set up between businesses can be extremely complex. Finally, any good purchasing agent is always on the lookout for alternative sources of supply.

Purchasing management had been a fairly staid profession in past years, but several trends are revolutionizing the field. One difference is the ease of obtaining materials from abroad; for example, a freeze that destroys Florida's orange crop instantaneously creates demand for juice exported from Brazil. Purchasing managers now find their suppliers all over the world.

Another trend is the growing interdependence between suppliers and producers. The major automotive companies, for instance, now spend considerable time at the factories of their suppliers, checking the quality of components before they are shipped to the assembly plants. Purchasing agents can find themselves spending more time at their suppliers' plants than at their home plants. The purchasing agent must also be able to translate upper-management's requirements for improvements, and decide whether or not to pay more for higher quality. Computers are also changing the purchase function. Bills are often paid by electronic-funds transfer rather than by check, for example.

Experience, rather than a college degree, had been the qualification for the purchasing agent, but college degrees, even MBAs, are becoming more common. About two-thirds of the members of the National Association of Purchasing Management (NAPM), according to a 1986 survey, had a college degree. The most powerful combination for manufacturing purchasing agents is an undergraduate degree in engineering combined with an MBA. This survey also showed that the medium age for purchasing agents was 46 years, and the average salary around $35,000 (starting salaries are around $20,000). These agents are responsible for the distribution of $6 million to $10 million per year. Projected growth in purchasing is 15%, the average for all professions.

**National Association of Purchasing Management**
PO Box 22160
Tempe, AZ   85282
(602) 752-6276

# RADIO/TELEVISION ANNOUNCER

### Communications, English, Performing Arts

The pinnacle of the announcing profession is a regular appearance on a nationally televised show, whether it is the evening news or a morning talk show. Thousands of experienced announcers compete for these positions. Just as newspaper journalists start at local papers and move closer to the big-city dailies, announcers start at local radio or television stations and keep moving toward bigger or more prestigious stations.

A synonym for radio/television announcer is a communications "personality," which describes one of the key qualifications. Visually and audibly, the announcer's force of personality must be able to engage the viewer or listener.

Getting ahead in the profession, however, calls for a broad array of skills, because most announcers start as generalists in the radio or television station, acting as reporters, news editors, and even technicians.

The virtual explosion of new communications channels, including cable, short-distance radio, direct satellite broadcasting, and videocassettes, is creating new opportunities for announcers. One such opportunity is taped or recorded information—whether it be an exercise cassette or a wildlife documentary.

The Bureau of Labor Statistics projects a 19% growth, to 67,000, for announcers by the turn of the century.

**National Association of Broadcasters**
1771 N Street, NW
Washington, DC   20036
(800) 368-5644

---

# REAL ESTATE SALES BROKER

**Architecture and Urban Design, Business Administration,
Political Science**

In most states, you can be certified to sell real estate just by passing a not-too-difficult examination. However, college students shouldn't ignore real estate sales. A strong educational background can be good preparation for the more complex, sophisticated sales projects, and, depending on the initiative of the agent, the path to management or proprietorship can be shorter with higher education. There are three specialties in selling real estate owned by someone else: the agent, the broker, and the appraiser.

The agent is the entry-level position. Advancement is tied to sales success. This kind of selling requires excellent communication skills. Remember that buying a home or business location is the largest decision an individual or business makes. The agent has to be able to understand the needs of potential customers, then find the appropriate building or land. The agent works for the seller, not the buyer.

The broker has a contract to represent the owners or operators of buildings in sales or rentals. A broker is often a small businessperson who has successfully sold real estate in a certain territory. Brokers employ agents and share the commissions from the sales. A broker must spend time developing ties to local businesspeople, and of course, must have a group of successful sales agent. Some brokers act as building managers (see **Property Manager**), and some, having had experience in what makes a local real estate market trick, are developers themselves.

The projected growth rate for real estate agents is 16%, just above the average for all professions. There are a lot of real estate agents—the Bureau of Labor Statistics counts 311,000. Many, however, are part-timers.

The projected growth rate for brokers is 20%, to 84,000 positions over the next decade. Brokers who handle commercial property as well as homes take advantage of business trends in both of these markets.

The last specialty, the appraiser, is a professional who has received training in the proper methods for assessing the value of a property. Appraisals takes into consideration local market conditions, the quality of construction, and the location of the property. Bankers depend on fair appraisals in order to decide whether or not the selling price of a property is reasonable; the bank requires reasonable selling prices in order to recover its investment in the mortgage should the owner default. There are about 41,000 appraisers; their projected growth rate is 20%.

The earnings of agents and brokers depend on their sales, and the earnings of appraisers depend on their number and complexity of evaluations. According to the National Association of Realtors, full-time agents earned about $19,000 in the mid-1980s; brokers and appraisers earned about $35,000.

**National Association of Realtors**
430 North Michigan Avenue
Chicago, IL 60611
(312) 329-8200

**Society of Real Estate Appraisers**
225 North Michigan Avenue
Chicago, IL 60601
(800) 819-2400

---

# REGIONAL PLANNER

## Architecture and Urban Design, Economics, Political Science

Regional planning applies the concerns and educational background of urban planning to a broader field. Large combined metropolitan areas, and most states, now have a planning commission that attempts to coordinate economic and developmental issues. Unlike urban planners, regional planners are concerned with more than one city, county, or state. Regional planners also need a stronger background in economics and public administration.

According to federal data and membership surveys from the American Planning Association (APA), about 26% of today's planners work for counties, regions or states, and another 3% for the federal government. Another quarter work in private practice, some concerned with regional or state affairs; the rest are spread through private industry, teaching, and non-profit work.

The regional planning profession enjoyed a tremendous upsurge during the 1980s as states sought to attract business investment. The model was Silicon Valley in California, which combined a major research university, Stanford, with a group of entrepreneurially-minded companies (such as electronics firms), with the appropriate public works and training facilities. The result was an economic powerhouse that created thousands of jobs, increased the value of property in the region, and boosted the fortunes of the university as well.

From the experiments in Silicon Valley, Research Triangle Park in North Carolina, and the Route 128 band around Boston, regional planners learned which mix of economic incentives, worker training, real estate, and public facilities are needed to attract private investment. These lessons have reshaped many regions of the country.

During the early part of the 80s, many states engaged in fierce bidding contests to win a contract to host a new factory. The bidding became even more intensive for foreign investors, such Japanese automobile factories or German chemical companies. States also vied for federal projects such as a new military base or national laboratory.

This bidding war has settled down because some states realized that winning a new factory investment sometimes cost more than the jobs and investments would earn the state. Overall, however, states and regions are much more sophisticated in their analysis and marketing of economic opportunities.

Because regional planning involves extensive interaction with real estate developers and private industry, some executives go back and forth between the public and private sectors.

Regional planners sometimes start out as urban planners. They often have more experience and training than urban planners.

Just as the scope of responsibility for the regional planner is larger than that of the city planner, so is the salary. APA reports that the median salaries earned by state planning executives, or those working for the federal government, are 10–15% higher than for city or county planners; the median is $34,000 at the state level, and $38,000 at the federal.

Students envisioning a career in regional planning should consider advanced education—either a master's degree in planning or a law or MBA degree. They should also leave themselves open to opportunities in the private sector, such as with real estate development firms, insurance firms, insurance companies (who invest heavily in real estate), and business consulting. Overall growth during this decade is 15%, just under the average for all professions.

**American Planning Association**
1313 East 60th Street
Chicago IL   60637
(312) 955-9100

# REGISTERED NURSE

### Allied Health Professions

In the late 1980s, there was an acute shortage of nurses. Ironically, in 1982 the National Academy of Sciences announced that the shortage of nurses in the 1970s would end shortly.

It is unclear whether or not the shortage will last for many years. Two trends may put a lid on dramatic numerical or salary growth: efforts by medical establishments to lower the educational requirements (and, implicitly, the status) of nursing, and the need for the entire health-care system to reduce costs. The short-term career prospects look very good, however. The Bureau of Labor Statistics projects a 39% growth in the profession during the 1990s, reaching a total of 2.2 million by the year 2000.

For the best starting salary and opportunity for advancement, a nurse should pursue the 2 to 4 years' training for the Registered Nurse (RN) or RN plus baccalaureate (BSN). As in most professions, the more advanced one's degrees are, the more opportunities appear.

Today's nurses are expected to be familiar with a wide range of medications, therapies, and sophisticated diagnostic tools. Like physicians, nurses can specialize in a variety of areas, including intensive care, geriatric care, pediatric nursing, and others. Some nurses expand their career horizons by studying hospital administration see **Hospital Administrator**) or another master's level health-care specialty.

Starting salaries vary widely with local supply and demand. Median earnings are about $24,000 to start; specialization, or the willingness to go to parts of the country where nurses are in short supply, can boost that by 25% or more.

**National Student Nurses Association**
Box 56
North Woodbury Road
Pitman, NJ    08071
(609) 589-2319

# RISK MANAGER

## Business Administration, Chemistry, Mathematics

Risk managers, who work for companies with large insurance policies, are the client-side counterparts of insurance underwriters. Their goal is to reduce the liabilities and insurance costs of corporations through better use of training, technology, and management.

Some kinds of insurance have become so expensive (for example, protecting chemical companies from their liabilities for toxic-chemical spills) that companies have turned to "self-insurance." Instead of buying a policy, they salt away enough money to cover themselves for accidents and other liabilities. Risk managers set up and run such programs.

Risk management is a fairly new career, although the business-insurance industry has been around for decades. Many insurance companies themselves employ risk managers to act as consultants to insured clients. There is also a growing business in providing consulting services in the risk management field, opening up entrepreneurial opportunities.

Several related specialties are now being brought under the risk management umbrella. Both insurance companies and the insured employ loss-control specialists to minimize the hazards of workplace accidents, fire, or theft. Others, with technical or engineering training, perform similar work under the title of safety engineer (see **Safety Engineer**).

In addition, many companies have brought their security specialists, ranging from guards to private police forces, under the direction of the risk management office. Finally, because medical insurance is such a big part of the insurance-premium cost of corporations, medical-claims representatives, who gather the paperwork when a claim is to be filed with the insurance company, or with government authorities, also report to risk managers.

Risk management is a growing field. The American Society of Safety Engineers, only one of the professional organizations, has grown over 50% since the beginning of the 1980s.

Most risk managers rise through the ranks of the various specialties; the "director of risk management" tends to be a senior-level executive. Earnings are commensurate with experience; the top managers at large corporations earn $50,000 or more.

Certification is available from a variety of organizations, including the Board of Certified Safety Professionals, whose procedure requires at least 4 years of experience and the passing of two examinations.

**Risk and Insurance Management Society**
205 East 42nd Street
New York, NY   10017
(212) 286-9292

**Public Risk Management Association**
Suite 400
1120 G Street, NW
Washington, DC   20005
(202) 626-4650

---

# SAFETY ENGINEER

### Biological Sciences, Chemical Engineering, Chemistry, Industrial Engineering

Workplace safety has become more important in recent years. An earlier driving force was the US Occupational Safety and Health Administration (OSHA), the federal agency charged with monitoring the work practices of America's industries. More recently, the spur has been money:   with insurance premiums and awards for industrial accidents zooming upward, it behooves any reputable business to provide a safe working environment for its employees.

The safety engineer is the expert called on to carry this out. Safety engineering is taught at relatively few schools, often as part of industrial hygiene, industrial engineering, or engineering management or technology programs. In practice, many safety engineers find their professional identity as members of the American Society of Safety Engineers (ASSE).

A prime responsibility of a safety engineer is to make sure that the OSHA's complex rules for workplace safety are rigorously followed. The engineer also has to keep up with constantly evolving technology for protecting workers, from face masks for purifying dusty air, to complex automatic controls for warning about hazardous material releases.

Another area of concern for safety engineers is equipment design. Many factories are brimming with high-speed rotating equipment, conveyor belts, furnaces, and other units which, while powerful and efficient, are also dangerous to be around. The safety engineer works with equipment suppliers, labor representatives, and production engineers to establish the proper use and maintenance of such equipment.

A field closely related to safety engineering is fire protection engineering. Here, obviously, the emphasis is on establishing systems that monitor, sound warnings, and even extinguish fires automatically.

A major employer of both safety and fire protection engineers is the insurance industry. To control costs, insurance companies send these engineers to clients' worksites.

Salaries range from $26,00 to about $30,000, depending on the type of employer.

**American Society of Safety Engineers**
1800 East Oakton Street
Des Plaines, IL   60018
(708) 692-4121

---

# SHIPPING MANAGER

### Business Administration, Industrial Engineering

A company's job is done once the order is received, the product boxed, and the trucker called, right? Wrong. Distributing products causes a significant portion of the cost and the headaches of a manufacturer. While companies have always had shipping departments, these days their managers are senior executives with a large say in how the corporation functions. Shipping—or, as it's called today, "physical distribution management"—has come of age.

Wal-Mart Stores, Inc., a major housegoods retailer that is now spreading throughout the United States, is a good example of how complex shipping and logistics have become. Products are barcoded when they are stocked on shelves; as they are sold, a computer keeps track of inventory. Regularly, the inventory data is transmitted via a satellite link to the chain's headquarters, and restocking is completed and trucks sent out overnight. The company prides itself on its ability to deliver a wide selection of goods in regions where major retailers have stayed away because of low population density.

The change may even be more dramatic in business-to-business selling than in retailing. All major equipment manufacturers, such as auto and computer companies, now practice some version of "just-in-time" inventory control. Rather than stocking months' worth of raw materials in a warehouse (and thereby tying up money and space), these firms now want their supplies delivered in smaller quantities practically daily. The manufacturers are also trying to reduce the backlog of inventory of the completed equipment, but at the same time to speed up delivery of products to customers. The auto companies, for example, would like to be able to take a customer's order for a car with a custom list of color, accessories, and components, make that car on the assembly line, and deliver it within days of the initial order.

Successful companies today are coping well with all these conflicting pressures. The importance of shipping and physical distribution has risen with this change in inventory-control, however. The Bureau of Labor Statistics counted 137,000 dispatchers at work in 1988, and projects a 16% growth during this decade (about average), but this job title is only one of several used.

At the top levels of the physical-distribution field, training in operations research is desirable; this academic specialty provides math tools for analyzing the most efficient means of transporting items over a broad area. Otherwise, training in business administration, combined with experience in shipping (even if it is the lowly stocking clerk in a store or warehouse) is appropriate. On-the-job training is also extensive.

Starting salaries are in the $20,000 to $25,000 range for entry-level positions; with rising responsibility at the larger corporations, the job can pay above $50,000.

**Council of Logistics Management**
Suite 380
2803 Butterfield Road
Oak Brook, IL   60521
(708) 574-0985

---

# SOCIAL WORKER

### Business Administration, Psychology, Sociology

It has been said that the best measure of a society is how it care of its weakest members—the poor, the handicapped, the homeless, the sick or aged. Social work is the profession that addresses these concerns, and it has a long and honored history of providing life-saving services to the needy. Professionals seeking to enter the field know to expect relatively low pay, but also to expect a large amount of psychic compensation in the form of helping others. These days, with the crises of drug addiction, homelessness, AIDS, and other social problems, many social workers feel that they are at the forefront of defining where American society is going, and providing guidance toward mending these problems.

Over the current decade, the number of job openings in social work is expected to rise at a faster rather than the average, with 495,000 openings in the year 2000 (an increase of 29% from 1988), according to the Bureau of Labor Statistics. Two out of five social workers are employed by federal, state or local government; the remainder work in the healthcare system, for private charities, and in consulting and teaching. Salary surveys from a variety of sources show that pay usually begins at around $16,000, and rises to around $28,000 with experience.

With a projected half-million social workers, it is no surprise that the field is specialized into many subcategories. Most social workers identify themselves in terms of the recipient of their services: family care, child care, healthcare, and more. Faster-growing specialties in the 1990's are expected to be care for the aged, for children, and for the drug-addicted.

The possession of a baccalaureate degree (BSW, bachelor's in social work) is the usual entry point for professionals. Most quickly discover that in order to move into managerial roles, or higher-paying specialties, an MSW is needed.

**National Association of Social Workers**
7981 Eastern Avenue
Silver Spring, MD   20910
(301) 565-0333

---

# STATISTICIAN

**Computer Science and Engineering, Economics, Mathematics**

Numbers provide a fundamental way of analyzing the world around us. Whether the topic is baseball or the effects of diet on health, statistics offer a way to quantify the best, worst, or most important.

Statistical science is booming these days, because of the general need for better analysis of what is going on, and the specific need for manufacturers to control the quality and cost of their products. The statistician provides these answers.

Of the 46,000 mathematical scientists that the Bureau of Labor Statistics has counted, about 15,000 are statisticians. The profession is projected to grow about 22% over this decade. About one out of five work for the federal government; the rest work in industry and education.

It seems that every day we are told about a new medical study that tells us about the value of lowering cholesterol, eating different foods, or engaging in different activities. These studies arise from a specialized group of statisticians known as biostatisticians. The ballooning cost of health-care in American will all but guarantee new employment opportunities for biostatisticians.

One area that will be extremely hot during 1990, and for a couple of years thereafter, is the work generated by the US Census, which is performed every 10 years. As the results come in, statisticians and demographers (see **Demographer**) will be compiling mountains of data into a profile of the American population. While this data is essential for such purposes as delineating the appropriate representation in Congress, private industry will spend millions of dollars analyzing the results for market-research needs. The targeting of advertising and marketing campaigns depends on such data.

In industry, one of the buzzwords at the moment is "statistical quality control" (SQC), part of the effort to upgrade the quality of manufactured products. By analyzing finished products rigorously, statisticians can identify faulty machinery or operating procedures. Although many of the techniques were originally developed in the US, American industry is learning them today from manufacturers in Japan and Europe. Statistical consultants are setting up the necessary quality control programs, and statistical teachers are showing factory workers how to apply the principles.

In a 1989 survey of new graduates, the American Mathematical Society found that salaries for doctorate-level statisticians ranged from a low of $29,500 in academic research to $44,000 in business and industry.

**American Statistical Society**
1429 Duke Street
Alexandria, VA   22314
(703) 684-1221

---

# STOCKBROKER

### Accounting, Business Administration, Political Science, Psychology

Stockbrokers, sometimes called account executives, are the sales people of the securities industry. The products they are offering, stocks, bonds, or other "financial instruments," are usually acquired by individuals purely for financial reasons—the better-performing ones will appreciate faster or provide more secure returns. Most brokers are selling the instruments that were devised by others, such as investment managers, at their firm. As a result, being a good stockbroker is mostly a matter of being a good salesperson; brilliant financial insight is not obligatory.

This is not to say that selling stocks and bonds is simple. The best brokers can translate the financial goals of their clients into the appropriate mix of investment categories, and then make a convincing presentation to the client. The client will be watching overall performance of the investment package closely, and if it falls short, will dump the investment and probably the stockbroker as well.

The securities industry has undergone enormous turmoil in the past decade. The traditional form of selling—to wealthy individuals or to investment companies—was altered dramatically when fixed commissions for sales were dropped in the late 1970s. The new "discount" brokerage firms simply execute the purchase or sale for the client, without offering any analysis of financial goals or investments. Then, during the roaring 1980s, a fast-growing stock market, combined with lowered taxes on investment earnings, led to the proliferation of all sorts of new financial instruments. Companies began trading in futures options (which are a guaranteed right to buy a stock, bond or commodity product at a future date, not necessarily with the intent to actually purchase the stock or bond). "Junk" bonds, which offered high yields and somewhat higher risk, also became popular.

Much of this financial thrashing stopped on October 19, 1987, when the New York Stock Exchange plummeted in value. Although its indexes have risen since then, things haven't been the same. The New York financial services industries lost over 15,000 jobs in the weeks following that day, and thousands more have been dropped since.

But the beat goes on. Regularly every year, the leading investment houses hire groups of trainees and put them through a series of seminars. Part of the training is to prepare for the tests provided by the National Association of Securities Dealers, Inc., to meet mandatory licensing requirements. Those passing the tests are then set up with a desk and telephone. The successful salespeople earn higher pay and bigger offices; the less successful are stuck or, since salaries are highly dependent on sales commissions, drop out for lack of income.

Salaries are highly variable, depending on the sales volume the broker can build up. Trainees' pay is in the $25,000 to $30,000 range, but it can go up quickly if one is successful. Top performers can earn over $100,000.

The aging of the United State population (with more middle-aged people presumably needing savings and investment plans), together with the continuation of new types of investments, is expected to generate considerable job growth, according to the Bureau of Labor Statistics. Projected growth is 55%—reaching 289,000 by the turn of the century. By no means are all or even most of the current and future jobs in New York; there are exchanges in Chicago, San Francisco, and other cities, and most national firms have local offices spread around the country.

The means of entering this field are varied. Some type of college degree is usually mandatory, and certainly a facility with math is a bonus. Some firms like to see MBAs, but they are not essential. Most securities dealers prefer trainees with some type of business experience, which makes them more credible salespeople. A winning personality and strong selling skills are key to success.

**National Association of Securities Dealers**
1735 K Street, NW
Washington, DC   20006
(202) 728-8000

# TEACHER, K–12

### Classics, Education, History, Home Economics, Modern Languages, Performing Arts, Psychology

Added together, the teachers at the preschool, kindergarten, elementary, and high school levels form one of the largest professions. The total in 1988, according to the Bureau of Labor

Statistics, was 2.76 million. That figure is projected to rise by 18.2%, to 3.26 million, by the year 2000. The growth rate is fastest for preschool teachers (30%), and lowest for the K–elementary group (15%). High school teaching is expected to grow by 19%. Because funding for education is rising faster than ever before, growth may be even stronger than projected.

Certainly it is true that teacher salaries have been rising rapidly in many part of the country. From a low of around $14,000 for preschool teaching, salaries can go up to the $50,000 vicinity for top-rated, experienced teachers in well-to-do school districts (bear in mind that this is for less than a full year's work). A number of school districts across the country are experimenting with high-incentive pay to keep the best teachers.

As of 1988, according to the National Education Association (Washington, DC), the states with the highest average salaries (high school level) were California, New York, Rhode Island, Connecticut, and Alaska (topping them all with an average of $40,700), while the lowest paying were South Dakota, Arkansas, Louisiana, Mississippi, and North Dakota (all around $19,000 to 21,000).

Teaching at any grade level usually requires a college degree which can be obtained in almost any type of major, including education. As part of the college program, the candidate teachers must spend time in a classroom setting under the supervision of an experienced teacher. Each state has its own certification procedures, which must be followed before one can be hired in that state. Some states require testing for basic competency in teaching certain subjects. For the teachers of the youngest pupils, training also usually requires courses in child psychology or counseling.

Having passed through the educational system, we all know what teachers do: instruct at the blackboard, hold one-on-one talks and discussions, and maintain some sort of order in the classroom.

Many of today's teachers feel that they are entitled to combat pay, especially those working in inner cities. Teaching is physically and mentally demanding, and many teachers burn out after several years. Luckily, numerous positions are available outside the school systems for those who tire of the public-school hassles. (see, for example, **Corporate Trainer** or **Vocational Teacher**)

National Education Association of the United States
1201 16th Street, NW
Washington, DC   20036
(202) 833-4000

---

# TECHNICAL WRITER

### Biological Sciences, Chemistry, Classics, Computer Science and Engineering, Philosophy and Religion, Physics

The term "technical writer" carries two meaning:  one who writes about technology in general, and one who writes documentation for computer programs. Both kinds of technical writers are in high demand in our increasingly technological and computerized world.

The majority of technical writers work at corporations and consulting firms. One of their primary tasks is to write proposals or plans for soliciting new business for the firm. An equally important function is to write the necessary documentation for operator's or assembler's manuals for complex equipment.

In the computer software field, many programs hardly exist until the instruction manual is prepared. Computer programs, especially large ones, would be gibberish to many users without a manual. Documentation for computer programs is so essential that sometimes a program succeeds commercially simply because the user's instructions are so good.

Technical writers are lumped together with all other writers and editors in the Bureau of Labor Statistics data; that group as a whole will experience a 25% growth during this decade. While a number of schools, especially institutes of technology that train large numbers of engineers and scientists, have now organized "technical communications" programs, other academic backgrounds are also suitable:   liberal arts, education, journalism. Experience is critical, as is the ability to extract information form technically-oriented people and translate it for the ultimate reader or user.

Pay scales are slightly ahead of general writing or journalism careers, at least initially. Starting salaries are in the range of

$18,000 to $24,000; with experience, they grow to the $40,000 to $50,000 range.

**Society For Technical Communication**
815 15th Street, NW
Washington, DC   20005
(202) 737-0035

---

# TELECOMMUNICATIONS MANAGER

### Accounting, Communications, Computer Science and Engineering, Electrical and Electronics Engineering

Perhaps no business changed more rapidly in the 80s than telecommunications. Not only did new technology create new business opportunities, but the deregulation of the telephone companies (the creation of the "Baby Bells") realigned the business.

Both AT&T and all the startup firms like MCI and US Sprint employ thousands of technicians, staff managers, maintenance specialists, and administrators. A key position, however, is the telecommunications marketing representative, who combines skills in technology, marketing, and selling.

The telecommunications manager is concerned with keeping existing customers of long-distance and other services happy, while developing approaches to gain new ones. This seems like a simple question of offering the best price and availability, but the technical issues are much more complex. In particular, these managers need to keep abreast of rapidly changing technologies and communication standards. The acquisition of outmoded technology can have a lasting, harmful effect on an organization.

Corporations and government agencies want not only long-distance "telephony" (to use the perferred industry term), but also many other types of telecommunications. These include digital communications, to enable computers to "talk" to one another; cellular telephone services for the car or travel; and intracompany voice and data messaging, which uses telephone equipment to keep staff personnel and computer equipment in communication.

On the telephone-using side, too, there is change and opportunity. Because of the myriad types of communications services, corporations hire a "chief information officer" to select and manage the services, and to design the right type of system for specific purposes. This work usually requires a technical background in electronics engineering or technology, combined with an MBA.

The number of electronic technicians and technologists alone (a category that includes those working with other types of electronic equipment in addition to telecommunications) is slated for a 38% growth over the coming decade, according to the Bureau of Labor Statistics. That's well over double the rate of all professions.

Pay averages around $29,000 to $31,000 for those with an engineering or science degree, and around $25,000 for accounting or business majors.

Even more changes are in the works for this field. The US, indeed the world, is shifting to a communications standard known as ISDN (Integrated Services Digital Network). This standard will enable the same piece of copper wire (or fiber optic cable) to carry multiple voice signals, computer data, television and radio signals across a building or around the world. Through standardization, many different types of communications equipment—from computer modems to fax machines, from traditional handsets to picturephones—will be used on the same network, thus expanding revenues, customers, and opportunities for new growth.

Telecommunications is a field creating new job opportunities, and new job titles, practically overnight. An exciting future is ahead.

**North American Telecommunications Association**
Suite 550
2000 M Street, NW
Washington, DC   20036
(202) 296-9800

**United States Telephone Association**
900 19th Street, NW
Washington, DC   20006
(202) 835-3100

# TEMPORARY WORKER

**With so many options in this field, there is no specific academic preparation.**

"Temps" used to be only secretaries, clerks, and perhaps retail salespeople during the holidays. Changes in workplace practices, the rising professionalism of the American workforce, and personal career goals, however, have made temporary work a viable, and sometimes lucrative, type of work for certain people.

The big change in temporary work that occurred during the 1980s was the addition of prestigious professions: accounting, computer programming, engineering, editing, legal services, auditing, and tax preparation. Over a million workers (roughly 1% of the US workforce) can be classified as temps, according to the National Association of Temporary Services (NATS).

Before you can be a professional temp worker, it is practically essential to have experience as a full-time practitioner of that profession. Temporary work should be an element in your career-planning portfolio, however. Temp work might be a good stepping stone for your career. The most obvious example being that temp work can provide income until a entrepreneurial venture takes off.

In some careers, temp work can provide a foot in the door, or at least relevant experience. More than a few temps have been turned into full-time employees once an employer has had a chance to see them in action.

According to NATS, about one out of three temp workers has a college degree; 5% have graduate or professional degrees. Almost 60% are under 35 years of age; 12% are retirees from a full-time job.

Most temps sign up at an agency, which keeps a resume and other personal information on file. When a company calls in with an assignment, the agency attempts to match the assignment with the appropriate person. The agency receives payment, and after taking a percentage, gives the temp a paycheck. Some agencies even offer health-care benefits or pension plans, just like a full-time employer.

Pay depends on the city or region and on the specialty. Most temps are paid by the hour; however, some projects pay a lump sum.

Trying to develop a permanent career as a temp worker has its drawbacks, since your commitment to a field would usually be questioned, but as a transition between one employer and another, or during the early years of parenthood, or when one doesn't need to be the sole breadwinner in a family, temporary work has many pluses.

**National Association of Temporary Workers**
119 South Saint Asaph Street
Alexandria, VA   22314
(202) 789-2424

---

# TRAVEL PLANNER

### Art History, History, Home Economics, Modern Languages, Performing Arts

The travel industry was on a bumpy ride for most of the 80s, as airline deregulation created new airlines, new travel routes, and new ways of doing business, but the resulting confusion may have made the travel agent more important than ever.

Travel and tourism is a huge business. The total of all the receipts for airline tickets, hotel stays, bus tours and souvenir-buying is over $330 billion, according to the US Travel Data Center. The tourist industry is the largest employer in 13 states, and is among the top three in 26 others. Over 5 million people are employed in its various facets.

Key personnel among those 5 million are the travel agents and brokers that help sell tourist packages, and arrange the trips and hotel reservations of business travelers. Most travel agencies are small, independent businesses, but there are similar agents and managers working for airlines, hotel chains, and community business-development agencies.

Training in foreign languages and cultures will become essential in the future. In 1989, according to the Department of Commerce, foreign visitors to the US, for the first time, spent more than did American travelers abroad, to the tune of $1.2 billion. During the period of 1983–1989, while the volume of US travel abroad grew by 50%, the equivalent in visitors here grew by 129%.

Travel planners engage in a range of activities. Airline ticketing is perhaps the most obvious; most agencies are now equipped with computers that connect them with the reservations databanks of the major airlines, and even some hotel chains. The agent works to arrange the most economical means of transportation while maximizing convenience for the business traveler and enjoyment for the personal traveler.

Agency managers and managers at hotels and airlines need good marketing skills today, because there are so many possible destinations and so many means of getting there. Travel providers must convince the buying public to spend their dollars with specific airlines or hotel companies, or in visiting particular resorts or cultural centers.

The Bureau of Labor Statistics estimated the number of travel agents in 1988 at 142,000, and projects an eye-popping 54% growth through the year 2000. Pay is low to start—around $14,000—but can rise as the business volume, and level of responsibility, increases.

Travel agents can seek certification from the Institute of Certified Travel Agents.

**American Society of Travel Agents**
1101 King Street
Alexandria, VA   22314
(703) 739-2782

**Institute of Certified Travel Agents**
PO Box 82–56
148 Linden Street
Wellesley, MA   02181
(617) 237-0280

**US Travel Data Center**
2 Lafayette Center
1133 21st Street, NW

Washington, DC    20036
(202) 293-1433
(This organization is affiliated with the Travel Industry
Association of America.)

---

# UNDERWRITER

## Accounting, Economics, Mathematics

Insurance sales agents sell policies, but the sale isn't complete until an underwriter examines all the details of the policy. The underwriter looks at the coverage being provided, assesses the risks involved, and reviews corporate policy for the cost of providing this coverage. Underwriting is thus a key element in the overall success (and profitability) of an insurance company. If underwriters set the policy costs too high, they may price their company's products out of the market; if they set them too low, they expose their employers to too much risk.

Successful underwriting combines business acumen with a good understanding of finance and statistics. Because the knowledge required is unique to the insurance industry, such professional organizations as the Life Underwriter Training Council have set up extensive educational programs for underwriters.

According to the Bureau of Labor Statistics, there are currently about 100,000 underwriters. The projected growth is 29%. Starting pay for underwriters is around $20,000 to $25,000, rising to $40,000 for experienced managers.

About 40% of underwriters work for independent insurance brokers and service organizations; another 40% work for insurance firms specializing in fire, marine, and casualty insurance; and the remainder work for life insurance firms and related businesses.

There is no specific academic training for underwriters, but a college degree is usually obligatory. Underwriter trainees work on standard types of insurance (i.e., life or property), gaining experience in performing assessments. A strong candidate will show an ability to work with numbers, an attention to detail, and insightfulness in perceiving the needs and risks of a diverse array of businesses and individuals.

With a background in the usual types of insurance practices, and the training provided by the insurance companies, the underwriter can move into the more specialized areas of insurance, such as professional liability. Underwriting experience can also lead to the upper-management of insurance companies.

Sometimes the underwriter's assessments are passed along to the insurance purchaser, to suggest how the cost might be reduced. By assessing the reliability of a fire-protection system, for example, the underwriter can help a building owner justify the system's cost through lower insurance premiums.

**National Association of Life Underwriters**
1922 F Street, NW
Washington, DC   20006
(202) 331-6001
(The Life Underwriter Training Council is affiliated with this
  organization.)

---

# URBAN PLANNER

### Architecture and Urban Design, Biological Sciences, Civil Engineering, Sociology

Why are some cities "in," and some "out?" What makes one city more livable than another? These abstract questions are behind the work of the urban planning profession.

Urban planners combine a knowledge of sociology, history, architecture, and economics to determine the best way to renew, enlarge, or improve cities and regions (see also **Regional Planner**). One of the key tools in guiding a city's progress is zoning codes, which determine the placement of commercial and residential buildings, the arrangement of transportation, and the density of development.

The urban planner is often thought of as the person who says

''No!'' to over-ambitious land developers, or to homeowners who want to knock down a historic house and build a new one in its place. Urban planners aren't just naysayers; they have an active role in helping create an environment for growth in cities. Obviously, people need a place to live; but they also need places to work, shop, and enjoy recreation. They must have means of getting from one place to another, so the city must plan for highways, parking lots, mass transit, and airports or bus terminals.

The glory days of the urban planners were the 1960s, when ambitious city managers, flush with federal monies, sought to redesign and rebuild many cities. Tighter budgets and lowered expectations in the 1970s stopped much of this work. Then a boom on commercial construction during the 1980s reshaped many cities' cores. Planning is emerging as a critical part of managing the growth that has occurred in the past decade, and regenerating the regions that have not grown in the recent past. Today's cities also have to plan to meet the critical needs of the homeless and economically disadvantaged.

There are several specialties within planning, according to the American Planning Association: city management (the actual running of cities, as opposed to planning for them), housing and human services, small-town and rural planning, urban preservation, and information technology.

The last shows the affect of the computer on urban planning work. Urban planners are using architectural programs that let them ''walk through'' a project by viewing it on a computer screen, as well as sophisticated modeling programs that calculate the effects of various economic and demographic trends on a city. These models, derived from econometric studies, can show how, for example, a change in taxation policies might affect the construction of low-income housing.

The long-term growth in the planning profession is about average for all types of employment, according to the Bureau of Labor Statistics. It counted 20,000 planners in 1988, and expects that to rise to 23,000 by the turn of the century. Currently, nearly 90% of all planners work for government.

A 1987 study by the American Planning Association (APA) revealed some of the trends in the field. Starting salaries were around $21,500; they go up with experience, advanced education, and the size of the region that the planner is responsible for. Top salaries, around $52,000 on average, went to holders of a PhD or law degree. The median salary for all planners was $36,000. APA provides certification, which can also boost salaries, through a subsidiary organization, the American Institute of Certified Planners.

The American Planning Association survey also showed that the planning profession is graying—"For the first time in the history of the . . . salary surveys, planners with more than 10 years' experience account for more than half of the respondents," it said. The profession is also becoming more open to women and minorities; 27.1% of the respondents were women, and 1.5% were members of minority groups.

**American Planning Association**
1313 East 60th Street
Chicago, IL   60637
(312) 955-9100
(The American Institute of Certified Planners is at the same
  address.)

# VETERINARIAN

### Biological Sciences

There are 55 million pet dogs in America—more than children. Our close relationship with animals has a commercial aspect, too; farmers and breeders invest substantial amounts of money in the care and development of livestock.

For commercial or personal reasons, we turn to the veterinarian to keep our animals healthy. The Bureau of Labor Statistics estimates that there are some 46,000 vets in the country, and projects above-average growth to 57,000 by the year 2000.

However, veterinary science has become less popular among students, so there may be real shortages developing in the next few years. It is hard to say why this decline has occurred; perhaps the steady bad news in the agricultural sector of the economy is dissuading students from any career associated with it.

According to surveys by the American Veterinary Medical Association (AVMA), just over half of today's vets have a "small animal" (i.e., pet) practice. Some of the rest have livestock or "large-animal" practices, and others combine the two. Although more than one out of two veterinary students is female, only about one out of four practicing vets is a woman.

The typical vet does many of the same things that medical doctors for humans do—running tests, making diagnoses, providing medication. Most have a private practice (that is, they are self-employed), and thus have the worries of running a business and keeping the books. Unlike medical doctors, though, many vets do make house calls, usually to farms. (Imagine trying to bring a herd of cattle to the vet's office!)

It takes 7 years of post-high school education, at least, to win the necessary degree, Doctor of Veterinary Medicine (DVM or VMD), from one of 27 schools. Starting salaries are around $23,000, and can rise to an average of over $50,000, depending on how successfully the practice is maintained.

**American Veterinary Medical Association**
930 North Meacham Moad
Schaumburg, IL  60196
(708) 605-8070

---

# VOCATIONAL (ADULT) TEACHER

### Anthropology, Art History, Education, Home Economics, Philosophy and Religion, Psychology, Sociology and Social Sciences

Vocational schools and programs of adult education represent an alternative to high school followed by college. Many vocational programs are geared toward recent high school graduates who want training in a specific skill. Adult education tends to be for older people who are contemplating a second career or who want to broaden their skills and expertise.

In either case, the primary student goal is job improvement. That makes the students very motivated. On the other hand, some vocational programs have a remedial nature that can make the work less exciting.

The Bureau of Labor Statistics projection for this field is slightly below-average growth—12%—to around 545,000 teachers. Many vocational/adult teachers work part-time; full-time teachers earn about $25,000 annually.

The range of teaching positions is quite large. Governments and private industry sponsor programs that re-train the unemployed, give technical training for manufacturing jobs, and provide remedial help for high school dropouts. Because there has been an upsurge in adult attendance at colleges, many college-level programs are taught, especially in accounting or business administration.

Greater attention is being paid to vocational/adult education today as part of the upsurge in interest in education. For the US to compete in the international economic arena, it needs a better-trained workforce. Paradoxically, industry is having a harder and harder time filling technical and administrative positions with high school graduates, due to the decline in educational quality, so partnerships between industry and vocational/adult schools are increasing.

**American Association for Adult and Continuing Education**
Suite 420
1112 16th Street, NW
Washington, DC    20036
(202) 822-7866

# INDEX